Why History?

P9-DMT-677

'I think this is a very important book because of its radical aim . . . the disestablishment of the whole conceptualisation . . . of the past-as-history. As an intellectual undertaking it is quite breathtaking. . . . It is likely to be one of the most significant commentaries on the nature of history published this decade.'

Alun Munslow

'Keith Jenkins is determined to drag historical studies (or their successors) into the twenty-first century . . . [this book] constitutes another splendid Jenkins tirade . . . what particularly appeals is the sense of engagement that comes through the commitment to an intellectual position which has enormous practical possibilities.'

Beverley Southgate

Why History? is an introduction to the issue of history and ethics. Designed to provoke discussion, the book asks whether a knowledge and understanding of the past is a good thing to have, and if so, why? In the context of postmodern times, *Why History?* suggests that the goal of 'learning lessons from the past' is actually learning lessons from stories written by historians and others. If the past as history has no foundation, can anything ethical be learned from history?

Why History? presents liberating challenges to history and ethics, proposing that we have reached an emancipatory moment that is well beyond 'the end of history'.

Keith Jenkins is Reader in History at University College Chichester and author of *Rethinking History* (1991), *On 'What is History?' From Carr and Elton to Rorty and White* (1995) and *The Postmodern History Reader* (1997).

Why History?
Ethics and postmodernity

Keith Jenkins

London and New York

First published 1999
by Routledge
11 New Fetter Lane, London EC4P 4EE

Simultaneously published in the USA and Canada
by Routledge
29 West 35th Street, New York, NY 10001

Routledge is an imprint of the Taylor & Francis Group

© 1999 Keith Jenkins

Typeset in Sabon by BC Typesetting, Bristol
Printed and bound in Great Britain by
TJ International Ltd, Padstow, Cornwall

All rights reserved. No part of this book may be reprinted or reproduced
or utilised in any form or by any electronic, mechanical, or other
means, now known or hereafter invented, including photocopying
and recording, or in any information storage or retrieval system,
without permission in writing from the publishers.

British Library Cataloguing in Publication Data
A catalogue record for this book is available from the British Library

Library of Congress Cataloging in Publication Data
Jenkins, Keith, 1943–
    Why history?/Keith Jenkins.
        p.   cm.
    Includes bibliographical references and index.
    1. History – Philosophy. I. Title.
    D16.8.J387   1999   98-39237
    901–dc21   CIP

ISBN 0–415–20632–4 (hbk)
ISBN 0–415–16416–8 (pbk)

For Maureen, Philip and Patrick

I confess I do not believe in [historical] time. I like to fold my magic carpet, after use, in such a way as to superimpose one part of the pattern upon another. Let visitors trip.

V. Nabokov, *Speak Memory*

Contents

Acknowledgements

Over the last few years I have had many conversations with members of the School of History and the Centre for Postmodern Studies, University College Chichester, about the detailed arguments and the general position I have tried to express in this text, and I thank them for their interest. Beverley Southgate generously took time out to read the final typescript and made invaluable comments which I have endeavoured to take on board, as did Michael Stanford whose opposition to many (if not all) of the things I have tried to say here gave me some uncomfortable 'second thoughts'. Alun Munslow very kindly read both the original typescript and the final proofs, as did – with her usual critical eye – Routledge's History Editor Heather McCullum. Above all, however, I am indebted to Philip Jenkins, whose interminable capacity to make me think again and differently I have failed to do justice to in the following pages. I am sure that the text is much better after the 'interventions' of all the above, its no doubt still numerous failings being nobody's fault but my own.

Particular thanks are due also to Carole Farnfield who, against all the odds, managed to turn my handwriting into an acceptable typed script.

A slightly different version of the section on Jean Baudrillard appeared in *Literature and History* in the Spring of 1999, and I thank Philip Martin and his fellow editors for publishing the essay.

The author and Routledge would like to thank Professor Elizabeth Deeds Ermarth and Princeton University Press for permission to reproduce extracts from her *Sequel to History*, Professor F.R. Ankersmit and the University of California Press for permission to reproduce pages from his *History and Tropology*, and Professor David Harlan and the University of Chicago Press for permission to reproduce extracts from his *The Degradation of American History*.

Introduction: Living in time but outside history; living in morality but outside ethics

This book is written primarily as an extended polemic; it is overtly positioned. It may be impossible to write today in any other way. The idea of writing an objective, neutral, disinterested text, where explaining, describing and 'introducing' something is done from a position that isn't ostensibly a position at all, is a naive one. For to put something 'under a description' in what might appear to be the most innocent of ways is still to privilege that description over another; it thus throws down a challenge; it stakes a claim; its 'objectivity' is spurious. To do this is to forget that nothing is given to a gaze, but rather is constituted 'in meaning' by it. This text is thus polemical and partisan in that it is an engagement with other ways of positioning 'certain objects of enquiry', in the main aligning itself with them through an appropriate vocabulary and speaking in an appropriate register.

I want to show, through a series of case studies of Derrida and others, that postmodern ways of thinking probably signal the end of history – 'history' especially when taken in either of two forms. These are: the 'upper case' or metanarrative history on one hand, and the 'lower case' or the professional, academic form (the kind usually met by undergraduates) on the other. By 'upper case history' I mean the consideration of the past in terms that assign objective significance to what are actually contingent events. It does this by identifying their place and function within a general schema of development; the past is used to advance a specific point of view. Examples are the more orthodox forms of Marxism or Whig progressive theories of history. By 'lower case history' I mean the 'disinterested' study of the past for its own sake, on its own terms, as objectively, impartially and thus as 'academically' as possible. This kind normally regards itself unproblematically as 'proper' history and thus as being non-ideological and non-positioned. But I take lower case history to be just as ideological and positioned/positioning as any other: history is always for someone.[1]

It is not only history whose end is signalled by postmodern thinking, but, thanks to postmodernism's celebration of the moral 'undecidability' of a decision, traditional ethics also. I explain what I mean by this more fully in Section 1b of this Introduction and in the chapter on Derrida, whose argument I tend to follow. In brief it goes like this: for a decision to be 'ethical' it has to pass through a moment of 'undecidability' (the *aporia*) when, because there are no unambiguous, apodictic, algebraic foundations on which to base *the* right decision, a choice between more than one equally (logically) possible decision has to be made. For Derrida, an ethical choice is thus only ethical if it passes through this moment of radical undecidability. If one refers back to a previously worked out or putative 'ethical system' – that is, if the decision is merely the application of a previous rule or code – then no ethical decision has been made.[2] I depart from Derrida in using the term 'ethics' for 'ethical systems' only, however, and 'moral' (not 'ethical', as he does) for ungroundable, *aporetic* decisions. So my argument is that we are now in a situation where we can (and do) live *outside* of 'ethics' but *in* 'morality'. And just as 'ethics' has now ended as a viable approach to 'moral decisions', so history has ended as a groundable (epistemological/ontological) discourse, and we are left in a condition allowing or necessitating only ungroundable temporal stylisations *in infinitum*.

As a consequence of this desirable collapse of history and ethics comes a reconsideration of the nature of the discourses going under these names. But do we still need to, or should we, reconsider them at all? For perhaps we are now at a postmodern moment when we can forget history and ethics altogether. Perhaps we are now under conditions where we can live our lives within new ways of timing time which do not refer to a past tense articulated in discourses that have become historically familiar to us. And perhaps we can now start to formulate new moralities without recourse to moribund ethical systems.

I shall argue, in Section 1 of the Introduction, that we can think of letting history and ethics go because postmodern thinking has provided all the intellectual resources we now need to think in future-orientated, emancipatory and democratising ways. We have rich 'imaginaries', by which I mean the 'feats of the imagination' that come out of 'political', discursive practices, and which open up possibly new ways of thinking and being,[3] matters that I explore in Section 2. The title of this Introduction points to a conclusion that is not only logical and the way things actually are, but also desirable: this way of putting things ('living in time but outside history, living in morality but outside ethics') points to possible future imaginaries exfoliating forever.

For no matter how ingeniously constructed the past has been in modernist (and other) historical/ethical practices, it is now clear that 'in and for itself' there is nothing definitive for us to get out of it other than that which we have put into it. That 'in and for itself' the past contains nothing of obvious significance. That left on its own it has no discoverable point. That it expresses no intelligible rhyme or reason. That it consists of nothing independent of us that we *have* to be loyal to, nothing we *have* to feel guilty about, no facts we *have* to find, no truths we *have* to respect, no problems we *have* to solve, no project we *have* to complete. It is clear that the past doesn't exist 'historically' outside of historians' textual, constructive appropriations, so that, being made by them, it has no independence to resist their interpretative will, not least at the level of meaning. However irreducible, stubborn, painful, comic or tragic the past may have been, it only reaches us through fictional devices which invest it with a range of highly selective and hierarchical readings which are 'always subservient to various powers and interests'.[4] Consequently, the past as history always has been and always will be necessarily configured, troped, emplotted, read, mythologised and ideologised in ways to suit ourselves. There is, as Hayden White has put it, 'an inexpungeable relativity to every representation of historical phenomena' such that one must simply face the fact that 'when it comes to apprehending the historical record, there are no grounds in the historical record itself for preferring one way of constructing its meaning over another'.[5] Accordingly, it is the recognition of this relativistic bottom line that has made Tony Bennett write

> if narratives are all that we can have and if all narratives are, in principle, of equal value – as it seems they must be if there is no touchstone of 'reality' to which they can be referred for the adjudication of their truth claims – then rational debate would seem to be pointless. If the non-accessibility of a referent means that the theorist is drawn into labyrinths of textual 'indecidability' where any kind of truth claim would only tell the story of its own undoing – then why bother?[6]

Bennett intends his question to be read rhetorically. He will go on to justify the study of history for his own purposes in impressive ways.

But I think that it is actually here, at this precise point where the study of the past is seen as being enormously problematic both in terms of the various 'metaphysical', 'ontological', 'epistemological', 'methodological' and 'ethical' claims made for it,[7] and in terms of its putative, normative utility, that we might begin to think about not trying to keep the ramshackle phenomena of history and ethics going (even when constructed in highly reflexive ways). We should put our best efforts into working the intellectual potentialities provided precisely by the postmodern theorising that has helped bring about their current moribund condition. For this may (though it cannot be guaranteed and certainly cannot be entailed) help us to construct new imaginaries of radical emancipation.

Now, it will already be obvious from what has been said that this is a positioned text designed to provoke discussion; I would never claim that in it I make much attempt at 'disinterested objectivity'. When I began to think about writing this book I asked myself what imaginaries 'we' might now need to enable us to re-think the possibility of emancipation, now that the Enlightenment, modernist projects had failed in their own terms.[8] I took it initially as a plausible hypothesis and then as an axiom, that the phenomena of postmodernity and postmodernism can best be thought of as coming *after* modernity, and that 'postist' thought can be best construed as representing a kind of *retrospective* of it. It does so in a way to at least raise the questions of what, *vis-à-vis* emancipations, we are to do now and what, if anything, we want from the past appropriated through modernist (and other) historicisations to help us to do it. In posing these questions, I originally came up with a positive response, because I had long had in mind – to the extent that it almost seemed to be common sense – George Steiner's observation that it is not the literal past that determines our present and our future but 'images of the past'. Such images, as selective as any other myth, give each 'new era' its sense of identity, of regress and of new achievements such that 'the echoes by which a society seeks to determine the reach, the logic and the authority of its own voice, come from the rear'.[9] But I am no longer so sure about this. For the sorts of reasons already briefly intimated in my opening paragraphs, I no longer feel able to treat Steiner's commonplace unproblematically, nor Bennett's rhetorical question rhetorically. It seems – and this is put forward hypothetically – that actually the 'myths' that may take us from the present into the future might best be *of* the present and *of* the future. Perhaps we not only do not need – and maybe never have needed – to measure our 'changes' against always highly selective images from the rear. Perhaps such practices are positively damaging in their restrictive cloyingness. There may be no reason at all why we cannot gather together the strength, as Nietzsche put it, to unburden ourselves of the past and past ethics, and to build future measurements of radical emancipation from current imaginaries and, more particularly in our own time and space, from postmodern ones.

And yet, having arrived at this re-stated 'thesis', a whole range of questions still seem to be left unanswered. For example, if you extend Bennett's query of 'why bother with the past' to why bother with history and why bother with ethics, why stop there? Why bother with literature, or art, or science, or politics, or philosophy . . . or life? If we stop bothering about ethics then why bother about morality? If we stop bothering about yesterday then why bother about today or tomorrow; why bother with, say, human emancipation? Again, if the past, despite all our 'historical' efforts, remains ultimately unfathomable as a whole and inexpungeably relativistic in its interpreted parts, then how can the present and future – similarly constructed and similarly unsutured – help us any better? If every reading of the 'real' world is ultimately an effect of that constitutive/ performative reading, then why should we bother with postmodern 'readings' rather than the modernist ones we've got used to . . . in the end, why bother with anything?

There are obviously no unproblematical answers to questions of this kind. Certainly there are none (though many have imagined that there were and some still do) at ontological and epistemological levels; at the level of 'truth'. Nor are there definitive answers (though again they have been sought) at the level of the metaphysical which, while constructed 'separately' as an 'ideal', can only be 'known' to us (i.e. reduced to us) as ontology and epistemology, which means that it cannot be 'known' at all. Thus, in response to the questions motivated by Bennett's query, I think that in the end the only thing we can fall back on *vis-à-vis* 'why bother?' is that, taken in the round, human beings just do.

This may seem an utterly trite response. But it may be the only one we can ultimately make, in that, just as, say, stomachs do the kinds of things that stomachs do, and spleens just do the kinds of things that spleens do for reasons we cannot fully fathom, so human beings *qua* human beings just do seem to be of a kind that wants to find answers to these kinds of impossible questions which they just happen as a species to be able to formulate in ways that affect their practices. Going back to George Steiner, Steiner argues in similar vein at the end of his *In Bluebeard's Castle* that it appears that we humans will open up the successive doors of the castle simply because 'they are there'. For to leave 'one door closed would not only be cowardice, but a betrayal . . . of the inquisitive, probing, forward-tensed stance of our species. We are hunters after reality [*sic*] wherever it may lead.'[10] We apparently cannot, adds Steiner, choose the dream of unknowing, so that it would appear that Nietzsche was right: 'we would rather will nothing than not will at all.' And Steiner goes on to argue further that conceiving the human condition in this way makes him choose one of two options. The first is that offered by what he calls 'Freud's stoic acquiescence'; his tired 'supposition that human life was a cancerous anomaly, a detour between vast stages of organic repose'. The second is that 'Nietzschean gaiety in the face of the inhuman, the tensed, ironic perception that we are, that we always have been, precarious guests in an indifferent, frequently murderous, but always fascinating world'.[11] Steiner's choice is for Nietzsche, and I think that he is right. Not because he is 'really right' of course, but because such a 'cultural' choice appeals to me as well; this is the ungrounded choice (the aporetic 'madness of the decision' choice) that I have decided to make here so as to try and 'make sense' of other things. And having made it, I have gone on to interpret it in such a way that it finds expression, for now, in the interconnected arguments I have already said I will be trying to make 'attractive' in this text; to repeat, arguments to the effect that, because of our postmodern condition, we now have the exciting possibility of forgetting moribund history and ethics in favour of a radical postmodernism appropriated to suit emancipatory aims. Yet, given that any such 'position' is inevitably ungrounded and cannot be justified, these arguments obviously cannot be put in a manner that suggests that I may be 'getting things right', or that what is being said corresponds to the way things definitively are; to the truth. Rather, the method I have tried to adopt here is one I have taken from Richard Rorty, a method he describes thus:

> The method is to redescribe lots of things in new ways, until you have created a pattern of linguistic behaviour which will tempt the rising generation to adopt it, thereby causing them to look for appropriate new forms of non-linguistic behaviour – for example . . . new social institutions. This sort of philosophy does not work piece by piece, analysing concept after concept, or testing thesis after thesis. Rather it works holistically and pragmatically. It says things like 'try thinking of it in this way' – or more specifically, 'try to ignore the apparently futile traditional questions by substituting the following new and possibly interest-

ing questions.' It does not pretend to have a better candidate for doing the same old things which we did when we spoke in the old way. Rather it suggests that we might want to stop doing those things and do something else . . . Conforming to my own precepts . . . I am going to try and make the vocabulary I favour look attractive by showing how it might be used to describe a variety of topics.[12]

The structure of this book 'reflects' the position I have just been sketching out. Thus in Part I, 'On the end of metanarratives', I look at the contribution made by postmodern theorising to bring that end about. Of course, for some readers, this 'sense of an ending' may be very familiar; maybe today we all have towards metanarratives that 'incredulity' so famously essayed by J. F. Lyotard in *The Postmodern Condition*.[13] But the way this incredulity has been instilled and, more particularly, the collateral impact the collapse of the upper case has arguably had on lower case history and the possibilities then opened up, has not been attempted in the way developed here. What I have tried to do in Part I is to draw on three major postmodern theorists who are not used very much by historians when considering 'the nature of their discourse'; namely, Jacques Derrida, Jean Baudrillard and Lyotard himself, in such a way as to try to kill two birds with one stone. For I hope that my use of Derrida, Baudrillard and Lyotard will serve not only to support my primary argument that meta-narrative history is so incredible that it ought to be forgotten, but will also allow me to 'introduce' Derrida *et al*. to students of history in accessible and stimulating ways. They can then inform their perspectives on 'the discourse of history and beyond' to suit their own purposes, irrespective of whether or not they accept my overall thesis.

In Part II, 'On the end of "proper" history', I look at the fatal impact postmodern theorising is arguably having on the viability of lower case (professional/academic) 'proper' history. Here the situation is not like that of the upper case and calls for a different approach. For whilst few people today defend metanarrative histories, a lot of people defend the lower case genre. Indeed, for many the collapse of metanarratives not only seems to have left lower case history intact but has bolstered its claims not to be just a genre but 'the real thing' – and to defend it as such. But I see this defence not in any way as a defence of 'history'. If it were genuinely that it would surely have to include metanarrative and 'postist' histories as interesting ways of making sense of the past which would add variety and stimula-tion for adventurous historians to open up new ways of thinking and doing things. Rather, in its bitter opposition to precisely these innovative ways of appropriating the past, it is merely an ideological/sectional defence of a particularly narrow (minded) professional code, and the fact that its defenders and champions don't much see it in this way adds only pathos to their beleaguered positions.

Now, these are very general comments and the detailed thinking behind them is unpacked in Part II of the text. But it might be useful to indicate in general terms at this early point just what it is that 'proper' historians find so threatening about postmodern critiques so that it can be kept in mind right from the start.

I think that in the end the perceived threats boil down simply to concerns about scepticism and relativism. For lower case defenders are not unaware of the power of that radical scepticism about metaphysical, ontological, epistemological, methodological and ethical foundations (anti-foundationalism) that has helped collapse the upper case, and it doesn't take much to work out that such critiques can also be applied to all of those categories when they are held in 'certaintist' lower case ways. That is to say, the critiques that have undercut the foundations to knowledge of the upper case can be applied with equal effectiveness to the lower. And second, such anti-foundationalism, when combined with relativism, unprivileges any claim that lower case history may harbour along the lines that it alone is 'proper' history. For relativism suggests that the past can be legitimately appropriated in a multiplicity of ways and for a multiplicity of purposes such that lower case historiography becomes just one more variant amongst others, a genre without a higher or a different status. Consequently, this means that anyone can have a history to suit themselves, anyone and anything – and thus 'everything' – is permitted. And it is the spaces opened up – in these democraticising days – by this kind of thinking that has allowed various types of historians and theorists, including postmodern ones ('barbarians' of varying degrees of ferocity according to Richard Evans)[14] to breach the defences of 'proper' history, a history which is now no longer seen as 'proper' at all but as just another ideological expression. Accordingly, what we now have is the ideologisation of *all* histories, such that we can begin legitimately to address to the lower case all those questions it itself likes to address to, say, the 'ideological upper case' or feminism or postmodernism, questions that in the end come down to just one: 'in whose interests?' Thus does lower case history now appear to be just one more foundationless, positioned expression of interests in a world of foundationless, positioned interests – which, of course, is what it is.

Given that this is the case, then, it may seem late in the scepticist/ relativist day still to raise one's own very time-bound, local and very peculiar craft – one's own *species* activity – to a status identical to that of its putative genus . . . and it is indeed too late. Yet if you look at what history 'really is' for people such as Geoffrey Elton, Gertrude Himmelfarb, John Tosh, J.H. Hexter, C.B. McCullagh, Lawrence Stone, Richard Evans and other defenders of the professional code you find that this is exactly what they do. For example, if one were to ask Richard Evans (as I shall be asking) what 'proper' history is, then he would and does unreflexively reply that, in effect, it's just what he does. It is the craft that he practises. To ask Evans what 'proper' history is is to invite him to produce his job description. In this way Evans *et al.* re-enact to the letter that universalising trait of all ideology, in that a sectional defence is presented as being in the interests of everybody, and that it is not *their* history that is in danger at all but history *per se*. Thus Evans *et al.* seem to be generously offering their services to everyone – a common but all too unlikely story.

It is fittingly ironic, then, that Evans *et al.* have inadvertently stumbled across what actually is the situation; that is, that it really is history *per se* that radical postmodernism threatens with extinction (a point not fully appreciated by postmodern historians themselves; I shall try to show this when I argue that we can now 'forget history' for postmodern imaginaries *sans histoire*). Of course, this doesn't mean to say that the lower case (and other histories) are already dead and buried, rather that an argument can be made that history *per se* is just slipping out of conversations; that it does not seem urgent or much to the point any more. And it is, of course, my argument that this is a *good thing*: that the optimum conditions for the creation and sustaining of history now lie behind us, and that we should now forget such configurations and embrace a non-historicising postmodernism.

It is to further this argument that Part II is thus designed. It has three sections. In the first I have chosen to critique a recent and representative polemic – *In Defence Of History* – by the aforementioned Evans. Using Evans to 'stand in for' the current state of the art, I conclude that his defence is inadequate and therefore that Evans's very typicality indicates a fatal failure in the viability and thus life of this particular genre. In the second and third sections I introduce and look at relevant aspects of the writings of Hayden White and Frank Ankersmit. Here I conclude that, adding their critiques of the lower case to my own, the genre is again radically undercut and found wanting, such that it would now be a kindness to just let it slip away in peace.

In Part III, 'Beyond histories and ethics', I examine aspects of the work of Elizabeth Deeds Ermarth and David Harlan. In her *Sequel to History: Postmodernism and the Crisis of Representational Time*,[15] Ermarth essays what it might be like to live in postmodern rhythmic *time* and thus outside of history; in temporal modes that eschew modernist (linear) histories in particular and history *per se* in general. To the question of whether or not it is possible to live outside history Ermarth's answer is an unequivocal *yes*: 'Women know – they have existed there.' To the question of whether it is possible to live outside ethics and in a relativist 'madness of the decision' morality, her answer is more qualified – but it needn't be. This is where Harlan comes in. For I want to appropriate Harlan in such a way that in his book *The Degradation of American History* he can be read as offering a way of living in morality but outside of ethics in stimulating ways. On the other hand, to the question of whether one can live outside history, Harlan's answer is still – but needn't be – too historical. Consequently, what I want to do in Part III is loosely to combine Ermarth's willingness to forget history (for new timings of time) and Harlan's happiness to forget ethics (for new moralities of ungrounded choice) so to suggest what 'living out of history but in time, and outside of ethics but in morality' might begin to look like when constructed through precisely postmodern imaginaries *sans histoire*.

Yet, although I have said it several times by now, the idea of forgetting history *per se* for postmodern imaginaries may still require further brief comment at this point; it may still ring very strange to some ears because it is still *very much* an expectation – not least amongst postmodernists – that after the end of modernity (and modernity-styled histories) we might well expect to see as a constituent of postmodernity, postmodern histories. This is the thinking that lies behind the insistent demand by modernist historians for postmodernists to explain 'what exactly would a postmodern history look like?' Because it is after all, the threat of postmodern histories superseding modernist ones that makes Evans *et al.* rush to the barricades; it is, after all, in the space created by the now withering hegemonic bulk of the lower case that, as has already been suggested, new histories – including embryonic postmodern ones – are now situating themselves. But it is my argument that to move into the future in radical, emancipatory ways, postmodern imaginaries *sans histoire* are all we need. Postmodern histories are not necessary for this task and my reasons for saying this can be put in preliminary ways thus . . .

So strong has history been in the formation of our culture, so central was its place in the bourgeois and proletarian 'experiment of modernity', that it appears as if history is almost a natural phenomenon: there is always a past so what is more natural than that there should always be histories of it. But, of course, history is not a natural phenomenon at all, and there is nothing eternal about it. In a culture, nothing cultural is, by definition, of 'a natural kind'; consequently, no discourse is anything other than a contingent phenomenon. Thus there is no need to think that *time* needs to be expressed historically. Although we apparently live in time (and time in us) the timing of time has been (and is) only articulated historically in certain kinds of social formation. So there is no reason why, in 'postist' social formations beyond modernity, 'postmodernism' need drag modernity's habit of historicising time with it. Indeed, so radioactive (a term Ermarth uses) with old upper and lower case connotations is history that to think radically 'new' it is arguably a distinct handicap still to think through categories that are 'old'. Accordingly, if an emancipatory politics is to be put onto the agenda, to cast it in the mode of a history (or to try to provide legitimations for a trajectory of a historical kind) is unnecessary. At the moment there are, as I read it, two sorts of recognisable and 'together' histories still in an (albeit moribund) existence – the old upper and lower cases. But the old upper case meta-narratives are now too decrepit and discredited to be wheeled out again; surely nobody believes in such teleological imaginaries any more. On the other hand, whilst lower case history once had – as befitted it as bourgeois ideology – emancipatory ambitions (as expressed in upper casist Whig and progressivist narratives) it has long been politically conservative, has long withdrawn from the world, has long been 'studiously academic'. Thus, broadly speaking, little in the way of emancipatory politics can really be expected of it. And so it is for this reason that, as I have noted, it looks to some as if postmodernism may well have to invent its own type of history given the uselessness of the other two – and hence the anxious query 'what will it look like?' But why need it look like anything? Why need it exist? For if postmodern critiques have shown that the past will go with anybody, if it will support everything in general and thus nothing in particular; if, moreover, historical 'knowledge' has been fatally undercut by postmodern scepticisms and relativisms and pragmatisms anyway, then not only is the question indeed raised as to what would a 'viable' postmodern history look like, but the question of why bother with one at all looks not only attractive but positively compelling; I mean, why bother historicising a past any more? Thus it will be my argument here that we might as well forget history and live in the ample imaginaries provided by postmodern type theorists (say, Roland Barthes, Michel Foucault, Gilles Deleuze, Jacques Derrida, J.F. Lyotard, Jean Baudrillard, Luce Irigary, Julia Kristeva, Gayatri Spivak, Judith Butler, Ernesto Laclau, Chantal Mouffe, Stanley Fish, Richard Rorty, Hayden White, Frank Ankersmit, Elizabeth Ermarth, David Harlan *et al.*), theorists who can provide between them enough intellectual weight to go forward *in* time but not *in* history. To be sure, such thinking about time may need to refer to what one might call 'philosophies of history', but such theorising need not be derived from, nor be predicated on (any more than it is now) the kind of historical knowledge of the past provided by empirical historians: 'theory' will come of age here then; here a postmodern, *posthistoire* future seems a desirable possibility in this construction.

The three parts of the book I have now finished describing make up the majority of its pages, and I hope that readers will see that, put together, they constitute an extended argument on the possible end of history and ethics under the impact of the postmodern – and what might possibly stem from this impact. But, as I have already mentioned, although I have tried to harmonise the three parts so as to explicate my general argument, I want to stress again that they can be read separately: as positive introductions to aspects of the work of Derrida, Baudrillard and Lyotard (in Part I), of White and Ankersmit (in Part II), and of Ermarth and Harlan (in Part III) that will be relevant to the needs of historians. Alone in this text Richard Evans appears as a negative figure, courtesy of my general thesis.

Finally I must point out that my summarising comments at the end of the book are intended, not only to rearticulate briefly some of what I have said, but to orientate the text towards the future – to beyond my present conclusions and to hint at further 'promisings'.

Such, in brief, is some of the general thinking that lies behind this book and its organisation. What now follows in this Introduction are two subdivided sections in which I enlarge upon the rather cryptically expressed assertions I have been essaying thus far. In the first section, I develop my reasons for thinking that we are now coming to the end of history and ethics and that this ending can be read positively. In the second, I explain in more detail for whom, and why, I have written this book and why the imaginaries of the postmodern should be read positively.

The first paragraph of the first section may, until I 'unpack' it, seem strange or even incomprehensible. For in it I shift into the type of discourse that Derrida and the others live in or refer to. I do so for good reason. We need to become familiar with their vocabulary right from the start so that the postmodern thinking they espouse throws into relief the rather different (and differently expressed) 'modernist' takes on history and ethics as exemplified in this text by Richard Evans.

Section 1a Locating histories

Let us begin by stipulating, then, as metaphysics, the givenness of existence (the *gift of the world*, of being) as something that just existentially is (we don't have a choice about accepting this gift). And let us say that this given, this gift-in-itself, is eternally unfathomable, sublime. Then let us stipulate ontology as the effort to bring this given within the closure of meaning, to try very precisely to make it fathomable and thus known (epistemological). Let us go on to say that this restriction, once ongoing, then performs those constant methodological and normative/ethical appropriations by which we seek to enlarge our meaning(s) until the metaphysical is exhausted, its apparent unintelligibility and indifference reduced to our discursive categories and concepts, domesticating its otherness until it finally seems to correspond to the same – to us. Then let us add that, of course, this attempted series of ontological, epistemological, methodological and ethical closures cannot ever be fully achieved. Let us add that there are always remainders, always something outside that should have been inside, a necessary supplement, an excess; that what Bataille calls the inexhaustible 'general economy' of metaphysics resists our most persistent cultural and intellectual drives towards the production and grounding of 'reality' and 'meaning' (the attempt to eliminate the excess, the surplus) within our 'productivist economy'. And then let us recognise that this struggle between the metaphysical sublime and the ontological-epistemological-methodological-ethical gestures (between the infinite general economy and the finite productivist one) constitutes at precisely one and the same time both the possibilities of meaning – which can only ever exist (as difference) in the (theoretical) space between the same and the other – and the impossibility of total meaning (full presence, self-identity, etc.). Thus we talk of the 'impossible conditions of the conditions of possibility'. We recognise that the gap between the *idea* of the thing-in-itself (the other, difference, radical alterity, the object...) and our theoretical/ metaphysical appropriations of 'it' remain, no matter how apparently close(d), infinitely and eternally open.

[handwritten marginalia:] impossible possibility ... Derrida / Booth ... "inconceivable Grace ... overcoming impossible possibility of Sin ....

Now, much of this can be put rather more simply by saying that, in a culture, 'nothing knowable is of a natural kind'. Everything to be meaning-full and productive for us has to be brought within our thinking ('our productivist economy') our logic, its excesses cordoned off and kept on the outside from whence to haunt it (haunt it with the thought of its always imperfect closures and the possible revenge of 'the other' – the outside(rs)), an economy which, to be shared, to be communicable, is necessarily coded, necessarily symbolic. Accordingly, to live *in* a culture is to live meaning-fully in and through a code, a language; it is to be literally constituted within imaginaries that produce what passes for reality such that residence in a language just is residence in reality. And this includes, of course, the imaginary of that metaphysical given/excess and whatever characteristics we performatively confer upon it; it includes the imagining of what, outside our thinking, the excess may be hypothesised as. That is to say, the 'necessary idea' of the excess is not any more 'really real' than that which inhabits the cultural inside; it is just another concept, another useful fiction, a massively productive silence. In fact, just like the (interdependent) inside it is, logically, 'anything you want it to be'.

Seen from this perspective, the *idea* of the historical past can thus be considered as just one more example of the many imaginaries we have fabricated to help us make some sense of the apparent senselessness of existence and to protect us from the possible trauma occasioned by having to face radical finitude. Of course, the past *per se* is not imagined in the sense that 'it' didn't actually occur. It did occur, and in exactly the way it did. But it is an imaginary with respect to the historical meanings and understandings, the significances and purposes it has been deemed to have for us, both as a whole and in its parts. For no matter how much we may have 'imagined' that such meanings and significances – both general and particular – have been found by us in the past, in fact the current generation of interpreters, like previous ones, constitutes the only semantic authorities there are: it is we who do the dictating in history. Put simply, we are the *source* of whatever the past means for us. Accordingly, we are now in a position reasonably to stipulate that the past as constituted by its still existing traces is always apprehended and appropriated textually through the sedimented layers of previous interpretative work(s), and through the reading habits and the categories/concepts of our previous/current methodological practices and our previous/current ideological desires. And such a worked-up historical past has rarely let us down. In its untiring availability and promiscuity, the historical past has gone along with anybody who has wanted it – Marxists, Whigs, racists, feminists, structuralists, empiricists, antiquarians, postmodernists – anybody can have it. Having no meaning-full existence independent of historians' textual embrace, being constructed by them, the past constituted as historicised text has ultimately no choice but to go along with whatever purposes are desired. Thus, in it we have almost invariably 'found' those origins, roots, teleologies, trajectories, lessons, facts and values we have been looking for. In our various historical turns (tropes) we have turned (the tropes of) contingency into necessity, the random into the patterned, and have transformed the accidental and the ephemeral into expressions of essences, continuities and inevitabilities. Historians have met few insuperable problems while giving form to the apparently formless, shape to the apparently shapeless, and narrative structure to the serendipitous, while 'straightening out' with their arguments, emplotments, tropological poetics and ideological agendas the arguably indifferent 'crookedness' of actuality, projecting on to the 'corroborated' once-occurring (yet inevitably selected) phenomena of the past, rhymes and reasons that no appropriation of them as 'raw data' could ever unproblematically suggest or sustain. It just seems to be a fact, then, that the past in its actual singularity has massively underdetermined our fertile, historicising imaginations: one past – many histories. Consequently, given that the past itself has nothing *intrinsically* historicist about it, then our various historicisations can come to stand as yet a further testimony to our human ingenuity for 'creating something out of nothing' – the story of our lives!

The historical imaginaries I am most critically interested in in this book are, as already noted, modernist upper case (metanarrative) and lower case 'proper' (professional/academic) histories. Sired and developed within the experiment of modernity (say from the late eighteenth to the late twentieth century) and shaped as normative projects in overwhelmingly bourgeois and proletarian forms, with the coming of the end of modernity so these forms – these bits of modernity – are also ending. Thus we have arrived at what might be called 'the end of history'. By this phrase I obviously do not mean that life as such is ending, nor that the past might not continue to be variously recalled. What I mean particularly is that what we are currently witnessing is the end of the very peculiar ways in which modernity conceptualised and carved up the past; the ways we made sense of it in metanarrative and lower case discursive practices; crazy, fabular ways that came to be seen in our culture as normal and, for a time, of a universal type and even 'true' . . . their time is now passing.

We should not be surprised at this sense of an ending. It has happened before. For, if I can briefly run a historical argument (whilst recognising the irony in doing so both here and at other places in this text in that, in arguing for the end of history you still – at the moment – need to employ historical arguments) historians of all stripes generally have little trouble (it is their stock in trade) in making connections between the end of an era (or 'culture' or 'civilisation') and the end of its constituent parts. For example, they generally see that, with the albeit ragged ending of, say, the classical world, classical conceptions of history ended too. They accept that with the end of the 'medieval', medieval takes on the past passed away. They accept that the types of history 'sired and developed' in the Renaissance effectively ended when it did. And so why not just as easily accept that histories constructed within and for modernity will come to an end as it does? For despite being characterised by that ideological gesture of universalising their own practices as if their species actually corresponded to its putative genus, we really ought to know better than that. No. Modernist histories are just modernist histories, are just local and very time-bound genres. Consequently, given that this is the case, if we are now beginning to live quantitatively and qualitatively postmodernist lives, I expect to see – with the transformation of the power bases that infused such histories with a relevant life – the transformation of such genres into irrelevancy and moribundity. Of course there will be resistance to such change on the part of traditional exponents of both upper case historiography – say unreconstructed Marxists – and lower case die-hards of the type aptly described as having 'reconstructionist' and 'constructionist' habits.[16] And this is what can be seen. And I also now expect to see a proliferation of 'postist' ways of representing the past ('postist' histories of a type that, still embryonic, are a kind 'that have not yet been') and arguments, such as the one I am developing here, that we can now forget the historical imagination and concentrate on a historically unburdened future.

Now, in the pages that follow, some of the particular ways in which modernist histories are being variously deconstructed will be detailed. But staying for the moment at the level of introductory remarks, it is useful to note that contemporary postmodernism is arguably a phase which is as 'concrete' a phenomenon as any empirical historian could ever wish for. Postmodernism (as signifying the best way of making sense of various expressive intellectual changes at the level of theory contingently refracting the socio-economic-political condition of our times – postmodernity) is no modish blip which will go away if it is ignored. Rather, it is the deeply disturbing removal of those protective covers, those fictive shelters that modernist historians have constructed to help keep us away from the abyss of the interminable, interpretative, relativistic flux. Ripping off the totalising carapaces of the upper case and subverting the realist, empiricist, objectivist, craft-based shibboleths of the lower case, postmodern critiques alert our consciousness, and confront us with the fabulous and fabular means by which we have tried to come to terms with the imagined 'other'. Nietzsche's argument in the timely entitled *Twilight of the Idols* – that the 'real' world has now been recognised as a fable – doesn't mean that once it wasn't but now it is fabular, or that in the future it won't be, but that it always has been and always will be the case that

> the world as such is only a fable. A fable is something which is told, having no existence outside of the tale. The world is something which is told, an event that is narrated; it is therefore an interpretation. Religion, art, science, history, are so many diverse interpretations of the world, or rather, so many variants of the fable.[17]

It is from a recognition of the fabular nature of 'our' world and the easygoing acceptance of the coming to the end of our thinking that we might know 'it' rather than our versions of 'it', that Richard Rorty can say that, whilst there may indeed be an actual 'world' underlying all such versions, we can now accept that the world is inaccessible and that versions are all we have. But that doesn't matter, since versions are all we have ever had, so that we can conclude that the putative world-before-all-versions (like the putative history-before-all-historiography) is one 'well lost'.[18] It is this easy acceptance of fabular versionality that informs so many postmodern attitudes; here is Vincent Descombes essaying just a few of them:

> there being *no original*, the model for the copy is itself a copy, and the copy is the copy of a copy; there is no *hypocritical mask*, for the face covered by the mask is itself a mask, and any mask is thus the mask of a mask; no *facts* only interpretations, and any interpretation is itself the interpretation of an older interpretation; there is no *meaning proper* to words, only figurative meanings, and concepts are therefore only dissembled metaphors; there is no *authentic version* of a text, there are only translations; no

truth, only pastiche and parody . . . If all discourse is considered to be a narrative, whoever were to claim that his discourse was absolute would invite mockery, for the properties of the narrative are as follows: (1) It has always already begun, and is always a story of a previous story; the referent of narrative discourse is never the crude fact, nor the dumb event, but other narratives, other stories; a great murmur of works preceding, provoking, accompanying and following the procession of wars, festivals, labour, time . . . (2) It is never finished, for in principle the narrator addresses a listener . . . who may in his turn become the narrator . . . Thus it is that the story (history) never ends. Or perhaps one story (one history) does; *one narrative comes to an end*, the dialectical narrative [Marxism] . . . but what power it must have had, to have hypnotised its narratees for so long![19]

Now, while the bulk of this summary of so many postmodern characteristics can be seen as forming a critique of all narratives and thus historiography *per se*, the last few lines point especially to the fatality of metanarratives after the collapse of their 'hypnotic' power. And the point I want to reiterate and develop very briefly here is that there is little doubt that the constant repetition of the way that the upper case has succumbed to critiques has given the wholly misleading impression – not least to lower case historians – that 'proper' history is unaffected by the collapse of its 'other' and thus remains intact; there is no doubt that in the bulk of the literature metanarratives are seen as postmodernists' major, and sometimes only, target. But as I have said, I think this is a profoundly mistaken view. For if postmodern critiques are really as irrelevant to lower case historians and their practices as it is sometimes said, then there is some difficulty in explaining why their champions and defenders are so hostile to them. Why should they take every opportunity to attack postmodernism, construct crude *ad hominem* criticisms against its advocates, and generally demonise it? I think the obvious reason why they do this is that postmodern critiques do impact upon the lower case and do remain unanswered. A little later in this Introduction and in detail in Part II, the poverty of those speaking on behalf of 'proper' historians will be considered. But I will now quote from Ankersmit's manifesto-like summing up of the sort of critique to which, if they can, 'proper' historians will have to attend in comprehensive detail. For these are arguments that undercut the viability of the lower case in no uncertain terms – as we shall see. For Ankersmit, then,

Narrative language has the ontological status of being . . . opaque; that it is self-referential; that it is intentional and hence . . . aestheticist; that the narrative meaning of a (historical) text is undecidable in an important sense of that word and even bears the marks of self-contradiction; that narrative meaning can only be identified in the presence of *other* meanings (intertextuality); that as far as narrative meaning is concerned the narrative text refers but not to a reality outside itself; that criteria of truth and falsity do not apply to historical representations . . . that we can only properly speak of causes and effects at the level of the statement; that narrative language is metaphorical (tropological) and as such embodies a proposal for how we should see the past; that the historical text is a substitute for the absent past; that narrative representations of the past have a tendency to disintegrate (especially when many rival representations of a past are present). All these postmodern claims, so amazing and even repulsive to the modernist [historian] can be given a . . . justification . . . I am convinced that underneath the postmodernist fat the thin man really is there and that we ought to listen to him since he can tell us a lot about the (historical) text that we do not yet know and that the modernist never bothered to tell us.[20]

Section 1b Locating the end of ethics and the morality (of the madness) of the decision

As I said in the opening paragraphs, this book is not just an argument against modernist histories but is also a welcoming of the collapse of ethical certainties, because that allows us to embrace a radically undecidable morality that is ultimately relativistic, and thus open up new possibilities. In the parts that follow I shall be spelling this out in detail, but I want now to sketch in some of the thinking behind my remarks on ethics and morality.

There are many ways of explaining how ethics (ethical systems) are currently being problematicised. Here I will outline just three examples, all of which I shall refer to later in passing. The first can best be seen as arising in the tension between elements of Judaic and Greek thought leading to the *aporia* of the moral decision, an argument particularly associated with Derrida and Levinas. The second stays much more within Greek thought as it influences the mainstream of western philosophy, and is expressed in the antagonism between two philosophical positions: foundationalist (of, say, a Platonic type) and rhetorical (of, say, a sophist type); it is an extended argument, which sees the rhetorical as currently in the ascendant, and claims that we now live in a post-foundational, rhetorical world. The third is based on arguments mainly derived from Baudrillard; namely, that loosed from 'real reality', symbolic exchange is (currently) free to construe equivalencies 'relativistically'.

Put briefly, the Judaic-Greek problematic can be expressed in the somewhat gnomic formula, 'Jewgreek is Greekjew'. What does this mean? There is an irreducible tension, an interminable struggle, between (aspects of) Jewish and Greek thought (such that the exchanges between the two are what Levinas calls 'philosophy' and Derrida 'différance').[21] The Judaic is metaphysical; it opens up an (imaginary) space which is God's and which can never be fully entered or known, or like the face of God, be depicted by humans. The Jewish God is the eternal other beyond all ontological and epistemological closures, beyond all economy (value, logic). Yet this unknowable other calls to me to act ethically towards others. How can I respond? What is required to be ethical? How do I know for sure? When called upon to make an ethical decision affecting an other, when called upon by the other to take full responsibility for my decision and all possible consequences flowing from it, how shall I act when no ultimate criteria are available? Called to an ethical act, called to a responsibility by the affected other, this 'undecidability of the decision' might be called the Jewish side of the Jewgreek dialogue.

The Greek side, simply put, is ontological and epistemological. Whereas the Jewish philosophy opens up the Event – the necessity of the decision – the only conceptual language available in which to figure a response is the Greek *logos* of reason. Unable to respond to the call of the metaphysical in anything other than the finitude of the (constructed) ontological, I find myself in a position of violence as the Greek *logos* cuts through the metaphysics of the ethical by a (moral) choice. Responding to the Jew I answer in a Greek that is 'never good enough', with no guarantee that my best will really be what the metaphysical opening requires. This dilemma is eternal. It can be called the *aporia* of the decision. A decision has to be taken in a moment of radical indecision, so ultimately taken in 'blindness'. It is a gamble, a risk, an ultimately 'mad' decision (after Kierkegaard . . . the 'madness of the (undecidable) moral decision'), one that must be taken *outside* of ethics yet *in* morality in that the singular (moral) choice, if it is to be a real choice, if it is to pass through the *aporia*, can *never* be the application of a previously existing ethical system with claims to omniscience. For if that was the case, if I merely referred back to an ethical system as some sort of code or set of rules or an algorithmic ethical formula, then no aporetic decision, no moral choice would have been made: I would merely have been applying a rule *as if* that rule knew the required 'metaphysical' response. But no code knows that. Thus for a decision to be mine it has to be, in the end, ungrounded, mad. For my decision to be a moral decision then, ethical systems cannot provide the 'moral' answer any more than the moral choice can, but the moral choice is mine, is my responsibility. Thus, for my decision to be moral it has to go through the agonies – and the ecstasies – of the *aporia*, again and again, alone; an eternity of always 'original' decisions without surety. Here ethics (ethical systems) flounder before the unique choice. It is no good having a history here to 'tell you what to do', to apply one of its 'lessons'. It is no good falling back on previous decisions as if they could provide any sort of foundation: each decision has to be marked and re-marked as a singularity – forever. My decision, then, my *logos*, is thus *différance* in that it is a response to the other which is at the same time non-renewable. The Jew's call can never be answered in full in the Greek; it exceeds the most 'total' of closures. The *logos* of reason, despite its wish for purity, totality and full presence, always has to settle for less, always has to settle for the eternal *différance* between the Jewish call and the Greek response. Thus:

> Deconstruction sees the Greek in the Jew and the Jew in the Greek. The interminable dialogue between the two, the irreducible tension between ethics and ontology and their respective contamination, the one in the other (the inevitable invagination). This curious dialogue is designated by the term *différance*: a word that here comes to signify the deconstructive [moral] project. Hence: deconstruction as the thought of différance; ethics as the thought of différance; deconstruction as ethics [morality]; ethics [morality] as deconstruction; Jewgreek is Greekjew.[22]

A second way of thinking about how it is that universal, foundational ethical systems have given way to the non-foundational 'madness of the (moral) decision' is to see our current postmodern condition as embodying, in its scepticism, pragmatism and relativism, all the *virtues* of sophist rhetoric. In his book *Doing What Comes Naturally* Stanley Fish argues that whilst there are many ways of reading the history of western philosophy, one of the most illuminating is to identify the *motif* that runs through it from the Greeks down to the present day as a fiercely engaged antagonism between foundationalism (of a Platonic type) and rhetoric (of a sophist type). Of course Fish is aware of the important differences in the way this antagonism has been conducted and the relative weight its component parts have, on occasion, exercised. Nevertheless, in Fish's view, the quarrel between foundationalism and rhetoric

> survives every sea-change in the history of Western thought, continually presenting us with the (skewed) choice between the plain unvarnished truth straightforwardly presented and the powerful but insidious appeal of 'fine language', language that has transgressed the limits of representation and substituted its own forms for the forms of reality.[23]

In that sense, goes on Fish, the quarrel between rhetorical and foundational thought is itself a foundation of a kind, in that its disagreements form the basis for disputes over the notion of the 'nature' of the human; of whether we think of ourselves as members of the category *homo seriosus* (Serious Man) or *homo rhetoricus* (Rhetorical Man):

> What serious man fears – the invasion of the fortress of essence by the contingent, the protean, and the unpredictable – is what rhetorical man celebrates and incarnates. In the philosopher's vision of the world rhetoric (and representation in general) is merely the (disposable) form by which a prior and substantiated content [such as the past] is conveyed; but in the world of *homo rhetoricus* rhetoric is *both* form and content, the manner of presentation and what is presented; the 'improving power of the rhetor' is at once all creating and the guarantee of the impermanence of its creations: to make a thing . . . just or unjust, good or bad is both a human power and a sign of the insubstantiality of these attributes. Having been made they can be [unmade] and made [up] again [everything can be morally redescribed].[24]

It is Fish's estimation that, whatever the fortunes of Serious Man versus Rhetorical Man in that long history from the Greeks down to us, today Rhetorical Man is in the ascendancy. We live today, Fish believes, in an anti-foundational, rhetorical world, a fact which, 'as a card-carrying anti-foundationalist', he welcomes. For in discipline after discipline, discourse after discourse, sceptical and relativising arguments of an anti-foundational type are 'on the upswing', an anti-foundationalism that teaches that

> questions of fact, truth, correctness, validity, and clarity, can neither be posed nor answered in reference to some extra con-textual, ahistorical, noninstitutional reality, or rule, or law, or value; rather, anti-foundationalism asserts, all of these matters are intelligible and debatable only within the precincts of the con-texts or situations or paradigms or communities that give them their local and changeable shape . . . Entities like world, language and the self can still be named; and value judgements having to do with validity, factuality, accuracy and propriety can still be made; but in *every* case these entities and values, along with the procedures by which they are identified and marshalled, will be inextricable from the . . . circumstances in which they do their work.[25]

In short, goes on Fish, in a crucial few lines (crucial in that they so lucidly and unerringly draw attention to the poverty of all *extra*-circumstantiated notions of objectivity, truth, warranted assertiability, etc., so necessary for anti-sceptical, anti-pragmatic, anti-relativist arguments),

> the very essentials that are in foundationalist discourse opposed to the local, the historical, the contingent, the variable, and the rhetorical, turn out to be irreducibly dependent on, and indeed to be functions of, the local, the historical, the contingent, the vari-able, and the rhetorical. Foundationalist theory fails, lies in ruins, because it is from the very first implicated in everything it claims to transcend.[26]

And it is not only that. What Fish thinks is abundantly clear – *and this really is a crucial insight* – is that this long-standing struggle between Serious Man and Rhetorical Man has not actually been fought out by two separate positions at all, but by two positions both of which are rhetorical. That is, what we can now see is that the seriousness of Serious Man is itself merely a rhetorical construction; that 'seriousness' is just another rhetorical trope, an affectation to help him get what he wanted to get, a persuasive device. In other words, Serious Man has himself no foundations other than those constructed locally, con-tingently, 'rhetorically', etc.; he is, like all of us, an embodiment of rhetoric such that not only are we all sophists now, but that is all we have ever been . . . there is nothing else we contingent, finite beings can be. In that sense, as Fish concludes, a sceptical and relativistic rhetoric has actually always been – and always will be – 'the only game in town'.

A third way of problematising ethics in favour of 'rhetorical morality' takes its leave from a comment by Baudrillard in *The Perfect Crime*, wherein he notes that whereas the old philosophical question used to be 'why is there something rather than nothing', today the (postmodern) question is 'why is there nothing rather than something?'[27] And this latter formulation suggests to Baudrillard (and it certainly suggests to me) that if we are bound only by the interminable circulation of 'imaginary' signs all potentially (and thus actually) equivalent to each other in that there is no-thing to stop this, then any sign can be exchanged, can be equivalent, to any other. Of course, it doesn't seem to appear this way. Indeed, productivist economies (such as our own) have gone to great lengths to conceal this. In the productivist, modernist economy, ethical value was tied to and hence 'based upon' use-value, it being held that there really were (are) knowable *intrinsic* needs, capacities, natures, human natures, species beings, etc., and that these provided a foundation, a measuring rod for discriminating between symbolic exchange. But in the postmodern 'moral' economy, postmodern thinking having thrown out every last notion of any intrinsic value that purported to entail necessary behaviour, exchange can only take place at the extrinsic level, at the symbolic level. Accordingly, reference back to any 'actuality' or knowable criteria for entailed judgement being unavailable, any 'symbol' can be exchanged for any 'other'. Thus, for example, you can, if you like, exchange love and justice for liberal democracy (make them equivalent). Or you can, if you like, exchange love and justice for fascism (make them equivalent). And it is no good asking which of these two really is 'love and justice', because it is only and precisely in the extrinsic ascribing of such values to one or the other that 'it' has a value in the first place. Things in themselves – liberal democracy or fascisms – don't have value *in* them as if value is some kind of property. No. Things are just things ('the past' is just 'the past') and we can ascribe value(s) to things (to the past) as we wish. In that sense, the referent doesn't really enter into it 'except rhetorically'; it is symbolic 'all the way down'. We may, of course, wish that all this was not the case, that there really is an unproblematical entailment between what *is* the case and what we *ought* to do; between fact and value. But despite centuries of attempts to show an entailment of this type, arguably none have been successful.

Pulling together the above three arguments, then, it seems as if the idea of ethical systems grounded in 'real' foundations, which can provide a basis for an entailment and which can then be universalised in such a way that ethical decisions can always be 'read off', is an impossible one. Accordingly, today we must all surely recognise, as Richard Rorty calmly puts it, that there never has been and there never will be, anything

> like Truth or Reason or The Scientifically-Knowable Nature of Reality towards which we need be humble, or on which we can rely for support . . . that we are as friendless, as much on our own, as the panda, the honeybee and the octopus – just one more species doing its best.[28]

Opposing this are those (including many traditional historians of varying stripes) who defend foundationalism on the basis that not to have foundations is to lose just about everything necessary for what might be called rational enquiry, common cultural endeavours and even the continued existence of 'civilisation itself'; they fail to appreciate the point that has been put variously by philosophers as different as Wittgenstein, Rorty and John Searle. The point is this: the fact that we now recognise that there never has been or will be the sorts of foundations some people once thought there were – but that we have still created *moral* discourses – means that we didn't need such foundations in the first place, and that the unending and unrewarding search for foundations can now be called off. For if Fish is right when he argues that another word for anti-foundationalism is rhetoric, and if we can say that modern anti-foundationalism is 'old sophism writ analytic', then there is no reason why for us, as for the old sophists, scepticism and relativism so construed cannot be seen as providing the *best* ways of dealing with the actuality of the finite, the contingent, and the aleatory. Let me briefly explain what I mean by the *best*.

In those sophist days before the start of the Western Tradition, the suspicion that the finite and the contingent was all that there was, the idea that the phenomenal world was the only knowable world, the understanding that the only basis for living finite lives was indeed the contingent, the aleatory ('chancy') and the ludic (playful), led to attitudes and theorisations expressed in varieties of ontological, epistemological and ethical relativisms *vis-à-vis* the significances and meanings conferred on the metaphysics of the 'given', of existence.

And why not? If from the 'events', 'evidences' and 'the facts', no non-contingent *ought* unequivocally followed; if individual, social and individual life seemed interpretable interminably; if there seemed nothing immanent in anything or anybody (indeed, if it was realised that the 'secret' of the essence of the thing-in-itself was that there was no such essence) – then no other viable conclusion seemed available other than a relativistic 'anything goes' coupled with the ultimate acceptance that 'might is right'. This was a way of looking at life that enabled one to live with such an actuality, to not worry about it, and to be relaxed.

But such an attitude was not long to be. For it is here, against these perceptions, that the Western Tradition begins, in the refusal, by Plato, to see that sort of sophism (as opposed to his own 'serious' but actually equally imaginary 'sophism') not as the *best solution* to the problematics of the finite, the contingent and the aleatory, but as *the problem*, seen now very precisely as 'the problem of scepticism and relativism still to be solved'. Accordingly, because sophists and, later and somewhat differently, pyrrhonist and other sceptical solutions for living life relativistically were not deemed to be solutions at all, so the finite world – *whose 'anti-logic' actualities Plato well recognised as providing no basis for anything other than a relativistic morality* – had to be supplemented by something 'beyond the reach of time and chance', a sort of 'infinite fix' to bring temporary/temporal 'chaos' into some kind of permanent order. Living in the shadow of Plato, the history of the Western Tradition has thus overwhelmingly been the history of various articulations of this stabilising fantasy in the guise of eternal verities expressed in the now familiar Anglicised upper case (Forms, God, Essence, Nature, Human Nature, the Categorical Imperative, Spirit, Class Struggle, Dialectic, Reason, History ...) and/or in older linguistic expressions suggesting immanence and centrings that had an invariable presence: *eidos*, *archē*, *telos*, *energeia*, *ousia* ... imaginaries all bearing down upon us bearing the insignia of *Truth*.

Whatever else it may have done, postmodern anti-foundationalism has ended the plausibility of such absolute thinking. We are now well aware that there never has been nor ever will be any access to any kind of extra-discursive transcendental signifier, full presence or omniscient narrative/narrator. In fact, today the imaginaries of the anti-relativist Western Tradition have become so unpacked that we are effectively back at the beginning again – rhetorical neo-sophists *après* Fish. In an interesting kind of reversal, we postmodernists are, as it were, now *pre*-Western Traditionalists, *pre*-Kantians, *pre*-

Hegelians, *pre*-Marxists, *pre*-modernists, in that the attempts to put us in touch with various foundations having failed, we now have to face, at the end of the Western Tradition, the same metaphysical/existential situation the sophists faced before it began. Accordingly, we now have the chance to consider contemporary, sophistical rhetorical (sceptical/relativist) takes on these problems very precisely as *solutions* and – and I want to underline this point – *not* as 'problems still to be solved': that scepticism and relativism are not problems at all, but the *best* solutions we can come up with. And if we accept this, then it seems to me that we are in good company, that we can live alongside a whole range of pre/postmodernists – Barthes, Derrida, Baudrillard, Lyotard, Fish, Rorty, Butler *et al.* – 'no problem'.

Besides, our foundationalist desires have caused us too many problems, not least in modernity. For one way of writing the history of modernity is to write it not as the working out of the 'Enlightenment project' but *also* (and this partly accounts for its 'failure') as the history of the European nation state, perhaps the most efficient (rational) killing-machine that has ever existed, a killing-machine that includes amongst its manifestations the actuality of the Holocaust – that supreme, *modern* event. Accordingly, as Rorty points out to all who argue that neo-pragmatism and postmodernism gives us no absolute basis upon which to resist fascists and neo-Nazis, a modernist or any other type of absolutist thinking won't do the job either, simply because all absolutes can be claimed by just anybody and thus relativised with ease. Thus says Rorty:

> anti-pragmatists [and anti-postmodernists] fool themselves when they think that by insisting that moral truths are objective – are true independent of human needs, interests, history – they have provided us with weapons against the bad guys. For the fascists can, and often do, reply that they entirely agree that moral truth is objective, eternal and universal . . . [and fascist]. Dewey made much of the fact that traditional notions of 'objectivity' and 'universality' were useful to the bad guys, and he had a point.[29]

This is not to say, adds Rorty immediately, that such inability to answer the 'bad guys' occurs because pragmatism (or relativism) is a wicked or inadequate position, but philosophy is just not the right weapon to reach for when all discursive/conversational attempts have failed and when 'might is right' raises its head. For when opposing *beliefs* face each other, reason and argumentation will only take you so far – which is never as far as either side wishes to go. For it is possible, when facing a foundationalist adversary, to proffer a range of arguments all of which one's opponent can (maybe reluctantly) admit as correct, yet still believe that 'they are right', or that they 'just do not care what you say'. And this is because the best definition of a belief is exactly something that argument cannot reach; a belief *is* a belief by being very precisely 'beyond reason'. If anything is 'irrational' in this area, then, it is not postmodernists who recognise the inevitable *aporetic* moment when you have to make a choice between two incommensurable positions both of which are held by their proponents to be 'true' (the precise condition of Lyotard's *différend*). Rather, the irrationalism is of foundationalists who still think that there actually are foundations that all can/must agree on, and that *the* truth will win out. Clinging to a foundationalism that cannot work at the very moment when you need it to (the moment of *aporia*) really is absurd, so, in that sense, we might as well admit that we are 'all relativists now'. Again, Rorty spells it out:

> Pragmatists think that any ... philosophical grounding is ... as a wheel that plays no part in the mechanism. In this, I think, they are quite right ... No sooner does one draw up a categorical imperative for Christians than somebody draws one for cannibals ... [Accordingly, since] the time of Kant, it has become more and more apparent ... that a really professional philosopher can supply a philosophical foundation for just about anything.[30]

Scepticism and relativism, then, just do seem to be things we can accept and live with happily and self-consciously, just as the old sophists did and postmodern rhetorical sophists do – there doesn't seem to be any foundational alternative; this is what our 'self-consciousness' realises. Accordingly, it is for these kinds of reasons that I think that we can now begin to indeed live *out* of history and ethics and *in* time and morality in relaxed and, I hope, emancipatory ways.

Section 2a Structuring the text: detail

To summarize. Unable to refer meaningfully to anything beyond its own performativity (the 'object' of discourse is only ever the subject's discourse objectified/objectifying), thought has to be content with simulating its objects of attention, analysis and critique to become, in the end, auto-analysis, auto-critique. For notions of truth, the 'real', history and so on are not somehow naturally 'pre-formed' and attendant upon the viewer's gaze but are the product of that gaze. With no access to extra-discursive validity or to any natural/neutral points of reference, all discourse is bound to self-referential simulacra and to the realities (the effect of the real) that come out of it. Containing, as it does, all discourse, this human condition obviously incorporates morality too in its radical contingency and historicising.

Now, what this arguably adds up to is not only the end of modernity's dream of transparent knowledge beyond that of an ultimately rhetorical, endless conversation, but the possibility of new thoughts free of the shackles of history and ethics. For those reluctant even seriously to contemplate this, these endings may seem equivalent to a 'real' crisis. But given that facts (such as these types of ending) cannot entail how they *ought* to be valued, then this same situation can also be described as an opportunity: the beginning of an exciting adventure (or something else...). Accordingly, in this text I have chosen to reject the idea of there being a postmodern crisis in favour of a potentiality that might sustain radical, emancipatory politics (in place of something else). And one reason for going with *this* choice is that postmodernism offers the radical historian the space to write about the past legitimately looking at it through different lenses (post-feminist, post-structuralist, post-Marxist, etc.). The result is the production of reflexive histories that expose the ideological usages of objectivity, unbiasedness and balance (putative properties of both upper and lower case histories) and, openly partisan, signal and flag their (sometime confessional) standpoints. These are, if you like, 'histories that have come out'. And I think of these reflexive histories as being advances on previous modernist histories, it being productions of this type that I tried to discuss and advocate as appropriately as I could in *Rethinking History*, in *On 'What Is History?'* and in *The Postmodern History Reader*.[31] But as I have now said repeatedly, I no longer feel that this position really faces up to, nor exploits, the further challenges postmodern theorising can be construed as offering and that, to say it again, it may now be possible and desirable to think of non-historical timings of time and of relativistic, *aporetic* moralities.

Yet if this text shifts the agenda somewhat from previous concerns, the main audience for it remains pretty much the same. This is not meant to be a text for 'insiders'. It is not for, say, experienced Derrideans, Baudrillardians, Lyotardians or Ermarthians, nor for seasoned scholars of White, Ankersmit or Harlan. It is a text written primarily to be a popular and accessible introduction to an important aspect of our postmodern condition, for history undergraduates, post-graduates and their teachers, such that it might prove useful for courses on, say, 'the nature of the discourse of history today'; in that sense it has pedagogic intentions. Consequently, one of the main tasks I have set myself here – to try and make attractive the sorts of shifts and possibilities discussed in this Introduction and which express the 'position' of the book – will be done through a series of popularising readings of the ideas of often 'difficult' theorists so as to put them on the agenda for discussion. It is in this sense that I spoke before of the parts of this book as being relatively autonomous introductions to Derrida *et al.* irrespective of whether or not its general thesis is considered plausible.

I think that such an introduction to Derrida and other theorists is essential nowadays even if, as I say, the 'spin' I have given them here may be deemed not to be. For despite history being – like every other discourse given that no discourse is of a natural kind – 'theoretical all the way down', and despite 'history theory' coming on apace since the late 1980s as the crisis/opportunity postmodernism creates for historiography is increasingly recognised, history students are still not as well served by theoretical texts as are their contemporaries studying literature, architecture, cultural studies, philosophy and so on; there the names and works of, say, Barthes, Foucault, Lacan, Derrida, Baudrillard, Lyotard, Levinas, Kristeva, Irigary, Judith Butler, Richard Rorty, Gianni Vattimo and others (along with such forerunners as Nietzsche and Heidegger) are not met with the sort of hostility, indifference or incomprehension they generally receive from most 'proper' historians. Thus one of the 'subsidiary' objectives here is to try to show how Derrida *et al.* are relevant to history *per se* and why they might be considered whenever and wherever 'history' is being considered. Through this book I would like to make postmodern theorisations a commonplace in everyday discussions of history, time, ethics and morality. This may not be exactly revolutionary but it is arguably a useful and achievable ambition which fits inside my 'own' overall 'polemic'.

Section 2b On the postmodern imaginary

It is ironic that historians – who claim to know a lot about the conditions under which changes take place and who often argue that one of the main reasons why they study the past is that it helps us understand 'what is going on in the world today' – are amongst the last to spot those contemporary shifts that are actually bringing their own discourse to its end. It is understandable that people variously interested in history might think that everybody else ought to be, and that what is good for them is good for us all. But what is particularly myopic is for them to think not only that their particular way of looking at the past is essential, but that it also somehow escapes the ageing and displacing processes that affect everything. This seems to be one of the very few 'lessons' we really can learn from the past (and the present); that is, nothing is unequivocally 'proper' and nothing lasts for ever. Things just do move on. For example, it must have seemed to late nineteenth-century Christian theologians that a secular social formation was both unthinkable and undesirable; to late nineteenth-century classicists that Latin and Greek were – and always would be – fundamental disciplinary constituents of any 'educated man'. But today that undesirable/unthinkable condition is our everyday life, and Latin and Greek are simply forgotten when curricula are being discussed. Once elements at the centre of our culture, they have now been left behind. Similarly, I don't think that it is too fanciful to imagine that, two hundred years from now, in social formations that have developed new imaginaries which are apt for them, modernist upper and lower case histories which once played such a central role for 'us' won't much function for them, or even at all, and that a genre of discourse which – curiously and sadly it may come to seem if anybody bothers to recall it – some amongst us thought might last forever was, in fact, just a local, temporary phenomenon which postmodernists (and others) started taking apart in the latter decades of the twentieth century.

This sort of future-gazing is, of course, always a hostage to fortune. It might turn out that, whilst modernist histories really are being subverted by postmodern critiques, postmodernism may have a short shelf-life. Certainly it won't last forever! But even if it is a most temporary phenomenon, I still think that while postmodernist texts are still literally on the shelf, historians ought to engage with them critically, because, as intellectuals, if they do not do so then they are turning their backs on what is arguably one of the most momentous events in the history of intellectual endeavour.

This is a big claim which might need some explanation; mine goes like this. It could plausibly be said that postmodern theorising – leaving aside for the moment what its impact might be on history and ethics – represents one of the most concentrated outpourings of intellectual vitality in the 'history of the West'. The Western Tradition, stretching back over at least two and a half thousand years, produced in that time some fifteen to twenty intellectual giants; seminal figures.

Their names are well known, inscribed as they are in our culture, from Plato and Aristotle through to Aquinas, Descartes, Kant, Mill, Marx *et al.* Today it is possible to draw up another list of some fifteen to twenty intellectuals who, aided by the odd modernist precursor (Nietzsche, Wittgenstein, Heidegger ...) have, in the space of just thirty or forty years, undermined, reworked and gone beyond the whole of that Western Tradition. Again their names are familiar: Barthes, Foucault, Lacan, Derrida, Lyotard, Rorty *et al.* But it is the phrase 'in the space of thirty or forty years' that is important. For what we have here – occupying different positions but all capable of being put under the rubric of 'postist' discourse – is the phenomenon of publicly available intellectual brilliance. In that sense we are lucky, we late twentieth-century lesser mortals, to be alive in this culture to witness this. Accordingly, it seems almost incomprehensible that some people – including so many historians – can shrug off this probably unrivalled phenomenon of condensed intellectuality and, if they are 'interested in it at all', pejoratively dismiss some of its exponents as second- or third-rate minds,[32] as 'mere theorists'. Would they do that, do they do that with Plato, Descartes, Kant and Marx? Well, maybe they do!

This is definitely not to say that such 'postist' theorising should be uncritically accepted, least of all by those who can see much virtue in it. But to turn one's eyes from it, to close one's mind to it, to not be intellectually curious about this phenomenon so obviously alive and kicking in our social formation – despite how it might affect one's own life and work – seems to give at least a local lie to George Steiner's assertion that, though curiosity may well kill cats, we humans cannot – and must not – resist opening Bluebeard's 'seventh door'.

To return to the content of this text. Engaged with or not by historians, postmodernism seems to be a vehicle through which, at the end of the experiment of modernity, *a little bit of newness is entering our world*. Of course, as left-wing critics of postmodernism (say Jameson, Eagleton, Norris, Bhaskar) very correctly point out, the phenomena of postmodernity and postmodernism have emerged out of, and as integral parts of, the exigencies of late-capital, and do indeed provide it with at least a major part of that 'cultural logic' such late-capital needs. As the title of Jameson's famous text says, postmodernism *is* the cultural logic of capitalism; capitalism *is* culturally postmodernist.[33] Of course. And that actual situation – capitalism – may well mean that 'postist' discourses will not after all bear fruit in emancipatory politics. Of course. But on the other hand, capitalism is only 'contingently' postmodernist. Postmodernism doesn't *belong* to capital; it is not simply *a* or *the* property of capital. Capitalism's history seems to be characterised as one long episode of unintended consequences, of which the phase of 'modernity' has been no exception. If Lyotard is right – that modernity has been a social formation that has been able to control enormously high levels of contingency – postmodernity may usher in a phase when that is not the case. We'll have to see. But in the meantime, postmodernism, construed radically, at least offers the possibility of keeping emancipatory thought alive. For it is at least possible that postmodern critiques and imaginaries may provide enough resources for a newness that is not a mere replication of the old, and which cannot be recuperated by a capital that is now too late to still be modern. And such new imaginaries – of surprising things 'to come' – may well not include in their number history and ethics as we have got to know them, or even include them at all.

I'm afraid "late capital" is not "too late" but only the 'latest'... for an active flows ... a certain "spirit" — 'power' that most uncannily, resides in a host of postmodern sites or, perhaps, the parasite, the virus of the 21st century ... of which Revelation may have been pointing to or ... The Beast ... — the whore! ... the Anti-Christ !!

Part I

On the end of metanarratives

As outlined in the main Introduction, the purpose of this Part is to examine aspects of the works of Jacques Derrida, Jean Baudrillard and Jean-François Lyotard in such a way that they can be construed as helping to undercut metanarrative history and traditional ethics and as semi-autonomous introductions for new history readers. I also want to suggest, in passing, some of the collateral damage the overturning of metanarratives inflicts upon lower case 'proper' history, and to start to assess some of the opportunities that might be opened up 'after history and ethics'. These opportunities will be put more positively here than perhaps is allowed by the idioms adopted by Derrida, Baudrillard and (to a lesser extent) Lyotard.

1 On Jacques Derrida

I begin with Derrida. This is not an easy place to start. Derrida is a
phenomenally prolific writer and he has attracted literally thousands
of expositors, commentators and critics (though few of these are historians). Accordingly, the enormity of the 'Derrida industry', the sometime difficulty of its textual productions, and the occasional presence
of 'Derrideans' whose purism can inhibit the sort of 'creative reading'
gone in for by, say, Richard Rorty, makes the short, popularising and
appropriative approach undertaken here fraught with dangers.

Nevertheless, an approach, a style and a start has to be made somehow, and in choosing one I have been influenced by an (almost) throw-
away remark by Simon Critchley in his *The Ethics of Deconstruction*.[1]
Commenting (in parenthesis) on the 'undecidable hesitation' in so
much of Derrida's work, Critchley remarks how such qualifications
are missing in the straightforward 'Afterword' of *Limited Inc.*,
which makes him go on to wonder about the status of this text and
about those of its genre – interviews, transcribed debates, conversations – upon which so much of his own interpretation of Derrida
actually relies. Are they, asks Critchley, 'properly speaking deconstructionist' or are they political or critical texts? And, whatever they are,
why does Derrida put things so clearly and unambiguously in an
apparently 'non-deconstructive mode' when he seems unable to do
so (or refuses to do so) in a 'deconstructive' one?[2]

Now, Critchley's comments seemed pertinent to me because I had
also been struck when reading Derrida (and also, in fact, when reading
Baudrillard and Lyotard) by how 'transparent' they all appeared to be
in talking about what they were doing, about where they stood politically, and about what effects they hoped their writings would have
when being interviewed for example, and yet how hesitant, cautious
and qualificatory they were about 'committing themselves' in their
actual texts. Accordingly, because in this book I want to put forward

a popularisation of Derrida *et al.* so to introduce and make accessible some of their ideas to students of history, Critchley's own use of such 'direct' sources seemed to help justify the way I also wanted to write about them. That is, I wanted to write about them pretty much *at the level of the interview throughout.* Consequently, this decision about approach and style and register taken, I then decided to base my reading of Derrida on his remarkably frank *Remarks on Deconstruction and Pragmatism*, which were given in response to papers by Richard Rorty and others at a symposium held in Paris in 1993.[3] Three 'remarks' from Derrida's paper – which I shall quote at length (having slightly 'contextualised' them) – are thus used here to establish what I argue is a 'Derridean position', a position I then go on to develop. Derrida's 'three remarks' are as follows.

First Remark. Derrida admits that the way 'deconstruction' can be put to work is multifarious (given that it is an empty mechanism, an always 'unstable motif' which can be used legitimately to 'serve quite different political purposes' and is in that sense 'politically neutral' ('anyone can have it')). Nevertheless, Derrida hopes that 'as a man of the left', deconstruction

> *will* serve to politicise or repoliticise the left with regard to positions which are not simply academic. I hope – and if I can continue and contribute a little to this I will be very content – that the political left in universities in the United States, France and elsewhere, will gain politically by employing deconstruction . . . Deconstruction is hyper-politicising in following paths and codes which are clearly not traditional . . . that is, it permits us to think the political and think the democratic by granting us the space [to do so].[4]

Second Remark. Derrida is clear as to the workings of this 'deconstructionist hope':

> All that a deconstructive point of view tries to show, is that since convention, institutions and consensus are stabilizations (sometimes stabilizations of great duration, sometimes micro-stabilizations) . . . this means that they are stabilizations of something essentially unstable and chaotic. Thus, it becomes necessary to stabilize precisely because stability is not natural [*sic*]; it is because there is instability that stabilization becomes necessary. Now, this chaos and instability, which is fundamental, founding and irreducible, is at once naturally the worst against which we

struggle with laws, rules, conventions, politics and provisional hegemony, but at the same time it is a chance, a chance to change, to destabilize. If there were continual stability, there would be no need for politics, and it is to the extent that stability is not natural, essential or substantial, that politics exists and ethics [morality] is possible. Chaos is at once a risk and a choice, and it is here that the possible and the impossible cross each other.[5] *See* BARTH!

Third Remark. Derrida thinks that it thus 'follows' that he must be against absolute notions of foundational ethics that can legislate on choice for everybody and 'for ever and ever', and that he must favour interminable moral decisions. He must favour the 'undecidability of the decision', that *aporetic* moment all decisions have to go through to even begin to be moral at all (or even to be a decision *per se*) and which would make even the most desired closures only temporary stabilisations:

Every time I decide if a position is possible, I invent the who, and I decide who decides what . . . That is why I would say that the transcendental subject is that which renders the decision impossible. The decision is barred when there is something like a transcendental subject. In order to take things a bit further I would say that if duty is conceived of as a simple relation between the categorical imperative and a determinable subject, then duty is [the moral aporia is] evaded. If I act in accordance with duty in the Kantian sense, I do not [morally] act and furthermore I do not act in accordance with duty . . . I believe that we cannot give up upon the concept of infinite responsibility . . . if you give up on the infinitude of responsibility [by obeying an 'in place' ethics/rule/code] there is no responsibility. It is because we live and act in infinitude that the responsibility with regard to the other (*autrui*) is irreducible. If responsibility were not infinite . . . [chaotic whilst awaiting the next temporary settlement] you could not have moral and political problems. There are only moral and political problems . . . from the moment when responsibility is not limitable . . . And this is why undecidability is not a moment to be traversed and overcome. Conflicts of duty – and there is only duty in conflict – are interminable and even when I take my decision and do something, undecidability is not at an end. I know that I have not done enough and it is in this way that morality continues.[6]

This interminable indeterminacy of the moral decision thus means (for Derrida, and for Levinas whom at this point in his *Remarks* Derrida is following) that one always keeps open the possibility of difference, of newness, of surprise, of politics, of an infinite excess of possibilities; of the 'to come'; of the 'perhaps'; of freedoms beyond every attempted (contingent) closure of that 'natural chaos' that is our lot. Derrida is thus, as he says, a *quasi-transcendental* thinker in the sense that he refuses 'absolutely . . . a discourse that would assign me a single code, a single language game, a single context, a single situation; and I claim this right not simply out of caprice . . . but for ethical [moral] and political reasons'. For the notion of the quasi-transcendental, of that imagined metaphysical excess beyond all determinate discursive practices, is what keeps the promise of some 'newness entering the world' on the agenda. It is a newness about which Derrida has political and moral preferences and which, while not performing an impossible to accomplish closure is still the 'best' (the weakest, the least violent) sort of basis for living that Derrida can conceive of, the sort of basis in *différance* that might engender a certain type of human friendship (*aimance*). Derrida seems very clear on this:

> Something that I learned . . . from Husserl in particular, is the necessity of posing transcendental questions in order not to be held in the fragility of an incompetent empiricist discourse, and thus it is in order to avoid empiricism, positivism and psychologism that it is endlessly necessary to renew transcendental questioning . . . This is not the dream of a beatifically pacific relation, but of a certain experience of friendship, perhaps unthinkable today and unthought within the [history of] . . . the West. This is a friendship, what I sometimes call an *aimance*, that excludes violence; a non-appropriative relation to the other . . . I am very sentimental and I believe in happiness; and I believe that this has an altogether determinate place in my work . . . [Yet] I do not believe that the themes of undecidability or infinite responsibility are romantic . . . the necessity for thinking to traverse interminably the experience of undecidability can, I think, be quite coolly demonstrated in an analysis of the [moral] . . . or political decision . . . [Consequently] I refuse to denounce the great classical discourse of emancipation. I believe that there is an enormous amount to do . . . Even if I would not wish to inscribe the discourse of emancipation into a teleology, a metaphysics, an eschatology, or even a classical messianism, I none the less believe that there is no [moral] political decision or gesture without what I would

call a 'Yes' to emancipation . . . and even, I would add, to some messianicity . . . a messianic structure that belongs to all language. There is no language without the performative dimension of the promise . . .

Do you promise . . . to love me
. . . Forever !!?

Thus, continues Derrida:

when I speak of democracy to come this does not mean that democracy will be realised, and it does not refer to a future democracy, rather it means that there is an engagement with regard to democracy which consists in recognising the irreducibility of the promise when, in the messianic moment, 'it can come' . . . there is the future. . . . there is something to come . . . that can happen . . . This is not utopian, it is what takes place here and now . . . And from this point of view, I do not see how one can pose the question of [morality] . . . if one renounces the motifs of emancipation and the messianic. Emancipation is once again a vast question today and I must say that I have no tolerance for those who – deconstructionist or not – are ironical with regard to the grand discourse of emancipation. This attitude has always distressed and irritated me. I do not want to renounce this discourse.[8]

Now these three 'remarks' are, as I say, remarkably clear statements on Derrida's general position; I have given them at length so that they can almost be left (but not quite) to speak for themselves. For on the basis of them I will now move gradually towards Derrida's importance for critiques of metanarrative histories seen very precisely as 'closures' (and the implications of this for all certaintist histories). I want also to address, via his notion of the 'undecidability of the (moral) decision', the development of his ideas about the openness of future *times* which offer in their emancipatory claims a move towards 'the impossible to actually achieve' but beckoning idea of Justice. These ideas are about a future *beyond* '*historical closures*' *in whatever case*, and of new moralities beyond ethical systems, moralities that do not take responsibility (in the face of the other) away. With Derrida's 'remarks' kept firmly in mind, then, let us begin by looking at Derrida's theory of 'natural language', which, I think, underpins his views on language *per se*, binary oppositions, textuality, the historical and the political.

For I take Derrida's talk of 'natural actuality' as being 'chaotic' to include as a constituent part of it the phenomenon of language. Consequently, I think it is possible to read Derrida as having what might be called (following his own perhaps surprising invocation of the 'natural') a theory of *natural language* which, because it is necessarily part of the 'chaotic', has itself this characteristic. For Derrida, then, 'by its nature' language is permanently unstable (chaotic) and never self-sufficient (identical to itself) in terms of words (signifiers) whilst, in larger linguistic constructions, it is never meaningful in itself outside of contexts – and you can always get another context. Thus, to start developing this by way of an example, if you take the word (the signifier) 'iterability' and ask somebody who has never met it before what it might mean, no knowing answer could be forthcoming. And if the person asked then went to a dictionary to look it up and the entry was effectively self-explanatory (i.e. identical to itself) so that it simply read 'iterability = iterability', then the person would still be no wiser. And this is because for Derrida (as for Saussure) words (signifiers) only mean something relative to other signifiers. They always need supplementing by other signifiers; they always depend on the presence of other signifiers that are different from them (that are *not* them). Thus, as Simon Critchley has pointed out (and I follow him intermittently for a while here), meaning only arises in so far as it is inscribed in a systematic chain of different signifiers such that this 'play of differences' (which is constitutive of meaning) actually is constitutive of what Derrida calls *différance* itself. As Critchley explains:

> This is why *différance* is neither a word nor a concept, but rather the condition of possibility for conceptuality and words as such. *Différance* is the playing movement that produces the differences constitutive of words and conceptuality. There is no presence outside or before semiological difference . . . all languages or codes [are] constituted as and by a weave of differences. This is what Derrida means when he claims that 'It is because of *différance* that the movement of signification is possible' . . . [so that] each 'present' element in a linguistic system signifies in so far as it differentially refers to another element [which] . . . is not itself present. The sign [is thus] a 'trace', a past that has never been present. The present is constituted by a differential network of traces. In order for the present to be present, it must be related to something non-present, something *différant*.[9]

Now, this something that is 'absent' but the trace of which is necessary for the signifier to signify anything, is an absence not just in a spatial sense (i.e. in the sense that it doesn't occupy the same space in the chain of signifiers as the actually 'present' signifier) but also in a temporal sense (in that the meaning of a signifier is always deferred until another appropriate signifier 'arrives'), it being this space–time structure that Derrida calls 'archi-writing', which, as articulated in his *Of Grammatology*, opens up a 'new way' of generalising 'writing in difference' as the condition of possibility of language itself. Here is Critchley explaining this:

> The grammatological space of a general writing, that in which experience is possible, is the space of what Derrida calls 'le texte en général'. . . . a limitless network of differentially ordered signs which is not preceded by any meaning, structure, or *eidos*, but itself constitutes each of these. It is here, upon the surface of the general text, that . . . deconstruction takes place.[10]

Now, I shall shortly develop Derrida's idea of the 'general text', its connections to 'context', including his (in)famous phrase 'there is nothing outside the text' (or better still, 'there is nothing outside con-text'). But more immediately I want to reformulate Critchley's summary of Derrida's position by saying that we can now see why no signifier is a meaningful island unto itself any more than any event or context or person is, and begin to see its implications. For people, like events and contexts, need other people to define themselves against; their identities come from outside themselves, and construct and deconstruct themselves in interminable trans-actions relative to interminably different contexts ('history never repeats itself'); these are never, in turn, definitively circumscribed.

Similarly, linguistic (and thus social) meanings are always performed 'relativistically' in the play of differences without end – without definitive closure – such that a total(ised) meaning is always deferred: you can always get another signifier. For meanings get grafted first on to one signifier then another, live parasitically off one another; get dubbed and re-dubbed, mixed and re-mixed, cited and re-cited, sometimes in relatively systematic ways and for lengthy periods (*Second Remark*: 'sometimes stabilizations of great duration'), sometimes not (*Second Remark*: 'sometimes micro-stabilizations'). New chains of signification come into the world fresh with new couplings, including metaphors of an emancipatory type: of future possibilities, of democracy to come. Consequently, it is this interminable, re-inscribing flux (i.e. iterability) that keeps open new possibilities never fully described and thus never fully satiated because full-presence, total self-identity is – short of our becoming God –

EXACTLY !!

impossible. And all of this 'political stuff' is arguably derived from Derrida's view of 'nature' and 'natural language' as being 'chaotic', to which he takes the (political) attitude that language *ought* to be kept loose and playful and 'chaotic' if one wants to be in a condition of non-totalising/non-totalitarian freedom. For Derrida, to long for a fixed meaning, for absolute certainty, to crave the Truth, is to wish for the end of enquiry; for death.

Accordingly, it seems Derrida's desire for a certain kind of democratisation of life makes him come to the decision to 'choose' to valorise interminable semantic flux as *natural*. So it might be said that he holds as natural what might be called a *horizontal* (democratic/egalitarian) 'surface' theory of language, *in that the endlessly circulating signifiers have nothing in them of a vertical kind which could, under their own volition, stop their incessant play.* In which case, anything that might stop this play is – whether relatively temporary or relatively permanent – an arbitrary blockage; natural chaos (play) is violated by fixity. To be sure, Derrida knows that to get around in the world 'we' need some fictive stabilisations to (albeit imperfectly) occur (*Second Remark*: 'thus it becomes necessary to stabilize precisely because stabilization is not natural'). But it is the task of deconstruction constantly to deconstruct such *verticals of authority* so to restore – despite the risk (*Second Remark*: 'chaos is at once a risk and a choice') – language to its 'natural', horizontal, egalitarian/democratic possibilities. For of course deconstruction is, as Derrida has always (but lately much more explicitly and persistently) said, a political project, in that the deconstruction of the verticals of (linguistic) authority is necessary given that such verticals underwrite (legitimate) socio-economic verticality (hierarchies), and especially those of western elitism. As a democratic 'man of the left', on the reading that I am 'making' here, it is easy to see why Derrida deconstructs every logocentric/phallologocentric closure he meets; why his deconstructivist play problematises every (fixed) essence, every notion of immanence, every Truth ('the first and last word') and thus every *binary opposition, the 'empty mechanism' that works to freeze over the natural flow of the contingent and the aleatory.*

Now, Derrida's deconstruction of the weft and weave of variously attempted vertical closures and stabilisations through binary oppositions cannot be detailed here. But the deconstruction of binary oppositions can perhaps be briefly introduced and summarised in ways that, if not always to Derrida's own letter, cast light on the sometimes 'rigid designation' of history by some historians and which history students ought to be aware of in general terms. What then, in this context, are ① binary oppositions; ② how does Derrida deconstruct them; and ③ to reiterate the political point already made but to push it along a little, why does he do so and what are the implications for history and ethics *vis-à-vis* 'time and morality'? Three questions, then, to be addressed in that order.

First, then, what are binary oppositions? Well, Derrida can be read as arguing – again to recap for a moment – that binary oppositions are the main way in which naturally horizontal (democratic) free-playing signifiers are congealed into the verticals of authority. Thus, for example, Derrida sees (western) meanings fixed in binary oppositions wherein the first term in the binary is privileged over the 'supplementary' second term. And so we have – to rehearse some of the more common ones – such binaries as masculine–feminine, heterosexual–homosexual, white–black, rationalism–irrationalism, mind–body, reason–emotion, knowledge–opinion, reality–illusion, subject–object, true–false, etc. And, moving into the discourse of history, it is binary oppositions that work to define and give characteristics to the upper and lower cases (the upper case *versus* the lower or the lower case *versus* the upper relative to one's preferences, being themselves binary oppositions). Thus with regard to a reading that would privilege the upper case, the following sort of binaries (with the first term always being the 'privileged' one) often goes as follows: absolute–relative, true–false, deductive–inductive, necessary–contingent, rational–irrational, etc., whilst within (and favouring) the lower case, the following are routinely juxtaposed: objective–subjective, balanced–unbalanced, fact–interpretation, realist–anti-realist, empiricist–idealist, neutral–ideological, professional–amateur, etc.

Now, such binary oppositions, once established, are hierarchically ordered in a process of superimposition, are 'piled up' vertically so that the dominant primary terms are typically put together and thus become associated. To give some very brief examples: in terms of general binaries the members constitutive of the privileged first term of every binary are superimposed on to each other to form a norm so that, for instance, what is privileged is not just masculinity but also heterosexuality, whiteness, rationality, truth and so on. Similarly, in the case of history, exponents of the upper case privilege histories that cluster together that which is absolutist, deductive, teleological, necessary, true, rational, etc., while in the lower case that which characterises 'proper' history is that which is objective, balanced, unbiased, factual, empirical, inductive, professional, etc., and the acceptance and further detailed working of such associations thus allows us to tell good histories from bad, the real from the fake, and the genuine from the ideological, with few problems. Or at least, there are few problems *if* we accept that the way that the binaries are set up are not always already themselves ideological verticals of authority – which of course they are. Consequently, because we can see very clearly now that binary oppositions are not of a natural kind, such artificial constructions can be quickly deconstructed in ways that expose those for whom they work. So to the second question: how does Derrida deconstruct such binaries?

It may appear that perhaps all you have to do is to relativise the binaries by reversing them, by privileging (or making equal) the unprivileged second term (so that the feminine is equal to the masculine, black is equal to white, etc.). But this, though a start, is not the way deconstruction works, for such reversals leave the binary *form* – and thus the oppositional thinking it engenders – intact. So, what do you do? Well, at least two things. First, you point out that there are a lot of cases (in fact it can be said that all cases are ultimately of this type) that are, strictly speaking, undecidable. Thus, you might point out that, actually, it is not at all clear what the characteristics of the masculine as opposed to the feminine 'really' are, that in fact what stereotypically pass for the feminine are characteristics that men have too – and vice versa. You point out that, in fact, it is by no means obvious what is necessary and what is contingent, or what is fact and what is interpretation, or what is disinterested scholarship and what is ideologically positioned, or what is inside and what is outside of any context. Consequently, in this way what may have initially appeared to be clear-cut binary oppositions become merely different ways of looking at things; matters of taste, style, stress, position. This is not to say such first term/second term (supplementarities) will not always have to exist, for this is the way language works (terms always have to be supplemented by what they are not in order to be anything, no signifier is an island, etc.), but what is 'arguably' *unnatural* is the *privileging* of one term over another as part of a *vertical* series as if such a series were 'natural'. It is in this sense that Derrida is against 'dualistic' thinking, a thinking that he frees up in order to think *différance*. In that sense, Derrida is not against 'binaries' but against 'binary oppositions' as 'natural' or 'fixed' hierarchically. This, then, is the first deconstructive move; the second is closely related and complements it.

It is Derrida's point that you can only hold together a stable first identity like masculinity, by displacing on to the second, feminine identity all those characteristics the masculine might want to regard as 'other'. Thus, the masculine typically displaces such attributes as caring, nurturing, being emotional, etc. on to the feminine, for only by there being two stable identities can binary oppositions work. But by showing that the masculine actually retains some/all of the displaced attributes to varying degrees, then the attempt to hold in place a stable first identity by virtue of a distinctive second breaks down: neither identity is now stable or secure. In which case, with the various attributes 'mixed up' it is no longer obvious what is being opposed to what. Accordingly, once clear-cut distinctions become blurred, their natural-ness is seen as being ultimately arbitrary and thus precisely 'unnatural'. Of course, distinctions have to be made, but no longer are they seen as being essential-ist; really foundational.

Turning to the third question, then, it should now be obvious why Derrida (as a man of the left) wants to deconstruct binary oppositions into ever exfoliating differences, into endless combinatories. Derrida wants to deconstruct the actualities of vertical power-political relationships that infuse such binaries with life (*Second Remark*: 'it is to the extent that stability is not natural, essential or substantial, that politics exists') thus opening up new 'horizontal' possibilities of, say, 'democracies to come'. Deconstructing binary stabilities into playful differences is thus only ever a chance, but it is one worth taking to put on the agenda democratic justice and 'infinite' moral responsibility (*Third Remark*: 'If responsibility were not infinite you could not have moral and political problems. There are only moral and political problems from the moment when responsibility is not limitable. And this is why undecidability is not a moment to be traversed or overcome.'). In the wake of Derrida's deconstruction of absolute political–ethical binary oppositions, then, comes the spectre of political–moral relativism (*Third Remark*: 'conflicts of [moral] duty – and there is only duty in conflict – are interminable'), a consequence of deconstruction I think Derrida accepts.

Now, the charge of moral relativism is levelled against 'postist' thinkers in such an accusing manner that it suggests they would like to deny it. But on the whole they don't because they can't; postmodernists cannot not be moral relativists. Contra Christopher Norris *et al.*, I think Derrida's arguments with regard to the *aporetic* (and thus in the end arbitrary) nature of the 'irreducibility of the madness of the decision' out of which moral responsibility and the idea of a never fully satiated justice stems, mean that, if every choice – to be 'a choice' – is one taken in conditions of maximum contingency then moral relativism is the fate of everyone – always. The choice is one made for the first time relative to a unique set of circumstances and not definitively decidable on the basis of previous experience and by reference back to a foundational ethical code. Of course, the details of the way in which the idea of moral relativism links up to the idea of justice – which for me signals the *end* of ethical systems/codes – is not one of the easiest to access. But fortunately Simon Critchley and Ernesto Laclau are, despite their 'differences', particularly helpful in this area and so, to clarify it before moving on, I follow their arguments intermittently for a couple of paragraphs. This is an important area and it needs a little further introductory discussion.

Derrida holds to the idea of justice as irreducible in that it cannot be reduced to (embodied within) any positive/empirical legal or ethical system. We can never say what exactly absolute justice is. Such a notion of justice defies closure, staying one step ahead of our finest grained analyses, in excess of all our 'ethical' codifications. But this idea of a never-possible-to-attain justice, this impossibility, is precisely the condition of possibility which makes moral positions both possible in the first place – they try to embody what they think justice is – and subject always to the possibility of critique in that 'for all we know' our best attempts at expressing justice always fall short. Thus is opened up forever that critical space between the notion of 'a never fully conceivable but necessary justice', and empirical 'justices', a critical space where deconstruction can work or, better still, where deconstruction (the possibility of deconstruction) *is* justice. What we experience when we make a moral choice/decision is the experience of having no unproblematic foundations (and thus excuses for) whatever choice we make. Laclau is helpful at glossing this condition. Precisely because, when faced with making the 'right' decision, there is no possibility of merely applying some kind of algorithmic formula, then the moment of decision always remains, says Laclau's Derrida,

> a finite moment of urgency and precipitation since it must not be the consequence or the effect of this theoretical or historical moment . . . since it always marks the interruption of the juridico- or ethical or politico-cognitive deliberation that . . . *must* precede it. The instance of the decision is a madness, says Kierkegaard.[11]

And as Laclau then goes on to comment, reinforcing Derrida's point, this decision exceeds anything – and to be a decision *must* exceed anything – containable within a calculable programme derived from both historical necessity and ethics. Derrida again on all of this:

> The undecidable is not merely the oscillation or the tension between two decisions, it is the experience of that which, though

heterogeneous, foreign to the order of the calculable and the rule, is still obliged . . . to give itself up to the impossible decision, while taking account of law and rules. A decision that didn't go through the ordeal of the undecidable would not be a free [moral] decision, it would only be the . . . application or unfolding of a calculable process [or rule].[12]

A moral decision thus escapes any and every rule; the decision has to be grounded only in itself, in its own singularity. And that singularity, as Laclau comments, 'cannot bring through the back door what it has excluded at the entrance – the universality of the rule. It is because of this that . . . the moment of decision is the moment of madness.'[13] Does that mean, then, that any decision that anyone might choose to make, so long as it goes through the undecidability of the decision is moral irrespective of the actual, substantive decision made? Can the Rorty bad-guys make moral decisions because of the process they go through to arrive at it? I think the answer has to be yes. This is the bottom line of relativism.

And I think Derrida can be read as reluctantly accepting this (though he is no 'happy relativist'). As noted (in his *First Remark*) Derrida states that the process of deconstruction is an empty mechanism, an 'unstable motif', which can be used to serve quite different political (moral) purposes. Thus Derrida can only, as he says, hope that in the process of deconstruction all those verticals of authority that are frustrating 'democracies to come', Derridean-type preferences will be chosen (*Third Remark*: 'Even if I would not wish to inscribe the discourse of emancipation into a teleology, a metaphysics, an eschatology, or even a classical messianism, I none the less believe that there is no [moral] political decision or gesture without what I would call a "Yes" to emancipation'). Consequently, it is Derrida's choice to take the side of emancipation, which gives him his position, an arbitrary but a 'good' one relative to his own lights and one from which he even considers the possibility of denying what the 'logic' of his position drives him towards; that is, of denying 'anything goes':

Not that it is good – good in itself – that everything or anything should happen [should be chosen]; nor that we should give up trying to prevent certain things [like Fascism] coming to pass (in that case there would be no choice, no responsibility, no ethics [morality] or politics). But you do not try to oppose events [choices] unless you think they shut off the future, or carry the threat of death: events [choices] which would end the possibility of event [choices], which would end any affirmative opening toward the arrival of the other.[14]

I hope it can now be seen why Derrida deconstructs any notion of a definitive history or ethics. By collapsing binary oppositions, subverting ostensibly stable entities, querying discursive species masquerading as identical to some putative genus (i.e. querying the equation of a transcendental gesture with an empirical manifestation), Derrida can be read as drawing a line under the *certaintist* experiment(s) of modernity. You cannot derive what you ought to do at the moment of decision from 'anything grounded in anything external to itself'. While from one's understanding of the historicised past one might indeed take some notice of it *relative* to what one chooses to give significance to, the choice that one makes remains one's singular responsibility. The moment of choice remains a contingent one since, to repeat one of Derrida's most basic points, it must very precisely 'not be the consequence of this theoretical or historical moment'. To put this once again to underline the point: a *decision that did not go through the ordeal of undecidability would not be a free/moral decision*. In that sense, at the very moment when it counts, history and morality have no entailment whatsoever; indeed, at this moment there must not be any. Here, any 'lessons' learnt from the past must *not* be the determining factor. At the moment of decision a historical consciousness is not to be drawn upon: history must not – just like the decision must not – repeat itself.

But it is not only that. For Derrida's deconstructionism has the effect of not only breaking apart any fact–value entailments, but also undercuts any idea that we can – irrespective of how we might want to consider and use it – get anything like true or objective history on which we might have thought we could base informed moral judgements in the first place. For while historical representations ostensibly refer to a past outside of themselves, that past, in the very process of becoming historicised (theorised, constructed, interpreted, read, written ...) loses its 'pastness', its radical alterity to us, and becomes totally textual, totally 'us'. The only way that the past can become capable of being analysed historically is for it to become 'historical'. It is in this sense that theoretical textuality/intertextuality thus 'goes all the way down' such that the truth of the past *per se* not only eludes us but makes no sense as a concept. Without 'us' the past is nothing; it waits for us to break its silence with our relativistic semantic desires: the 'relativised'/textual, historicised past is only always us – back there.

Few phrases seem to irritate 'proper' historians more than the phrase (and the implications of the phrase – which is what I have just been talking about) that 'there is nothing outside of the text'. So I want briefly to explain what he means by it and the more detailed consequences it has for traditional notions of history/historiography in both cases.

In his excellent *After Derrida* (which I have drawn on freely here) Nicholas Royle argues that the implications of Derrida's work 'for historiography in general are quite massive'. For Derrida views (western/modernist) history as a concept that is always determined 'in the last analysis as the history of meaning' insofar as it is

> not only linked to linearity but to an entire system of implications ('teleology, eschatology, elevating and intermingling accumulations of meaning, a certain kind of traditionality, a certain concept of continuity, of truth') . . . [it] has *writing* [in the most general sense of this term] as its condition of possibility. For it is writing which opens 'the field of history'.[15]

What does 'writing as the condition of possibility which opens up the field of history' mean here? What Derrida definitely does not mean is that history is simply determined by what has been written in the conventional sense and which forms the bulk of the traces/ sources of the past actuality used by historians – archival deposits, journals, books, etc. (although the literal textuality of the bulk of these traces does mean such phenomena are indeed texts). For Derrida has a second and main sense of writing wherein the terms 'writing' and 'text' are not used in their conventional way. What Derrida wants to show, Royle explains, is how these terms are necessarily subject to 'unbounded generalisation':

> To say that history is radically determined by writing, then, is to say that it is constituted by a general or unbounded logic of traces and remainders – general and unbounded because these traces and remains, this work of remainders and remnants are themselves neither presences nor origins: rather they too are constituted by traces and remains in turn.[16]

It is thus this unbounded situation that constitutes writing for Derrida – a situation wherein we never really know where to start or end our accounts; where the way those reminders and remnants are carved up, emplotted and troped is ultimately one of choice; where how to select, distribute, serialise, endow with certain meanings and not others isn't 'given'; where how to contextualise, combine, recombine, connect, disconnect is not in the 'things themselves'; where we get no definitive help from the 'seamless past' in these matters, and where any help we do derive from the always already 'framed' historicised past is actually always ultimately through encounters with it – with ourselves – as textuality. And these arbitrary ways of carving things up are compounded by the fact that we readers and writers are ourselves part of this process of the general and unbounded logic of traces and remains; we are ourselves textual. We too are the stuff of history, of textuality, unable to access any Archimedean point outside of ourselves from whence we might issue forth, omniscient narrator style. Thus to the question of where should we begin and end our accounts, our appropriative writings, Derrida's answer is clear: 'wherever we are; in a text already'.[17] It is in this sense that Derrida thus writes that 'there is nothing outside the text/context'. Accordingly – and seen exactly in this *context* – Derrida's statement does *not* mean that, say, the actual past never existed outside of literal texts, or that houses and factories, wars and concentration camps are literally texts. All this is so obvious that the point should not need to be made, but apparently it is needed, not least because this way of reading Derrida (and often postmodernism in general) remains common. Yet it stretches credulity to breaking point when Richard Evans can write, apparently in all seriousness against Derrida and postmodernists, that 'the insistence that all history is discourse diverts attention from the real lives and sufferings of people in the past. Auschwitz is not a text. The gas chambers were not a discourse. It trivialises mass murder to see it as a text.'[18] For these are not only extremely tasteless comments to direct towards a Jewish intellectual who has enough reason not to forget the actuality of gas chambers, but a complete misreading of the notion of textuality. As Simon Critchley has pointed out (to Evansists) Derrida's generalised concept of the text does not

wish to turn the world into some vast library; nor does it wish to cut off reference to some 'extra-textual realm'. Deconstruction is not bibliophilia. Text *qua* text is glossed by Derrida as the entire 'real-history-of-the-world', and this is said in order to emphasise the fact that the word 'text' does not suspend reference 'to history, to the world, to reality, to being *and especially not to the other*'. All the latter appear in an experience which is not an immediate experience of presence – the text or context is not present . . . but rather the experience of a network of differentially signifying traces which are constitutive of meaning. *Experience or thought traces a ceaseless movement of interpretation within a limitless context.*[19]

So important is this point that, despite Critchley's lucid and economical glossing, Derrida's own words can be given to supplement it:

What I call 'text' implies all the structures called 'real', 'economic', 'historical', 'socio-institutional', in short, all possible referents. Another way of recalling once again that 'there is nothing outside the text'. That does not mean that all referents are suspended, denied or enclosed in a book, as people have claimed, or have been naive enough to believe and to have accused me of believing. But it does mean that every referent and all reality has the structure of a différantial trace and that one cannot refer to this 'real' except in an interpretative experience. The latter neither yields meaning nor assumes it except in a movement of différantial referring. That's all.[20]

Finally, then, here is Royle pulling together several points in clarification of what I have just been referring to, after which the implications of Derrida for history really should be apparent. Here is Royle:

'The referent is in the text' as Derrida puts it . . . His concern [is] to elaborate readings which take rigorous account of the ways in which any text (in the traditional sense of that word) and any writer (the notion of the writer itself 'a logocentric product') are variously affected, inscribed and governed by the logic of the text, of supplementarity or contextualisation which can never be saturated or arrested. Every text (in the traditional sense) has meaning only on the basis of belonging to a supplementary and 'indefinitely multiple structure' of contextualisation and incessant recontextualisation. As Derrida declares . . . 'The supplement is always the supplement of a supplement. One wishes to go back *from the supplement to the source* . . . one must recognise that there *is a supplement always already at the source*' . . . Language, text and writing are [thus] constituted by supplementarity, by a network of traces and referents, references to other references, a general referability without single origin, presence or destination.[21]

Thus, no reading can, as Derrida puts it, transgress the text towards something other than it, towards 'a referent or towards a signifier outside the text whose content could take place, could have taken place, outside language; that is to say, in the sense that we give here to that word, outside writing in general'.[22]

'History as a text' as understood here, then, *can obviously never be finished*. All the limits erected by the historian – the world, the real, reality, the facts, teleology, immanence, essence – in opposition to the incessant and interminable exploitation of readings, are transgressed. History in general and in its modernist upper and lower case genres can never be stabilised, definitively known. Locked into the uncertainties of ontology and epistemology, methodology is no high road to the truth, to meaning. And Derrida is happy with this. Derrida hopes that histories of the future – of histories to come (if we still bother with them) – will be histories without end(s); histories of surprise, of risk, of democracies to come – and come again (*Third Remark*: 'There is the future . . . there is something to come . . . that can happen'). Royle brings all of this to his own arbitrary end:

> No supplementary asylum, then, no place of refuge from the ceaselessly disabling, dislocating power of the supplement. What we have instead are states of emergency . . . Not a state but states of emergency; but there can be no history, and therefore no states of emergency, without that which surprises and deconstructs every emergency . . . history, like deconstruction, is [thus] less about the past than about the opening of the future. Writing history has to do with states of emergency, states given both to an acknowledgement that 'the future can only be anticipated in the form of an absolute danger', and to a recognition that the past was never present.[23]

Here is a final thought on Derrida before we move towards Baudrillard and Lyotard, one which links all three of them. In *Derrida and the Political*, Richard Beardsworth makes the well-known claim that Derrida relates all his critical thought to deconstructing what he calls the 'closure of metaphysics';[24] that is to say, to opposing the attempted closure of the metaphysical excess; to opposing the possibility of the 'to come', of the promise, of the *aporia* of the decision and of the surprise, of the 'perhaps', by all forms of recognition (conceptual, logical, discursive, political, technical); to opposing the snuffing out of the democratising promise by the logic of technics. And I think that Beardsworth is right. For Derrida's uncoupling of time from western notions of linearity, from metaphysics and indeed from lower case certaintism, signals a way of envisaging the desirability of the *end* of History/history and ethics. For it is against such fix-ations that Derrida's own notion of a new type of future freed from older logics of economy, coupled with notions of an irreducible justice, a non-ossifiable morality and *aimance*, takes shape in order to think, beyond binary oppositions and stable identities, fresh emancipatory hopes that pull on the ineffable nature of the sublime, a chaotic 'nothingness' that can promise everything, including his own (always temporary) preferences.

I think that, in this broad respect, both Baudrillard and Lyotard occupy the same area. Beardsworth is therefore again to the point when he writes that 'a powerful thinking has thus emerged in French thought which links the "mourning" of metaphysical logic with a thinking of time and singularity which exceeds the politico-philosophical seizure of the "real"', which invokes ideas of the excess, of the sublime and of the radical otherness of the other.[25] It is thus to aspects of the works of Baudrillard and Lyotard and their 'critiques' of history, ethics and the currently contingent masquerading as the 'really real', that I now turn.

2 On Jean Baudrillard

I will approach Jean Baudrillard's thoughts on the 'end of history' by way of some preliminary remarks about aspects of his thinking that might make his views on history more easily understandable before going on to a more detailed reading. I shall end my reading of Baudrillard rather abruptly before contextualising his contribution to 'the end of metanarratives' in the section 'Final thoughts' which comes at the end of Part I. But here is Baudrillard now.

Currently in his late sixties and for many years Professor of Sociology at the University of Paris (Nanterre) and Visiting Professor at various American universities, Jean Baudrillard has been famous, or infamous, worldwide. A sometime columnist for the French daily *Libération*, a television personality, an acclaimed conference speaker, a web-site guru, the subject (object) of dozens of features in 'trendy' magazines (*Figaro Magazine, Les Inrockuptibles, The Face*), Baudrillard has all the trappings, and attracts all the hype, of a media star. Within academia he escapes easy categorisation as he ranges across vast swathes of intellectual territory: sociology, philosophy, literature, history, politics, architecture, etc. The author of numerous books (for instance *Symbolic Exchange and Death* (1976), *Simulacra and Simulation* (1981), *Fatal Strategies* (1983), *America* (1988), *Seduction* (1990), *The Illusion of the End* (1992), *The Transparency of Evil* (1993), *Cool Memories* (1995), *The Perfect Crime* (1995)), Baudrillard violates, in his ceaseless 'border crossings', the neat disciplinary boxes of scholarship to the discomfort, and sometimes to the disgust, of those firmly tucked up inside them. Accordingly, such an irritating transgressor is easy to characterise, and then dismiss, as a scholarly lightweight, a gadfly lacking propriety, seriousness and rigour; a joker, a charlatan, 'The Walt Disney of contemporary metaphysics', a representative of postmodernism at its emptiest and wackiest, a hyper-relativist who, according to Christopher Norris, 'is lost in the funhouse!'[1]

It is not my intention here to 'correct' these possible misreadings which seem to pepper the Baudrillardian literature. Besides, as Baudrillard himself comments, such corrective ambitions are always ultimately impossible. For as he insists, because every discursive analysis defines its own meaningful object of study relative to the analyst's interests, then any object – and in this case Baudrillard – escapes definitive closure. There is no definitive or 'comprehensive' Baudrillard in what follows, then; rather what I want to do is to explicate some of the reasons why he thinks we have now come to the 'end of history' or, more accurately, the end of the illusion that the past could be construed as if it had an end 'in it'. When Baudrillard, and most other people come to that, but especially postmodernists, talk about the end of history, they are not of course talking about the end of life or saying that the future won't come. Rather, what they are generally saying is that the peculiar ways in which the past was historicised (was conceptualised in modernist, linear and essentially metanarrative forms) has now come to the end of its productive life; the all-encompassing 'experiment of modernity' – of which metanarratives were a key constitutive part – is passing away in our postmodern condition. This means that the idea (which we now recognise as 'just an idea') of history having an end is an idea now behind us, in the sense that the modernist attempt to realise it has failed. And Baudrillard thinks that this makes everything different. In an interview with Scott Lash and Roy Boyne, Baudrillard says that, in understanding the idea of the end of history, we have to

> start out from the fact that something has happened – a break, a mutation has taken place – and that we are in a new world . . . Here, I think, there is a genuine break with modernity. This is perhaps the only case in which we can really take the term 'postmodern' seriously . . . We have really passed beyond something, perhaps even beyond the end – I've analysed this question in *The Illusion of the End* – and, in fact, there is no finality or end any longer, because we have already passed beyond. And there, the rules are no longer the same . . . We are not this side of finality. This is what I mean when I say everything is realised . . . And having to make sense of a world where the end is not ahead of us but behind us . . . changes everything.[2]

Of course, Baudrillard isn't the first to spot the absurdity of thinking that there was a knowable, immanent teleology in the 'historicised past', and of thinking that the events etc. of the past actually 'had the shapes of stories'. But what is arguably unique in Baudrillard is the way in which a whole battery of terms (simulacra, simulation, seduction, the object, reversibility, hyper-reality, etc.), as well as cross-disciplinary/cross-cultural analyses of 'our' condition, are brought to bear not just on the illusory idea of history as having an end, but also on the notion that any sort of meaning or significance can be 'found' in it as opposed to being imposed on it. Baudrillard conducts his analyses in such a way that they suggest to me the figure (an unusual one in the Baudrillard literature) of Baudrillard as a moralist, of Baudrillard as offering a radical, moral critique of our social, political, logical, ethical economies. This is a critique that I think opens up for him the glimmer of a future 'beyond history and ethics', a future of interminable ironies and reversals and temporalities; in it the 'excess' of any 'economic reduction' (that is, the reduction of the sublimity and indifference of existence to definite and definitive orderings which have about them the now moribund characteristics of 'foundationalism') is reactivated subversively.

This is not to say that Baudrillard thinks that he has 'real grounds' for his critique. Baudrillard's critique is – if I can put it this way – 'absolutely reflexive', in that the axioms he argues his position from are, of course, arbitrary and 'fictional', the outcome of a constitutive choice. But, having made that choice (a choice constantly refined and expanded over the years) his position, far from being an 'irrational' or 'nihilistic' one (common charges levelled against him), is recognisably 'rational', coherent and understandable. This general position, which I think informs all his work, can be understood – very briefly for now – in ways that go something like this.

For Baudrillard the world (as an object of enquiry) and the phenomenological objects and 'events', etc. that constitute it, are never fully captured in even the most finely grained analyses we conduct. The 'object' of enquiry always remains out of our reach, certainly inexplicable, skipping clear of all and every attempt to 'pin it down', so that Baudrillard talks of the 'revenge of the object' (the way it retaliates against our efforts to control it) and how it continues to seduce us into thinking that – next time – it will be ours; that its radical otherness/alterity will be reduced to the same, to us. But that time never comes. Beyond every analysis there is always something 'disruptive' left out; beyond even the most tightly sutured context there is a further context; beyond every closure there remains something that should have been inside, such that the world (and world's 'past') remains, as I have already said, sublime, ineffable, eternally other, interminably interpretable: everything can be put under another description, another constitutive performative. And Baudrillard likes this, because it means that no closure is ever a total closure, no attempt to achieve 'full presence' is ever 'full'. Thus no social form-ation is ever fully stable, ever immune from critique, ever free of destabilisation as those useful fictions – those simulations of reality that pass for reality *per se* and which pragmatically 'stabilise things' – are revealed as but ephemeral, discursive 'effects of the real' through yet further simulations. Consequently, Baudrillard is happy to accept that the world is not only unintelligible but that the task is to critique all and every attempt at 'making it' intelligible. As Baudrillard puts it, 'The absolute rule of thought is to give back the world as it was given to us – unintelligible. And, if possible, to render it a little more unintelligible.' To have to the world, then, an attitude not of nihilism (for there is never anything knowably there to really lose or feel nostalgic and remorseful about in the first place) but of *indifference* – this is Baudrillard's position, a position of indifference that is generative of endless critiques. Baudrillard expresses all this himself (in the Lash–Boyne interview):

> Ultimately, what might be closest to a morality would be a rule of stripping-away, the rule of the Stoics. This isn't [meant as] something positive . . . There is no ideality here, but an indifference on the part of the world and nature . . . The only task, then, would be to clear a space, as it were, around the object, to act so that it shone out resplendent in all its indifference . . . so that the subject himself can attune himself to the world in a kind of symbolic exchange of indifference . . . [I have not been] forgiven for [taking this attitude], for not according value, for not adding value to something, to some particular process and, ultimately, for offering no kind of solution, opening or ideal, or the like. It is in that sense, that I am indifferent. Not nihilistic but indifferent [to an indifferent world] . . . To come to terms with this situation . . . the rule must be *not* to try and escape this kind of profound indifference . . . by [trying to retrieve] value and difference, but to play with this indifference – this objective indifference which is our destiny – to manage to transform this fateful indifference into the rule of the game, if not indeed play with it. And to recover a sort of passion for indifference.[3]

Consequently, it is this attitude not of nihilism or irresponsibility or irrationalism or immorality but of indifference that metaphorically and heuristically 'underpins' Baudrillard's position, a position connected by him to the possibility of an emancipatory and democratic future. For

> where symbolic exchange, reversibility and the rest are concerned, everyone has the same potential. . . . We are not equal before the law, of course, the law is a principle of profound inequality. But everyone is equal before the rule [of indifference] because it is arbitrary. So there we find the foundations of a true democracy . . . though not by any means of the usual political type.[4]

I think that it is this (sort of) idea that gives Baudrillard the notion of a future beyond 'certaintism' and 'endism', however articulated; a future of relativistic, reversing ironies; of temporalities that reverse linearity and teleology – and then themselves. Over and over. As Baudrillard puts it – and this is my last (long) quote before I get directly to 'Baudrillard and history' –

> Our situation is a wholly pataphysical one; that is to say, everything around us has passed beyond its own limits, has moved beyond the laws of physics and metaphysics. Now, pataphysics is ironic, and the hypothesis which suggests itself here is that, *at the same time as things have reached a state of paroxysm, they have also reached a state of parody.*
>
> Might we advance the hypothesis – beyond the heroic stage, beyond the critical stage – of an ironic stage of technology, an ironic stage of history, an ironic stage of value? This would at last free us from the Heideggerian vision of technology as the effectuation and final stage of metaphysics, it would free us from all retrospective nostalgia for being, and we would have, rather, a gigantic objectively ironic 'take' on all this scientific and technical process . . .
>
> [Thus we would have for example] an ironic reversal of technology similar to the irony of the media sphere. The common illusion about the media is that they are used by those in power to manipulate . . . the masses. A naive interpretation . . . the ironic version is precisely the opposite. It is that, through the media, it is the masses who manipulate those in power . . . At the very least, let us agree that matters are undecidable here; that both hypotheses

are valid . . . [consequently] it is precisely in this reversibility that
the objective irony lies . . .

[Consequently] ironic hypotheses . . . being by definition unverifiable, let us [thus] content ourselves with the undecidable . . .
[such that] we are faced in the end with two irreconcilable
hypotheses: that of the perfect crime or, in other words, of the
extermination by technology and virtuality of all reality – and
equally of the illusion of the world – or that of the ironic play
of technology, of an ironic destiny of all science and all knowledge
[including history] by which the world – and the illusion of the
world – are perpetuated. Let us content ourselves with these two
irreconcilable and simultaneously 'true' perspectives. There is
nothing that allows us to decide between them. As Wittgenstein
says, 'The world is everything which is the case'.[5]

So much, then, for some prefacing remarks. Within the context
I hope they have established (and I shall recontextualise some of
them in what follows so to make their meaning more 'obvious'),
I will now go on to discuss Baudrillard's position on the end of
history and the way the possibilities opened up by the end of history
(modernist–linear–metanarrative style) might indeed suggest a radical,
moral, critical rethinking of time/temporality. It would be constitutive,
'beyond the heroic stage', of an 'ironic stage of history' beyond all 'the
old laws' yet congruent with the 'rules of indifference', of endless,
reversible simulacra, which for Baudrillard seems 'to be' actuality.
The reading I want to give (which is based on Baudrillard's book
The Illusion of the End[6] and, intermittently, his essay 'The End
of the Millennium or the Countdown') is organised around three
questions.

First, what sort of conditions does Baudrillard think existed for a
way of carving up the past 'historically' such that it offered us the
illusion of it having an end; that allowed linear histories 'without
irony' to emerge? Second, what sort of hypotheses does Baudrillard
play with to undercut such illusions, to suggest, as he does, that
'endism' is no longer before but behind us ('having to make sense of
a world where the end is not ahead of us but behind us . . . changes
everything'). Third, in this 'new situation' (our contemporary condition) are there new forms of troping the past that might suggest a
'poetic reversibility of events', of radically new, *ironic* modes not of
historicising but of 'timing time'? (This last point is a 'reading into'
Baudrillard something that is, despite my above comments, more

problematic given that Baudrillard's *métier* is *critique* and not anything suggestive of a positive beyond.)

So to the first question: what conditions have to be met to give rise
to the idea that events which occur contingently constitute a sense of
(modernist) linear histories? Baudrillard's answer is brief but constitutes his working hypothesis. A degree of slowness is required; that
is, a certain speed – but not too much. A degree of distance is required;
that is, a certain spacing – but not too much. And a degree of libera-
tion is required (an 'energy for rupture and change') – but not too
much. Together, these factors bring about 'the condensation or
significant crystallisation of events we call history, the kind of coherent
unfolding of causes and effects we call reality'.[7] It is such conditions
that, existing in their optimum condition in the nineteenth century
especially, arguably produced our now moribund linear/endist histories of meaning.

So to my second question: what hypotheses does Baudrillard use to
suggest that such histories are indeed moribund and behind us?
Baudrillard has (at least) three hypotheses and some general
comments.

First, Baudrillard draws on Elias Cannetti's 'tormenting thought'
that, 'as of a certain point, history was no longer *real*. Without
noticing it, all mankind suddenly left reality', a thought suggesting
to Baudrillard the idea of that 'escape velocity a body requires to
free itself from the gravitational field of a star or a planet'.[8] Staying
with this image, Baudrillard suggests that the accelerations of
modernity have given 'us' the velocity enabling us to hurtle free of
'the referential sphere of the real and of history'. Accordingly,
beyond this gravitational effect, which had kept bodies circulating
regularly and predictably, each atom pursues its own trajectory and
is lost in space. This, says Baudrillard, 'is precisely what we are
seeing in our . . . societies, intent as they are on accelerating all
bodies, messages and processes in all directions and which, with
modern media, have created for every event, story and image a simulation of an infinite trajectory'.[9]

Every political, historical and cultural fact thus possesses a kinetic
energy which 'propels it into hyperspace where, since it will never
return, it loses all meaning'. No need for science fiction here, adds
Baudrillard. In our computers, circuits and networks we have the par-
ticle accelerator to 'smash the referential orbit of things once and for
all'.[10] No human language can withstand the speed of light; no
event can withstand being beamed across the planet, no meaning
can withstand this kind of acceleration. And no history can with-

stand 'the centrifugation of facts or their being short-circuited in real time'; history has ended here precisely because that essential re-telling (re-citatum) has become impossible since it is, by definition, 'the possible recurrence of a sequence of meanings'.[11]

Baudrillard's second hypothesis 'reverses' the first: it has to do not with speeding up but slowing down. It is one he says he takes directly from physics. Matter slows the passing of time. Time at the surface of a dense body seems to be in slow motion. This intensifies as the density increases. In turn this increases the length of the light wave emitted. Beyond a certain limit time stops; the wavelength becomes infinite. The light goes out. Analogously, history slows down as it 'rubs up against' the body of the 'silent majorities', against the sluggish density of the 'mass of the masses'. This is of the utmost significance, the emergence, in the very course of the masses' mobilisation and revolutionary process, of an equivalent force of inertia. This inertia is not, perhaps paradoxically, produced by a lack of exchange or communication, but by the saturation of such exchanges: the hyperdensity of cities, commodities and exchange. Here events cascade over each other, cancelling each other out – where are they all leading to? Consequently, the masses, 'mithridatised by information', in turn neutralise history so that, unable to escape from this overdense body, time slows to a point where 'right now, the perception and imagination of the future are beyond us'. History (as modernist, linear progress and endism) ends here, not for want of activity but aimlessness: 'It is no longer able to transcend itself . . . to dream of its own end; it is being buried beneath its own immediate effect, worn out in special effects, imploding into current events . . . its effects are accelerating, but its meaning is slowing inexorably.'[12]

And this phenomenon, which Baudrillard calls 'the event strike' (incidentally the French subtitle of *The Illusion of the End* is 'the event strike' – *la grève des événements*), is a crucial part of his argument. What does it mean? It means "That the work of history has ceased to function. Thus the work of mourning is beginning. That the information system is taking over the baton from History and starting to produce the event in the same way that Capital is starting to produce Work, so that labour no longer has any significance of its own', just as the event produced by information has no historical meaning of its own. For what has been lost today is the prodigious event, the event that is measured neither by its causes nor its consequences but creates its own stage, its own dramatic effect. Events 'now have no more significance than their anticipated meaning, their programming or their broadcast'. This results in one of those ironic reversals Baudrillard is so good at spotting, namely, that it is this event strike itself that actually constitutes a 'true' historical phenomenon – this refusal 'to signify anything whatever, or this capacity to signify anything at all. This is the true [*sic*] end of history, the end of historical Reason.'[13] Yet this doesn't mean – and this has to be underlined – that history *per se* has finished. What has disappeared is, as Baudrillard puts it, the prestige of the event, the sense of purpose, meaning, significance. *Petit* events are still being manufactured in that abundance that is the very thing fuelling the end of those linear histories that had at least the illusion of meaning, of endism; of some point. For Baudrillard then, contemporary social formations look suspiciously like that postmodernism that *is* the cultural logic of late capitalism: everything is surface, effect and affectation; pastiche and collage are the dominant figures. What is lacking is depth, power, weight, gravity, and that gravitas only serious, non-ironists have. Consequently, rather than 'pressing forward and taking flight into the future we [now] prefer . . . blanket revisionism'.[14] Today we are condemned to an 'infinite retrospective' of historical cleansing. 'Our' societies are revising everything, laundering their political crimes, their dirty money, their dirty history. Today we are rifling through the dustbins of history looking for redemption in the rubbish. But it's worse than that. For the end of history is also the end of the dustbin of history. Consequently the problem becomes one of waste: of waste disposal. Where, asks Baudrillard, are we going to put our waste products, our defunct ideologies, bygone utopias, old regimes, old values: 'who will rid us of the sedimentation of centuries of stupidity?' As for history – 'that living lump of waste, that dying monster which, like the corpse in Ionesco's Amédée, continues to swell after it has died – how are we to be rid of it?' Well, maybe there is no problem. Maybe it has been resolved by incineration and recycling. Anything that won't burn is recycled such that, ironically, we may 'not be spared the worst – that is, *history will not come to an end* – since the leftovers . . . the Church, ethnic groups, conflicts, ideologies – are indefinitely, recyclable'. All that we believed over and done with, left behind in the inexorable march of progress, is not dead at all but festering in its revenge . . . here modernity has never happened, here reactionary conflicts which we thought had gone for ever are rekindled. What is stupendous, says Baudrillard is that all the old forms are ready to re-emerge, intact and timeless like viruses deep in the body and with utterly problematic potentialities which can, ironically, be read, and go, 'either way'.

Now, these two hypotheses (both of which are equally plausible or implausible – that is what is so ironic about them) of history speeding up or slowing down through what has happened to meaning, to 'events in modernity', are returned to by Baudrillard in the penultimate chapter of his book under the title 'Exponential Instability, Exponential Stability', and combined. Baudrillard's argument here is that in a non-linear, non-Euclidean space of history, the end is never locatable, realisable. An 'end' is, in fact, only conceivable in a logical order of causality and continuity, whereas today 'it is the events themselves which, by their artificial production, their programmed occurrence or the anticipation of their effects . . . are suppressing the cause-effect relation and hence all historical continuity'.[15] Consequently, this distortion of cause–effect, this cause–effect reversibility, engenders a disorder resembling 'chaos theory' such that

> perhaps history itself has to be regarded as a chaotic formation in which acceleration puts an end to linearity and the turbulence created . . . deflects [it] definitively from its end . . . this is one . . . version of Chaos Theory – that of exponential instability. It accounts very well for the 'end' of history, interrupted in its linear or dialectical movement by that catastrophic singularity . . . of contemporary events.

But that's not all. For there is another state – exponential stability – which defines a state in which, no matter where you start from you always end up at the same point. No potentialities develop. Consequently, there is once again no end, 'not from effects becoming excessive and unpredictable, but because everything is already there, everything has taken place'. But that's not all either. For, though incompatible, these two hypotheses are 'in fact simultaneously valid'. Our current condition ironically embodies both of them: 'It combines in effect an inflation, a galloping acceleration, a dizzying whirlpool of mobility, an eccentricity of events and an excess of meaning and information with an exponential tendency towards total entropy. Our systems are thus doubly chaotic.' And it is this chaos that, after the illusion of an 'endism' which 'straightened things out', we are left with: 'condemned to an intense metabolism . . . they become exhausted within themselves and no longer have any destination, any end . . . they are condemned, precisely, to the epidemic, to the endless excrescences of the fractal . . . . We know only the signs of catastrophe now; we no longer know the signs of destiny.'[16]

These, then, are the first two of Baudrillard's three hypotheses. What is his third? Baudrillard calls it the 'stereophonic effect'. He writes:

> We are all obsessed with high fidelity, with the quality of musical 're-production'. At the console of our stereos, armed with our tuners . . . we mix, adjust settings, multiply tracks in pursuit of a flawless sound. Is this still music? Where is the high fidelity threshold beyond which music disappears as such? It does not disappear for lack of music, but because it has passed this limit point; it disappears . . . into its own special effect . . . It is the ecstasy of musicality, and its end.[17]

Analogously, history's disappearance is of the same order. By dint of their efforts, historians mix and remix, dub and redub, interpret and reinterpret the past in pursuit of a flawless history. Is this still the past? Just as at the 'very heart' of hi-fi, music threatens to disappear, so at the very heart of news, history threatens to disappear . . . 'everywhere we find the same stereophonic effect; the same effect of absolute proximity to the real, the same effect of simulation'.[18] The passing of this point is, says Baudrillard, irreversible. We shall never get back to pre-stereo, pre-unsimulated music (except by additional, technical, simulation effects); we shall never get back to pre-news, pre-media history (except by additional, technical, simulation effects). Besides, what was that 'real' music, that 'real' history, but previous simulations anyway? Here the very idea of history dissolves into an interminable simulation mode.

For of course – and here I leave Baudrillard's three hypotheses to look briefly at his general remarks connected to them – the fact that we're now leaving history to move into a realm of simulation doesn't mean that history hasn't always been 'an immense simulation model'. Because it has. Not only in the sense – though this is an important sense – that it has only ever existed in the various (generally narrative) forms we have carved the past up into but, says Baudrillard, simulated in the sense of the concept of time in which the past was troped to unfold – in modernist, non-reversible, linear mode. And it is this – the simulation of history as 'linear endism', as the illusion of having an end – that has now ended. We are thus no longer 'this side of finality' (as an end to be fulfilled, an end 'still to come') but beyond finality. Thus, to recall parts of an earlier remark of Baudrillard's I quoted from the Lash–Boyne interview, which are now perhaps better 'contextualised':

having to make sense of a world where the end is not ahead of us but behind us and already realised, changes everything. Here, I think, there is a genuine break with modernity. This is perhaps the only case in which we can really take the term 'postmodern' seriously. There has been a kind of break . . . And I mean by this that we are now in a different world. We have really passed beyond something, perhaps even beyond the end . . . there is no finality any longer because we have already passed beyond. And there the rules are no longer the same.[19]

And so I come to the third and final question which is the following: in this new situation (our 'postmodern condition') is there anything suggestive of new forms of troping the past that might suggest new modes *not* of historicising 'time' but of 'timing' it in the *ironic* way Baudrillard considers favourably, as a critique of present arrangements? As I said at the start, this idea of Baudrillard having something positive to say may look as if it reverses the view of Baudrillard as 'always and only' a radical critic. But maybe it doesn't. For Baudrillard's more positive comments can still act as a critique of our current condition which is, very precisely, one beyond which 'we' cannot see; in that sense Baudrillard's 'beyond' only further problematicises any answers of a serious 'historical kind' by pointing to the simulacratic status of all such imaginaries – straight or ironic.

In answering my third question I depart from Baudrillard's summary of our current condition. Today, he says, we seem unable to dream of a past or future state of things. Things are in a state 'which is literally definitive – neither finished, nor infinite, nor definite, but de-finitive, that is, deprived of its end'.[20] Against which, he says, there remains – and this is a crucial sentence – 'the completely improbable and, no doubt, unverifiable hypothesis of a *poetic reversibility of events*, more or less the only evidence for which is the existence of the same possibility in language'.[21] And why should Baudrillard want this improbable thought . . . this 'perhaps', this hypothesis? The answer may well stem from his remarks, a few pages before the above lines, about keeping open the possibility of something akin to Nietzsche's *transvaluation of all values based upon the illusion of the world itself*.[22] In other words, to keep open the radical possibility of the *illusion* of the world's actuality that previous and current illusions have concealed in their various closures, their 'fictive shelters' of truth, becoming, meaning, etc. To these we can, as stated, 'only oppose the illusion of the world itself, whose rules, admittedly mysterious and arbitrary [for the world is, for Baudrillard, a *gift*] are nonetheless imminent and necessary'[23] and which seem expressible (hypothetically) in a form 'not far removed from poetic form'.[24]

Whatever the pros and cons of Baudrillard's hypothesis (is he drifting into ontology here?) I think that Baudrillard does outline at least some possible forms which, though they are (probably totally) 'illusory', may at least ('improbably') open up a mental space for something 'in excess'. So I will follow him through the last few pages of his text.

'The poetic form is not far removed from the chaotic form.' This is Baudrillard's starting point, then, and he seems to hold this view because both flout the law of cause and effect, there being a (metaphoric) affinity between the immanence of poetic development – 'which is ours today' – and the immanence of 'chaotic development' – 'the unfolding of events which are . . . without meaning and consequence and in which – with effects substituting themselves for causes – there are no longer any causes, but only effects. The world is there, effectively. There is no reason for this, and God is dead.'[25]

Consequently, if nothing exists but effects, we are in a state of total illusion – in the poetic. If the effect is in the cause, or the beginning in the end, then the catastrophe is behind us, thus liberating us from any future responsibility in that regard: 'We are free of the Last Judgement.' Which brings us, says Baudrillard, to a poetic, ironic analysis of events. Against the simulation of a linear (modernist) history as 'progress', we can thus privilege 'those backfires, those malign deviations'; those ruptures, breaks, reversals that, covered over by our language of continuity, we can now see as just other types of trope, *none crazier or more sensible than linearity but just 'different'*. All of which suggests, that not only has 'history' never actually unfolded in a linear fashion, but that 'perhaps language has never unfolded in a linear fashion' either: 'Everything moves in loops, tropes, inversions of meaning, except in numerical and artificial languages which, for that very reason, *no longer are languages*.'[26] We live in a world which just 'is' paratactic, which is to say asyntactic, which is to say, meaning-less. *We live today recognising that the grammar of our language created a 'grammatical history', it did not allow us to 'discover one'*.

Consequently, asks Baudrillard, 'might we not transpose new language games on to social and historical phenomena' of a different poetics from those we have got used to. Might we not read the past through 'anagrams, acrostics, spoonerisms, rhyme, strophe and catastrophe', and fabricate a temporality not just through the major figures of metaphor (metonomy, synechdoche, etc.) either, but through instant, puerile, formalistic games, the heteroclite tropes which are the delight of a vulgar imagination? And are there social spooner-isms, or an anagrammatic history (where meaning is dismembered and scattered to the winds, like the name of God in the anagram), rhyming forms of political action or events which can be read in either direction?

Is there a chance, Baudrillard asks, that history will lend itself to such a poetic convulsion which would even,

> beyond meaning – allow the pure materiality of language to show through, and – beyond historical meaning – allow the pure materiality of time to show through? Such would be the enchanted alternative to the linearity of history, the poetic alternative to the disenchanted confusion, the chaotic profusion of present events.[27]

In this way, concludes Baudrillard, we might enter, beyond the illusion of history and the illusion of the end of history, into that greatest illusion of all – *the radical illusion of the world* in all its apparent, radical *indifference* to our most ambitious attempts to fold it into our ontologies of closure. Again to recall, in the Lash–Boyne interview, Baudrillard talked about how the only task he has ever really had has been that of clearing a space around the object – the world, the past, history – so that it shone out in its indifference, so that, and I quote again, the subject 'can attune himself [*sic*] to the world, harmonise with the world in a kind of symbolic exchange of indifference'.[28] And I've not been forgiven, he adds, for taking this attitude,

> for not according value, for not adding value to something, to some particular process and, ultimately, for offering no kind of solution, opening an ideal, or the like. . . . In that sense, I am indif-ferent. Not nihilistic but indifferent . . . [one must] try to play with this indifference . . . which is our destiny . . . and to recover a sort of passion for indifference.

This recovery of a passion for indifference is, I think, what Baudrillard achieves in his final few pages. And again, I now think we can see what he means. Or, to put it another way, we can now understand Baudrillard's somewhat gnomic comments in *The Perfect Crime*, and which, slightly differently articulated and contextualised, I've also mentioned above where he stated, as a sort of *credo*, that

'The absolute rule of thought is to give back the world as it was given to us – unintelligible. And, if possible, to render it a little more unintelligible.'[29] For it is this unintelligible world that I think Baudrillard captures in the final paragraph of *The Illusion of the End*, with which I end:

> In this very way, we enter, beyond history, upon pure fiction . . . The illusion of our history opens on to *the greatly more radical illusion of the world*. Now we have closed the eyelids of the Revolution . . . now that the lips of protest are closed . . . now Europe – and memories – are no longer haunted by the spectre of communism, nor even by that of power, now the aristocratic illusion of the origin and the democratic illusion of the end are increasingly receding, we no longer have the choice of advancing, of persevering in the present destruction, or of retreating – but only of facing up to this radical illusion.[30]

3 On Jean-François Lyotard

In the foreword to the English edition of _The Postmodern Explained to Children_, the translators (Don Barry _et al._) pose the question: 'What would happen if thought no longer had a childhood?'[1] And their answer – which is Lyotard's answer – is that, today, it is post-modernism that maintains the possibility of thought happening in conditions where the old modernist faith in repairing 'the crimes of the past by guiding the present towards the end of the realisation of ideas' has itself ended. For what postmodernism does is to allow thought to be cast adrift 'from the chronophobia of the will which sets out to plot or master the course of time' by allowing itself to be very precisely 'thrown off course'.[2] Accordingly, what thought has to do is to

> set out without knowing its destination or its destiny, leaving itself open to the unfamiliarity of what ever may occur to it, and make rules in the absence of rules. The postmodern text will be in advance of itself: it will be writing written in the _what will have been_ of the future anterior. It will be both premature (without presumption) and patient (awaiting the event of thought).[3]

Consequently, Lyotard's _The Postmodern Explained to Children_ will not have fully explained the implications of postmodernism either to children or anyone else (for it has yet to be 'developed'). Rather, what Lyotard can do is show why and how it is necessary to approach the questions raised by the postmodern condition with both the afore-mentioned patience and with 'the mind of the child'. For childhood 'is the season of the mind's possibilities and of the possibility of philosophy'. A child is born totally future-orientated and (literally) pre-mature. It has no conscious anterior to hold it back, no baggage containing old imaginaries to weigh it down. It has to 'make things up' as it goes along. Analogously, postmodernism is future-orientated. It is what we might grow into if we can escape being constrained by either the past or by a past-based future teleology, or by pre-programmed schemas. Postmodernism is an iconoclastic invitation to go beyond old rules (and rulers) in emancipatory and democratising ways through imagining new imaginaries 'without end'. For

> it should be made clear that it is not up to us to *provide reality* but to invent illusions to what is conceivable but not presentable. And this task should not lead us to expect the slightest reconciliation between 'language games' – Kant, naming them the faculties, knew they were separated by an abyss and that only a transcendental illusion (Hegel's) can hope to totalise them into a real unity. But he also knew that the price of this illusion is terror. The nineteenth and twentieth centuries have given us our fill of terror. We have paid dearly for our nostalgia for the all and the one, for a reconciliation of the concept and the sensible, for a transparent and communicable experience. Beneath the general demand for relaxation and appeasement, we hear murmurings of the desire to reinstitute terror and fulfil the fantasm of taking possession of reality. The answer is: war on totality. Let us attest to the unpresentable, let us activate the différands and save the honour of the name [and the future].[4]

To 'attest to the unpresentable'; to 'activate the différands'; to 'save the honour of the name and the future'; to 'wage war on totality' – it is these explicit Lyotardian desires that I want to use as a way in and through aspects of his work(s), both as a basis for a reading of his general position (which can be arguably seen as constituted by them) and, more particularly, of Lyotard's critique – and the implications for lower case history of it – of those metanarratives towards which, in these postmodern days, incredulity is the only attitude we can plausibly adopt.

So, to 'attest to the unpresentable'. What is Lyotard getting at here? In summary form his argument – which plays on the theme of the sublime and in so doing 'defines' the postmodern – can be read in the following way.

Today there is no denying the dominance of 'techno-science', that is to say, the subordination of cognitive statements to efficiency and to the criterion of the 'finality of the best possible performance'. It is a technical, instrumentalist, means–end rationality especially prevalent within capitalist social formations wherein the 'reality rule' is that 'there is no reality unless it is confirmed by a consensus between partners on questions of knowledge and commitment'.[5] This rule, adds Lyotard, is indispensable to the 'birth of science and capitalism', having been installed at the expense of previous metaphysical, religious and political assurances as the basis on which to 'ground' the status of knowledge: 'modernity, whenever it appears, does not occur . . . without the discovery of the *lack of reality* in reality – a discovery linked to the invention of other realities' (imaginaries).[6] Accordingly, asks Lyotard, what would this 'lack of reality' signify if it were to be freed from a narrow 'historicising interpretation'. And his answer is that such a signification is to be best understood via 'the Kantian theme of the sublime'.[7]

What is the theme of the sublime according to Lyotard's Kant, and how does it lead to an understanding of postmodernism? For Kant, the feeling of the sublime is an 'equivocal emotion'; in it pleasure proceeds from pain as conflicts develop between the faculty to 'conceive' something and the capacity to 'present' it. As far as Kant is concerned, knowledge exists if a statement is intelligible and if cases that correspond to it 'can be drawn from experience'. For example, beauty exists if a particular case (a work of art) given first by the sensibility, arouses a feeling of pleasure which appeals beyond any specific interests to 'a principle of universal consensus (which may never be realised)'.[8] In this way, Kant says taste demonstrates that an accord between the capacity to conceive and then present an object corresponding to it gives rise to 'a reflexive judgement', which gives pleasure. For we now *know* what the beautiful really is; it is controlled, stabilised.

The feeling of the sublime is very different from such a stabilisation. It occurs when the 'imagination fails to present any object which seems to accord with a concept even if only in principle'. Thus, says Lyotard, we have (say) the 'Idea of The World' (the totality of what is) but not the capacity to show an example of it. Similarly, we can conceive of the absolutely great or the absolutely powerful, but we cannot definitely illustrate these (infinite) qualities with concrete examples. As with Derrida and Baudrillard, so with Lyotard, ideality or the object remains one step ahead: the fatal attraction for total presence is like unrequited love. Consequently, it is this idea of the infinite gap between ideality and any empirical substantiation that constitutes the *unpresentable* to which Lyotard 'attests'. For these ideas, for which there is no possible total presentation, therefore provide no ultimate knowledge of reality, and thus (also) prohibit the 'free accord' of the faculties that produce the feeling of the beautiful:

'They obstruct the formation and stabilization of taste. One could call them unpresentable.'[9]

Consequently, says Lyotard, he will call *modern* that art which devotes itself to 'presenting the existence of something unpresentable'.[10] Yet, he goes on to ask, 'how do we show something that cannot be seen?' Lyotard's Kant shows the way when he names 'formlessness' (*the absence of form*) as a possible index to the unpresentable and, speaking of the 'empty abstraction' felt by the imagination as it searches for a 'presentation of the infinite', likens this to 'negative presentation'. Citing the passage 'Thou shalt not make unto Thee any graven image' as the most sublime in the Bible (in that it forbids any presentation of the absolute/full presence), Lyotard says this constitutes 'an outline of an aesthetic of sublime painting' in that it will 'present something, but negatively'; it will 'make one see only by prohibiting one from seeing; it will give pleasure only by giving pain', the 'pleasurable pain' of knowing the uncrossable limits of the presentable . . . of which we always 'fall short'. And Lyotard concludes that a plausible formulation of the *modern* aesthetic would thus remain 'inexplicable without the incommensurability between reality and concept implied by the Kantian philosophy of the sublime'.[11]

Against this, then, what is the postmodern? Lyotard's answer now emerges out of his finessing of the concept of the 'modern' as he has portrayed it and the emergence of the postmodern from *within* it, for postmodernism is undoubtedly, on Lyotard's reading, 'part of the modern'.[12] So, how is that emergence argued? Lyotard begins by making what he calls a necessary distinction between two modes of emergence, for while it is the case that 'modernity unfolds in the retreat of the real and according to the sublime relationship of the presentable with the conceivable, we can . . . distinguish two essential modes in this relationship'.[13] First, the emphasis can be placed on the inadequacy of the 'faculty of presentation' and thus on 'the nostalgia for presence experienced by the human subject and the obscure and futile will which animates it'. Second, the stress can be laid on the capacity of human beings to 'forget' that nostalgia for that correspondence between 'what the imagination accords with what it conceives' and celebrate this instead by embracing uncertainty: by valorising 'the extension of being and jubilation which comes from inventing new rules of the game, whether pictorial, artistic, or something else'. (Lyotard cites the German expressionists as an example of the first ('melancholic') disposition, Picasso and Duchamp of the second.) To be sure, he adds, what distinguishes these two modes may only seem to be nuances, but actually they 'attest to a *différend* (an incommensurable difference of opinion) . . . a *différend* between regret and experimentation',[14] although this *différend* can be, and has been, containable within the overall structure of 'the modern'. For what contains both the regret and the experimentation – what makes modernist dealings with the sublime very precisely 'modernist' and not 'postmodernist' – is the continuation within the modern of a stable *form*. That is to say – *and this is the crucial, defining point* – whilst the modern aesthetic is an aesthetic of the sublime right enough, it nevertheless allows the 'unpresentable' to be invoked 'only as an absent content', while form, 'thanks to its recognisable consistency, continues to offer . . . material for consolation and pleasure'.[15] In which case, the feelings aroused do not amount to the 'truly' sublime. For while the 'truly' sublime is still a combination of pleasure and pain, it does *not* allow the unpresentable to be invoked only as an absent content whilst retaining form, but gets pleasure from the 'pain' of letting both content *and* the form go. And this 'letting go' constitutes the postmodern. As Lyotard puts it, the postmodern can now be defined as that which 'refuses the consolation of correct *forms*, refuses the consensus of taste permitting a common experience of nostalgia for the impossible, and inquires into new presentations – not to take pleasure in them but the better to produce the feeling that there is something unpresentable'.[16] The postmodernist is thus in the position of the philosopher in that

> the text he writes or the work he creates is not in principle governed by pre-established rules and cannot be judged according to a determinant judgement, by the application of given categories to this text or work. Such rules and categories are what the work or text is investigating. The [postmodern] artist or writer therefore works without rules, and in order to establish the rules for *what will have been made*. This is why the work and the text can take on the properties of an event; it is also why they would arrive too late for their author or, in what amounts to the same thing, why their creation would always begin too soon. *Postmodern* would be understanding according to the paradox of the future (*post*) anterior (*modo*) [post-modo].[17]

Now the implications of Lyotard's construction of postmodernism for history *per se* are quite devastating. After it, nothing definitive (or maybe nothing at all as currently/modernistically understood) can be said. Lyotard's own sketching out of his problematisation of history appears in numerous places throughout his works (Kerwin Klein has pulled many of them together)[18] but the gist of his position and its implications for 'history' can be summarised as follows.

For Lyotard (and I fully agree with him) the 'postmodern sublime' problematises not just the *content* of history but the *form* too. The content of history is something we are used to, so we can easily accept numerous interpretations both of the historicised past *per se* and aspects of it – say many interpretations of the French Revolution. What postmodernism calls attention to is that however well formulated the *form* of history as an idea might be, we cannot show a definitive example of it. Thus modernist historians of both cases have the comforting (pleasurable) thought (pleasurable in that it limits the extent of the sublime) that the sometime discomforting fact of countless interpretations *vis-à-vis* the *content* of their discourses can at least be lived with because they can all be recognised as being within the *form* of history (i.e. 'at least they're all historical'). But the problematisation of the form takes this reassuring 'pleasure' away. For it is now impossible to say what history really is given the 'sublime' gap between the ideality of history and any empirical manifestations. It is now not at all obvious (nor can it ever be 'obvious') what the *form of history* is, or whether what proper historians do when they do 'it' really is 'it', or that if other people want to do something different under the name of history that has not yet been done ('making up rules in the absence of rules') and call it history, they cannot legitimately do so. To continue this thought by linking it to Lyotard's *future-anterior* verb: this means that if we now have – at this postmodern moment – neither definitive *content* nor *form* for history (if history is now seen to be radically unstable 'all the way down' – a condition it has actually always been in and always will be in but which we can see now) then we are free, as postmodernists, to make up new rules as we go along, or to forget the discourse of history altogether. In this respect Lyotard's argument is congruent with Derrida's notion of the undecidability of the decision, the *aporia* in that, to recall, insofar as any judgement made is a judgement *made* and not merely the application of a previous rule, then that judgement is always 'to come'; is always a decision, a new rule, made in the absence of rules. Thus the question of 'what is history?' arises in postmodern discourse in ways that it doesn't do for modernist historians, in that an answer to the question calls for a decision for which no definitive answer currently in existence can be 'automatically' reached for and for which any new answer that will be given will prove 'not to have been good enough'. Consequently, the judgement will now – at this level of consciousness – have to be made and re-made (marked and re-marked) interminably – if the decision 'to bother' is taken. Thus, whilst the question of 'what is history?' may remain on the agenda for some time yet, what has now *ended* is at least the idea that any given answer – and certainly any answer provided by the modernist upper and lower case – will ever again suffice. For both the *form and the content* are now seen as being empty categories, non-rigid designators that have all the promiscuous characteristics of a wayward temporality (contingency, impermanence, ephemerality, difference...), this emptying out of *all* intrinsic meaning opening the category of history up to new forces beyond previous closures. From now on history really can be(come) whatever we want it to be(come) – or nothing at all.

It is Lyotard's argument that thus lies in great part behind my own position that history is nowadays either ① 'up for grabs' and that one desirable way of grabbing it is through more reflexive and inventive ways pre-fixed by the term 'post', which is thus overtly positioned in emancipatory ways or ② something we can forget. This second option is not advocated by Lyotard, but there is no reason why his attitude of 'incredulity towards metanarratives' might not be extended to 'incredulity towards the lower case' and then to history *per se*, thus raising the question of why we need discourses that we can only have incredulity towards.

But be that as it may, Lyotard's own thinking about why our attitude towards metanarratives in particular should be one of incredulity draws on arguments additional to those he uses to 'attest to the unpresentable' as outlined in part in the above paragraphs. For in his desire to 'wage war on totality' (included in which are totalising historical metanarratives in particular) Lyotard also 'activates the *différend*' in extremely interesting and pertinent ways. Thus it is to examine what Lyotard means by this phrase – and some of the relevant implications – that I now develop his position further.

Lyotard's arguments about the existence of the *différend* (a conflict, an irresolvable difference, between at least two parties, which cannot be resolved for lack of a rule of judgement equally applicable and acceptable to both of them) is straightforwardly political.[19] Lyotard likes the indestructability of the *différend* because it means that unresolvable disagreements, which he regards as issuing from the 'nature' of language, will always logically exist, thus preventing – at least logically – total(itarian) closures. As far as Lyotard is concerned there is no such thing as a total language ('language in general'). If there was, then in principle such a general language could provide

BARTH ... Except ... the One who is THE WORD of GOD ... in total freedom of Being ... "from perfection to perfection" ...

the basis for total knowledge (for the coming together of the idea and the example, the conceivable and the presentable, the same and the other) in which unhappy case the notions of subversion/critique – which always take place in the *aporetic 'différance'* between the 'whole and the part' – would end. But fortunately this won't (logically) happen, for reasons Lyotard expresses through his arguments establishing the linguistic 'basis' of the *différend*. What are some of these arguments?

Lyotard's starting point is his view that language is permanently unsettled because it is composed of what he calls phrase regimes: 'a phrase . . . even the most ordinary one', is constituted 'according to a set of rules (its *regimen*)'.[20] These phrase regimes are of different types (phrases that describe or question or command or request, etc.) and, as such, do not logically connect; they do not entail each other ('phrases from heterogeneous regimens cannot be translated from one into the other').[21] Consequently, such incommensurate phrase regimes guarantee, through their heterogeneity, that any attempted homogenisation or translation logically fails. This does not mean that phrases from different regimes are disconnected from each other all the time. Connections do in fact take place in accordance with 'an end fixed by a genre of discourse'. For example, 'dialogue links an ostension (showing) or a definition (describing) onto a question; at stake in it is the two parties coming to an agreement about the sense of a referent'.[22] But the point is that such linkages are neither natural nor entailed, but rather are contingent and, in the end, arbitrary: nothing necessarily connects.

Not only that. Such contingent pragmatics means that any specific linkages that have occurred may *never* take place again. The reappearance of any first phrase cannot ever guarantee that the previous second phrase will also reappear, so the future is radically open: it is not remotely necessary and even less remotely inevitable: who knows what will come next? Moreover – and expanding on the non-entailed nature of phrase linkages and moving into the area of genres of discourse (such genres of discourse being composed of variously allowed/needed phrase linkages) – such genres of discourse are also of a kind such that they themselves do not necessarily connect. For there is no possible entailment between, for example, descriptive genres and evaluative genres (thus you can describe what are, say, the facts of the situation, but the way such facts *ought* to be – or *have* to be – evaluated, doesn't follow). And nor is there any connection between the distinctive categories (faculties) of reason as adumbrated by Kant. That is to say, there is no necessary connection between the faculties of analytical, cognitive, practical and speculative reason, which again subverts the idea of there being any entailed passage between facts and values (between the cognitive and the speculative). And it is this situation that, as already noted, Lyotard wants. It is exactly this non-entailment between the faculties of reason that prevents – at the level of the *contents* of the genres of discourse – total knowledge/integration of difference, thus helping guarantee at least linguistic freedom – and, it is to be hoped, political freedom too:

> Given (1) the impossibility of avoiding conflicts (the impossibility of indifference) and (2) the absence of a universal genre of discourse to regulate them (or, if you prefer, the inevitable partiality of the judge) . . . [then the task is to] show that the linking of one phrase onto another is problematic and that this is a problem of politics.[23]

What politics is about, then, is 'the multiplicity of genres, the diversity of ends, and *par excellence* the question of linkage'.[24] Once again this is similar to Derrida's notion of politics in that because of the relationship between the quasi-transcendental gesture and the empirical (the Idea and the example of it) a perpetual space is opened up that might reasonably be called political insofar as it makes judgements necessary by disavowing any full cognitive grasp or possible programme or set of rules to do the deciding beforehand. Thus for both Derrida and Lyotard, total political closure is a linguistic and logical impossibility, an irreducible condition. For there is always the guaranteed excess beyond every closure, an 'imaginary' place where intellectual reserves can be replenished to challenge all and every claim to achieved totality. As Lyotard puts it:

> what distinguishes various kinds of politics is the genre of discourse . . . whereby *différends* are formulated as litigations and find their 'regulation'. Whatever genre this is, from the sole fact that it excludes other genres whether through interdiction (slaves and women) through autonymic neutralization, through narrative redemption, etc., it leaves a 'residue' of *différends* that are not regulated and cannot be regulated within an idiom, a residue from whence the civil war of 'language' can always return, and indeed does return.[25]

Consequently, for Lyotard (and this is, of course, a non-entailed value judgement he has taken) one's responsibility before any totalising thought consists in 'detecting *différends* and in finding the (impossible) idiom for phrasing them. This is what a philosopher does.'[26] From which position the idea of *justice* for Lyotard consists of keeping the political open, of keeping the *différend* (the *aporia*, the incommensurable) going. Against which one might ask: does this mean then that *any* political genre of discourse must be given a voice irrespective of what it says? It is a question Lyotard attends to in *The Différend* and extensively in his *Just Gaming*.[27] Does it mean – reversing the normal way of putting this *différend* – that a neo-fascist genre must not be silenced by a social democrat one because such a genre will help prevent the attempt of social democracy to become totalistic? Lyotard's answer seems as clear and as arbitrary as Derrida's answer to the same problem (as we saw above, i.e. the problem of whether, if the *différend* is 'natural', is any discourse that might clash with another allowed to do so whatever its substance?). Here is Lyotard's reply:

> What do we do with a thesis like 'it is unjust, I rebel'? How does one say this if one does not know what is just and what is unjust? [Well] . . . absolute injustice would occur if the pragmatics of obligation, that is, the possibility of continuing to play the game of the just, were excluded. That is what is unjust . . . that which prohibits that the question of the just and the unjust be, and remain, raised. Thus, obviously, all terror, annihilation, massacre, etc., or their threat, are by definition, unjust . . . [as is] any decision that takes away . . . the possibility of playing.[28]

Genres of discourse are thus allowed if and only if it is the aim of such genres – were they ever to become hegemonic – not to close down opposition genres, these oppositional genres in turn being committed to keeping the game of the *différend* in play. It is thus that Lyotard will wage his 'war against totality', including wars against total historical explanations (metanarratives) which themselves threaten to subsume and annul all that are different from them or which, as with the lower case, wish jealously to appropriate to themselves the status of the 'proper': for Lyotard both of these closures are unjust.

Applying these arguments very directly to history *per se* at this juncture, then, perhaps the best way to understand how the application of the *différend* to history radically problematises any certaintist claims is to see how Lyotard works the Kantian distinction between the different categories of reason, of which the most important is the *différend* between cognitive and speculative types.

For Lyotard, Kant was correct to see that there is an unbridgeable gulf between the various phrase regimes (faculties) that live under the names of cognitive and speculative reason; that the phrase regimes of one faculty cannot be either reduced to each other or logically entail each other. Thus Lyotard holds that the phrase regimes that constitute the faculty of cognitive reason (phrases about facts, specific events, etc.) cannot be used as a foundation for claims that come from the totally separate faculty of speculative reason (phrases about values, meanings, significance, etc.) such that from 'the facts' one can entail such speculations as, say, the desired direction or a meaning or a purpose for history. That is to say (as Christopher Norris says in his perceptive but severely critical discussion of Lyotard in his *What's Wrong With Postmodernism*) that there is

> no question of consulting past or present events as if to find grounds – probative grounds – for the continued belief in progress, democracy and other such enlightened or emancipatory interests ... To imagine otherwise – as if by looking to history for *evidence* of progress in this or that determinate respect – is to confuse the two 'phrase regimes' of cognitive and speculative reason . . . From which it [also] follows that to treat such episodes [as] . . . the French Revolution . . . as determinate stages in a world-historical progress towards meaning, reason or truth is the worst of all errors, a legacy of the old (Hegelean-Marxist) misreadings of Kant which ignored the difference between *Ideas of Reason* on the one hand and *contingent historical events* on the other, and which thus pinned its hope to various forms of delusive meta-narrative (or 'totalising') theory.[29]

Thus it is this simple category mistake – of imposing some speculative metanarrative on to the ultimately sublime events of the past and the past *per se* – that makes such impositions seem incredible and a positive attitude towards them as now provoking widespread incredulity: surely nobody can believe in such speculations any more? Accordingly, to assume that we can somehow equate matters of cognitive, empirical knowledge with regulative and normative notions also means (as Norris goes on to say) that the idea that we can, in some way, 'learn from history', is just another example of a category mistake or, as Lyotard would have it – a negative lesson in the sheer contingency of all such events. If there is one thing we should have learned by now . . . it is that . . . such thinking ignores the crucial difference between . . . judgements of an ethical, political or social-evaluative character – and those that claim a grounding in past or present historical realities [actualities] . . . So it can never be a question of justifying one's political hopes, convictions or beliefs by appealing to the witness of historical events as if by way of demonstrative proof. This would be an error of judgement similar to that which deludedly seeks a commensurate object (or phenomenal presentation) for feelings of the sublime.[30]

In his essay 'Missive on Universal History' Lyotard has little difficulty in arguing that it is thus impossible to still imagine that we can 'continue to organise the mass of events coming from the human and non-human world by referring them to the Idea of a universal history of humanity',[31] as had been the case with modernity. The modernity meant here is 'not as an epoch but a mode . . . within thought, speech and sensibility', a mode traced by him on this occasion via the first person narration chosen by Descartes through aspects of the eighteenth-century *Aufklärung* to the thought of the nineteenth and twentieth centuries as governed by an Idea (in the Kantian sense): the Idea of emancipation:

It is of course framed in quite different ways, depending upon what we call the philosophies of history, the grand narratives which attempt to organise this mass of events: the Christian narrative of the redemption of original sin through love; the *Aufklärer* narrative of emancipation from ignorance and servitude through knowledge and egalitarianism; the speculative narrative of the realisation of the universal Idea through the dialectic of the concrete; the Marxist narrative of emancipation from exploitation and alienation through the socialisation of work; and the capitalist narrative of emancipation from poverty through techno-industrial development. Between these narratives there are grounds for litigation and even for *différands*. But in all of them, the givens arising from events are situated in the course of a history whose end, even if it remains beyond reach, is called universal freedom, the fulfilment of all humanity.[32]

It is these failures of emancipation in the name of humanity (Humanity) that have been dashed in the twentieth century. Since about the 1930s or 1940s each metanarrative has had its foundations shaken, its principles de-legitimated. Lyotard gives a long list of signs indicating unfulfilment:

> *All that is real is rational, all that is rational is real*: 'Auschwitz' refutes the speculative doctrine . . . *All that is proletarian is communist, all that is communist is proletarian*: 'Berlin 1953', 'Budapest 1956', 'Czechoslovakia 1968', 'Poland 1980' . . . refute the doctrine of historical materialism: The workers rise up against the Party. *All that is democratic is by the people and for the people, and vice-versa*: 'May 1968' refutes the doctrine of parliamentary liberalism . . . *Everything that promotes the free flow of supply and demand is good for general prosperity, and vice-versa*: the 'crises of 1974–1979' refutes the post-Keynesian modification of that doctrine.[33]

Against such 'failures' Lyotard thus praises *petit narratives*. The postmodern is marked by a different kind of thought; by an ever-increasing number of incommensurable, irreducible and performative games (parologies) each with its own players, rules and ends, which keep, under their different names, difference and radical alterity alive. As Kerwin Klein comments, as distinct from little stories which received and bestowed names on their own, the

> great story of history has as its end the extinction of names (particularism). At the end of the great story there will simply be humanity. Hence the postmodern as politics: to denounce meta-narratives and applaud the proliferation of local narratives is to resist totalitarian universal history and political repression.'[34]

Accordingly, points out Klein, in his celebrated exchange with Richard Rorty, even Rorty's laid-back liberal cosmopolitanism was too totalising for Lyotard. Rorty argued that we can do without the fantasy of any transcendental or final grounds for our beliefs given that 'social consensus, persuasion, and pragmatic criticism are not only all that we have and all that we are ever going to get, they are all we need' (an argument that runs alongside my own position that we no longer need history (and ethics) given that the postmodern imaginaries may give us 'all that we are ever going to need'). He suggested that we just keep spinning 'first under narratives' about particular places and groups 'that will help us *imagine* a more cosmopolitan future in which all the world might conceivably enjoy the benefits of social democracy'. But by Lyotard's lights, Klein comments, Rorty's vision is too all-inclusive: 'No cosmopolitanism without mastery', he warns.[35]

In his perceptive *Postmodern Literary Theory* Niall Lucy makes much the same point that, in a nutshell, the message coming from Lyotard is that 'little' is better than 'big'.[36] For Lyotard it is the case of the smaller the better, since it is the smallest narratives and least imperial of genres whose rules and procedures are the least determined and determining. David Carroll agrees: 'The little narrative is, in this sense, a kind of 'zero degree' of differentiating discourse – the form discourse takes to express diversity and unresolved conflict and, thus, resist homogenisation.[37]

Of course, one could always say, as Lucy does, that for all that Lyotard goes on about genres of discourse being in interminable dispute, there is, for him, one thing that isn't disputable; namely, his own argument that 'everything is in dispute'. And Lucy goes on to argue that if this is the case, then it is difficult to see how this statement – 'everything is in dispute' – differs from a metanarrative as 'a genre of discourse that enjoys a universal authority to decide'.[38] But I doubt if Lyotard can be caught in this hackneyed 'performative contradiction'. For Lyotard takes the *différend* to be the case in the same way as Derrida takes deconstruction to be irreducible and Baudrillard the unintelligibility of the world, as working hypotheses not in the certaintist way that metanarratives suggest but as useful fictions that, until they can be refuted, stand as the best way of thinking through such matters. This is the old Pyrrhonist position Lyotard's sophist-pragmatic attitude finds amenable: the Pyrrhonist follows what appears to be the case without committing himself/herself to the view that 'what appears to be the case is the case'.

This, it seems to me, captures Lyotard's anti-totalising, anti-metanarrative and relativistic position and allows the point to be briefly made that it is the incommensurability of those phrases, genres, and discourses, attested to by the *différend*, that allows him to affirm moral relativism and to do so without incurring any damage from the usual critiques of relativism, which accuse it of being a self-contradictory or self-refuting position to hold. That is to say – and I think this is an important thing to say – that Lyotard's *différend* allows him to hold two opposing views of the same thing and at the same time in a way that is not contradictory (i.e. to put it in terms of logic, that rather than accepting that 'p' cannot be both 'p' and 'not p' at the same time, the *différend* allows you to do exactly that), and that the self-refutation argument also fails. That is, the argument that if one claims that it is true that 'everything is relative' then this statement refutes itself by virtue of the argument that if all truths are relatively true then it cannot be absolutely true that 'all truth is relative', just misses the point of what relativists mean.

Yet, because these are popular objections to relativism – and because I am arguing here for a relativistic morality – I want briefly to attend to such arguments in the context of Lyotard's *différend*. So let me begin by refuting the argument from formal logic that 'p' cannot be both 'p' and 'not p' at the same time and then, to conclude, look at the status of the alleged 'self-refutation' contradiction.

With regard to this argument, let us take the example of a person who is differently evaluated by two (or more) people. Let us call this person X. And let us say that according to the first evaluator, A, X has all the characteristics of 'depravity' and should be treated accordingly. Then let us say that according to the second evaluator, B, X has all the characteristics of sainthood and should be treated accordingly. It now looks as if X is both depraved and not depraved at one and the same time. Now, the usual way of resolving this apparent contradiction is to ascertain if X really is depraved or not. But how can this be done? For what we have here is an example of a *différend*; that is, two incommensurable views of the same 'agreed' object (that is, there is not a dispute over the existence of X or over X's characteristics, but over how to evaluate X). Thus the only way one might possibly resolve this would be if it could be shown to both A and B what X really was, 'in and for himself/herself'. But because such an essence is unavailable (so that anything purporting to be an essence could only be a third evaluation) this approach cannot work. Consequently, the only conclusion to be drawn seems to be that, in the absence of any resolution of this *différend*, X is indeed both depraved and not depraved at one and the same time. Thus this contradiction is not so much a contradiction as a relativist paradox. For a contradiction would only exist if we really could definitively know who the person was 'beyond dispute', and that *not* to admit this would commit one to contradict what was known to be the case. But because there is no such knowledge there is nothing to contradict. What we have here are just two non-entailed evaluations taken relative to the lights of A and B which differ and cannot be resolved. Here relativism wins against closure; here the *différend* helps Lyotard win his war against totality.

To help make the argument that such a relativist position is not only not contradictory but not a self refuting position either, let us use some comments by Stanley Fish.

In *Doing What Comes Naturally*,[39] Fish discusses why anti-foundational relativism is not self-refuting. For, for Fish, it is not that anti-foundational relativists think there are no foundations. Such people think it is obvious that there are. But, such foundations are not 'real'. Rather they are useful fictions which just pragmatically allow one to put the world under a description which then acts *as if* it were real. Accordingly, anti-foundational relativists are anti-foundational – are against foundationalists, those who take such 'reality effects' to be 'really real'. But if you don't do that, then you have no self-refutation problems. For because anti-foundationalists are happy to regard all foundations as simply useful fictions, then they are happy to extend this 'vulnerable status' to their own positions; that is, they are not saying that their own 'foundational' (useful fiction) relativism is 'really true', but that it is just a useful way to look at things until a better argument comes along. As Fish puts it:

> This vulnerability also extends, of course, to the anti-foundationalist thesis itself, and that is why its assertion does not involve a contradiction as it would if what was being asserted was the impossibility of foundational assertion; but since what is being asserted is that assertions – about foundations or anything else – have to make their way against objections and counter-examples, anti-foundationalism can without contradiction include itself under its own scope and await the objections one might make of it; and so long as these objections are successfully met and turned back by those who preach anti-foundationalism . . . anti-foundationalism can be asserted as absolutely true since (at least for the time being) there is no argument which holds the field against it.[40]

Here, anti-foundationalism/relativism, here Lyotard's *différend*, win the war against totality.

Final thoughts

In general terms I have argued that the premises that underlie the relativistic, anti-foundationalist stance of Derrida, Baudrillard and Lyotard are those of the performativity of the social and the finite. All three 'know' that there are no 'real foundations' but, on this basis, they 'deconstruct' the ways in which, in social formations like ours, we have tended to forget this. The ways in which the world has been (and is being) put under description (technics) has tempted us to mis-take such pragmatic heuristics for 'reality'. The critique of this blindness has been done in order to keep the fictional – and future – alive; to think the imaginaries of democracies and emancipation to come; to keep the excess and alterity in the frame. For all three (although I am using a Derridean vocabulary) this necessity to think beyond every conceivable closure is articulated as *logic*, as a series of logical arguments along the lines of 'the possibility of the impossibility of the ideality of the term Justice or Time or History': a quasi-transcendental gesture. The key notion of *différance* here is thus essentially a statement of not 'postmodern irrationalism' or some such common accusation, but logic; the logic of the possibility of the sign at the same time as the impossibility of its purity (the possibility of its constitutive repetition). With Baudrillard this is used to critique the economies of the political, the social and the ethical in the name of radical alterity. Baudrillard is interested in the way the future is prepared for so as not to be 'disruptive'; the way it is annulled, pre-arranged, rendered manageable – and how this can be subverted. Lyotard's anti-totalising thought is, again, a logical demonstration of the interminability of phrase-regime language games which are irreducibly incommensurable, while Derrida's *aporia* makes *différance* irreducible. Here the future is opened up. Here the past does not much figure.

Relating these concluding remarks more specifically to history, then, the application of the ideas of Derrida, Baudrillard and Lyotard should now be easy to see. Again the overarching logic of *différance* pretty much says it all.

To put it this way: *différance* is the tension between the idealised quasi-transcendental and the necessity of inscriptions in the phenomenal/empirical world. Every sign wants to say what it actually means, to refer transparently and wholly to its referent. That is the sign's motivation. This is the idealised gesture of the quasi-transcendental. However, for the sign to operate as a sign it must be irreducible to a single context; it must be repeatable in any context (iterability). Otherwise it simply wouldn't be a sign. But this necessity of inscription, of iterability, is also the very impossibility of the purity of the transcendental gesture. Nevertheless, the 'myth' of the realisation of full presence (the Truth) remains as the motivator of the sign of the Law, Justice, etc. and this is thus the site of the *aporetic* tension: the impossible yet necessary condition of possibility. Here the originary violence of the sign (the possibility of its iterability...) enables us to think the transcendental gesture, yet that gesture is not reducible to that sign at any given manifestation. In this context, *history* as a transcendental gesture is only thinkable at the level of the iterability of the sign (*particular* histories) yet it is also irreducible to it in that there will always be an infinite excess, an interminable gap and play between the ideality of history *per se* (the genus) and any specific history (species). In that sense, historical discourse *is différance*, at once an idealised gesture *and* iterable, i.e. subject to different inscriptions – *forever*. Thus the idealised gesture is always 'to come', is never reducible to iterable articulation: there never can be a 'definitive history', i.e. full presence. History as a transcendental realisable idea then – that of the *reconstruction* of the past – is thus yet another impossible 'myth', one that motivates historical work yet is never reducible to it. This aporetic tension of the quasi-transcendental structure between pure intention, presence and iterability is the site/ situation of all deconstruction and is, as such, undeconstructable.

But this logic is, of course, a formal logic. It will apply to historical discourse – as to other discourses – for as long as they exist. But this does not mean that they must exist forever, that history cannot drop out of the conversation, any more than its formal logic determines the substance that goes into it. This might mean at least three things.

First, insofar as we think about history, a definitive history will never be achievable; the logic of deconstruction guarantees this. Second, any discourse that takes as its subject the past and historicises it is currently 'a' *form* of history. As Hayden White puts it, it

> takes as its object of study any aspect of 'the past', distinguishes between that object and its various contexts, periodizes the processes of change governing the relationships between them, posits specific [if problematic] causal forces as governing these processes, and represents the part of history thus marked out for study as a complex structure of relationships at once integrated at any given moment and developing and changing across any sequence of such moments.[41]

It is a 'form' of history irrespective of the specific theories and methods producing from any particular traces of the past its *substantive* content. This means that postmodern histories, were we to want them, are as legitimate as any other 'form and content' fabrication (and as marked by *différance* in the same way). And third – to repeat somewhat the point about the possibility of any discourse dropping out of the conversation – this possibility means that postmodern imaginaries without 'historical back-up' cannot be ruled out – and, indeed, may now begin to be ruled in.

Geographical Imaginations

— Derek Gregory

It is this guaranteed failure then (there will never be a definitive history in terms of either form or content), and the possibilities potentially opened up by it, that is valued in slightly different ways by Derrida, Baudrillard and Lyotard. Yet, rather than this being a reason for despondency and gloom, the fact that history is problematic 'all the way down' is arguably a cause for celebration: it signals at least the end of metanarrative closures and the end of any lower case variant privileging its local expression as 'proper' history. And the same goes for ethics; its demise coincides with the rise of the 'knowledge' of the undecidability of the (moral) decision. Consequently, in the light of such theorising, we might look without nostalgia or anxiety on the benefits of scepticism and relativism for freedom, and for a future that might best realise it unencumbered by the burden of history modernist-style.

The notion of 'definitive history' is thus passé; we have arguably come to the end of history. And not least to the end of the lower case. Accordingly, it is to the lower case that I now turn, and I start by looking at a defence of it as 'real' history, as 'proper' history, by Richard Evans – a view by now surely archaic. And to do so – to enter the intellectual world of Evans – I need temporarily to shift out of the register I have been using (and will continue to use with White *et al.*) to engage with him.

Part II

On the end of 'proper' history

In his essay 'Michel de Certeau and the History of Consumerism', in his book *Cultural History and Postmodernity*, Mark Poster points to the seminal influence of Roland Barthes's 1968 text *The Discourse of History*. In it Barthes decoded the discursive operations by which historians produced the 'reality effects' of their works by pointing to the way the past was represented in history texts as the result of certain combinations of signifiers and referents, an operation that fascinated the theorist of history, de Certeau.[1] For how is it possible, Poster's de Certeau queried in amazement, for a discursive practice and an institutional structure to constitute a specific kind of writing that makes these very conditions of production invisible? How is it possible

> that a narrative form claims to produce not a fiction but a (past) real?. . . What peculiar kind of sustained, permanent ambiguity is it that historians practice, one by which a 'real' past is taken for granted, another 'real' past is represented in texts, and a 'real' present is effaced from their production?[2]

These are indeed good questions and de Certeau's answer hits the spot:

> The operation in question is rather sly . . . [For] the 'real' as represented by historiography does not correspond to the [present] 'real' that determines its production. A *mise en scene* of a (past) actuality, that is, the historiographical discourse itself, occults the social and technical apparatus of the professional institution that produces it . . . The discourse gives itself credibility in the name of the reality which it is supposed to represent, but this authorised appearance of the 'real' serves precisely to camouflage the practice which in fact determines it. Representation thus disguises the praxis that organises it.[3]

In his book *In Defence of History*,[4] Richard Evans does not systematically refute or even address the implications of arguments like this one concerning such modes of 'historical production that disguises the praxis that organises them'. It is the existence of this praxis that Barthes, de Certeau and Poster so unerringly expose. The 'professional' discourse whose plausibility depends on it has been undermined by postmodern critiques such as those of White and Ankersmit. Despite the blurb on the dust-jacket of Evans's book heralding it as a 'brilliant and compellingly effective defence' of history against the 'onslaught of postmodernist theory' which has plunged the profession into crisis ('its assumptions derided and its methods rejected as outmoded') it is, in fact, a poor thing. There are now much more powerfully argued and informed 'defences' of professional history at the level of praxis than Evans's (I am thinking here of recent works by Roger Chartier, Gabrielle Spiegel, David Roberts, Michael Roth).[5] But I have stayed with Evans because he arguably crystallises and articulates at a popularly expressed level (and in that 'accessible register' and no-nonsense style so beloved by 'proper' historians) the problems – and the solutions to these problems – that most typical historians would currently recognise, overwhelmingly concur with and similarly put, to their undergraduate and postgraduate historians. In that sense the level Evans operates at, the things he thinks postmodernists are saying, the defensive arguments he thinks adequate and the attacks he feels will be successful against them, can be regarded as absolutely typical. Evans's very ordinariness and his taken-for-granted assumptions can therefore be used here to 'stand in for' the 'proper' historian in ways other defenders cannot. Consequently, I want to read Evans 'symptomatically'; as representative of an attitude constitutive of contemporary lower case orthodoxy, a not unreasonable thing to do in the circumstances, given the way Evans has assumed the mantle of champion and the way most of his colleagues have cheered him on or tacitly supported him from the sidelines – not least (*pace* Evans's rejection of their sometime criticisms) in their reviews.[6] In what follows I am not going to attempt a word-by-word refutation of Evans, then; rather what I am going to do is, leaving the details precisely as details, put forward a series of arguments in four broad sections before going on to White and Ankersmit.

First, I identify two broad positions which, whether Evans recognises it or not, provide the assimilationist and ideological assumptions that largely determine his own view of history and the histories of others: I consider these assumptions narrow-minded and unattractive.

Second, I argue that, on the basis of these assumptions, Evans tries to make his sort of history invulnerable to critique. In effect Evans wants people to join his 'history club' (or the 'history tribe' as Roth puts it).[7] He has at least two ways of trying to retain/attract members. First, he spends some time trying to counter-attack postmodern arguments in particular. I review some of these attacks and find them slight, unengaged and unconvincing. Second, he defines the 'core' practices of 'proper' history and tries to make them look attractive. He fails in this too.

I then argue, third, that such a 'core' practice – effectively a version of some up-dated Rankeanism – is utterly problematic. My way of reaching this conclusion is two-fold. First, I critique in some detail the three basic elements of Evans's updated Rankeanism. I argue that, as empty mechanisms, they cannot provide the viable basis Evans wants. And second, I argue that if Evans wants to say his discourse is viable in his own terms, then he would have to provide some detailed epistemological and methodological arguments to some areas now commonly regarded as problematic – and he does not do so. I conclude that, on the 'evidence' of his book, Evans has no adequate answer to postmodern (and other) critiques so that, as a result, lower case history Evans-style – and by extension lower case history *per se* – is unviable as a way of convincingly explaining how the past becomes historical discourse 'in its own terms'.

Fourth – under the heading 'Ending Evans' – I move away from Evans towards some broader issues: the nature and viability of the lower case raised by Hayden White and Frank Ankersmit. I argue that their general critiques supplement and compound the more particular ones I shall have been making, for the following reasons.

Evans's text is concentrated very much on a defence of a history based on the viability of the working practices of the 'proper' historian, a professional historian who, with a revised Rankeanism, a lot of patience and a large supply of HB pencils, works on the traces of the past as found in the historicised 'archive' in such a way that they can be 'written up' as history. And it is here that perhaps the most fundamental weakness of Evans's position is made manifest. For Evans admits (and never effectively repairs the admission) on page 64 of his text that while there is plenty of training and rules and methods for assessing the factual reliability of the historical traces of the past, there is *no* training, *no* rules, and *no* definitive methods for the 'process of constructing a story out of the disparate pieces of evidence . . . When it comes to creating a coherent account out of these evidential fragments, the historical method consists only of appealing to the muse.'[8]

Yet it is precisely at this point that postmodernist arguments – those of White (who is incidentally no postmodernist 'as such') and Ankersmit (who arguably is) – kick in. But Evans never engages with this. And this is the fatal mistake. For what Evans has basically defended – the research practices of the archive (documentation, empiricism, objectivism, epistemological realism) are not really much attacked by postmodernists. Of course, postmodernists can and sometimes do – as I have tried to here a little – engage with 'proper' historians at the 'research' level, but White and Ankersmit *et al.* are not much concerned with this *phase* of the production of the historical text, but what happens *after it*: at the decisive level of the mysterious muse. Hence, if Evans had wanted to defend his genre, he need not have much bothered to defend the research phase – whose strengths and weaknesses postmodernists well know and just take as read – but the phase after that, attempting to rebut, *in detail*, the sorts of arguments put forward by White and Ankersmit to the effect that, considered as a finished product (a book, a text), history has all the characteristics of (in its narrative mode/substance) *fiction*. But Evans never examines *why* and *how* they argue this, never attempts a detailed refutation of what postmodern critics actually argue and do. In other words, Evans is defending in his book those historians' practices that most postmodernists do not bother to attack, and leaves undefended the very area that they do. Thus Evans spectacularly misses the point.

At that point I leave Evans to go on to two new chapters, one on White, the second on Ankersmit. After some general remarks on both of them, I look at aspects of their work most relevant to my own argument. My general conclusion, after considering White and Ankersmit, is that, like upper case history, the lower case is now a moribund discourse to be regarded with much incredulity, and that we should effectively abandon it for postmodern moral imaginaries 'beyond the end of histories'.

4　On Richard Evans

We now enter an intellectual world utterly unlike that of the generous quasi-transcendental, cross-discursive, playful, radical one of Derrida, Baudrillard and Lyotard. Here is a world of the flat-earth variety. It is pre-eminently that of practical, technical, 'Serious Men'; of those suffering very badly from the 'effects of gravity' as Nietzsche might have put it – and punned it. And this feeling of coming down to earth, of entering a more mean-spirited, often rather arrogant and dismissive discourse can be confirmed by working through Evans's purportedly sensible, ostensibly moderate and generally much praised book. For while Evans gives the (I think spurious) impression that he has actually read a lot of theory and that he is receptive to even some postmodern aspects of it, he remains adamant that any flights of fancy should be firmly grounded on the work-bench of the day-to-day experience of the jobbing historian.[1] Consequently, it is against the criterion of getting one's hands dirty in the archive (in fact the really rather precious 'artisan' side of the professional) that anything alien will be rejected or allowed. The first of Evans's assumptions which figure his position, then, is what I have termed *assimilationism*.

On assimilationism and ideology

Evans begins his book by making it clear that he speaks for *all* historians. Thus his first sentence is cast in the mode of the inclusive 'we': 'This book is about how we study history, how we research and write about it, and how we read it.'[2] And he also makes it clear that he is updating its basics by self-consciously improving upon those still crucial but now ageing mainstays of the profession, E. H. Carr and Geoffrey Elton, an updating he thinks necessary because of attacks by postmodernists who have caused many 'proper' historians 'at the end of the twentieth century' to be 'haunted by a sense of gloom' as

see Karl Barth

they abandon 'the search for truth, the belief in objectivity, and the quest for a scientific approach to the past'.[3] Yet this sense of a crisis, a crisis Evans sees as rippling beyond history as it compounds the 'much bigger problem of how far society can ever attain the kind of objective certainty about the great issues of our time that can serve as a reliable basis for taking vital decisions for our future in the twenty-first century'[4] (an extension allowing the fate and defence of history to be imagined as integral to the fate and defence of maybe even civilisation itself against postmodern scepticism and relativism) is something he thinks can yet be stemmed. And he thinks this general stemming can be done, in part, by a sturdy defence of the *existing* practices of the 'proper' historian against postmodern despoilers. Evans's task seems clear. 'We' must defend history against some of 'the intellectual barbarians at the disciplinary gates' who are 'loitering there with distinctively hostile intent', or, more accurately, 'we' must be very careful about selecting the one or two who might be let in. For historians 'should approach the invading hordes of semioticians, post-structuralists, New Historicists, Foucauldians, Lacanians and the rest with . . . discrimination . . . drawing up the disciplinary drawbridge has never been a good idea for historians' and some of them 'might prove more friendly, or more useful, than they seem at first sight'.[5] And the criteria for admittance are basically two-fold. First, postmodernists might be admitted if they really can help the profession positively to be more reflexive and intellectually curious in 'productive' ways. And second (and this is somewhat contradictory), they might be admitted if their theories can gird the *present* working practices of *the* historian. As Evans sums up in a style that rather sets the tone for much of the book:

> Practising historians may not have a God-given monopoly of pronouncing sensibly on such matters [as historical ontology, epistemology, methodology, etc.] but they surely have as much right to try and think and write about them as anybody else; and the experience of actually doing historical research ought to mean they have something to contribute which those who have not shared this experience cannot offer.[6]

Now, there are a lot of things going on here and I shall revisit some of them later, but I will begin in this assimilationist section by looking at Evans's characterisation of postmodernists as 'barbarian invaders', a rhetorical move replicating that typical (ethnic) gesture of insiders smearing aliens and demonising the other – in this case theorists of a postmodern type. But I put it to you, is Derrida – a man committed to future emancipation and democracy, a 'humanist' intellectual, a man not destroying but exploring the limits of reason and logic, a man absolutely saturated in ethical and moral concerns and whose close textual readings in several languages would relegate many professional historians' archive work to amateur status – really a barbarian? Is Baudrillard's invocation of a radical, symbolic excess, ironic reversals and his argument that it is the task of theory to never allow total/ totalising/totalitarian closures what one might expect of a man of the horde? Is Lyotard's defence of political difference and freedom precisely *against* totalitarianism and barbarism (*against* the shadow of Auschwitz and possible terrors 'to come') itself the remit of a barbarian invader? Are not the neo-Kantian White, the humanist Ankersmit, the feminist, emancipatory Ermarth, and the moral David Harlan trying to provide generous solutions to the great issues of our time rather than acting barbarically towards them? What kind of hyperbolic language is Evans using here? Well, it serves a purpose of course (a purpose like that of the *ad hominem* attacks Evans also regularly resorts to); it questions the integrity of theorists wrestling with the failure of the modernist project and raises acute questions about the status of discursive practices developed in new emancipatory ways and in new imaginaries (Evans never seriously considers the emancipatory, democratising thrust of radical postmodern arguments). It also re-plays the old strategies of divide and rule, 'us against them' and 'some of them against others of them': the really barbaric are kept out, while the more moderate and usable are let in to bolster the ranks. It is the typical assimilationist gesture so beloved of conservatives, and it permeates the whole of Evans's text. But its failing is that as a strategy it is 'beside the point'.

The assumption upon which all dominant assimilationism rests is that it takes for granted not only its hegemonic position but, when queried, argues that it is deservedly dominant because it is the 'real and proper thing'. As Allan Megill has pointed out, those firmly within a discipline most often do not think of its boundaries, instead they feel its constraints are 'simply those of good scholarship generally'.[7] Thus, what is in this case a historically unique species of history, an utterly contingent and local assembly of phrase regimes, is unreflexively taken to be history *per se* such that it is only natural that it should figure what it sees as counter-hegemonic gestures as fake, and their purveyors as sad charlatans. At the same time it attempts to assimilate recuperable expressions of this 'dissenting minority', which might then serve to portray (a) the dominant discourse as open, pluralistic and accommodating to sensible/rational newcomers and (b) justifiably destructive against all those still deemed to be dangerous. But what doesn't much occur in arguments of this 'qualified tolerance of the dominant discourse' type, indeed, what probably cannot occur if such arguments are to be plausible, is the possibility that those outsiders have a point when they say that such a protected discourse is both a mere genre and one positively harmful, intellectually myopic and non-emancipatory (the claims of some postmodernists).

Of course they do. And what also does not often occur to insiders is whether postmodern outsiders may well be asking – in an interesting reversal – the same sorts of questions about them. Which of course they are. So, for postmodernists who know their position, the question for them is not whether they have anything to offer the insiders so that they might be lucky enough to be allowed to join them, but whether 'proper' historians *are fit to join them* as they now move *not* towards those defended gates but away from them and into the future. Moreover, for postmodernists who have gone on intellectual adventures with Derrida and Baudrillard, Lyotard and Rorty, Ankersmit and White, Ermarth and Harlan, and many others, where they have been engaged in 'making up rules in the absence of rules', what possible attraction does the citadel of the stay-at-home lower case offer? No, what Evans has not realised is that the boot is now on the other foot. And it is not just that either. For Evans's time-scale is askew as well. For since the 1960s or so, postmodern 'theorists' have not only undercut the foundations of the Western Tradition – of which modernity is the latest 'certaintist' expression – but undermined those of both upper and lower case histories so that – for those who look carefully – little remains standing: the upper case is rubble, the lower case unsuitable for further development. Thus whilst one can understand Evans's thinking as a practitioner of the lower case variant in which he still has faith, and that he would indeed welcome any help he can get from friendly barbarians to shore things up for a bit longer, in fact such friendly barbarians are few and far between, and not much interested anyway, whilst the rest have simply moved on to develop their own thing(s). So Evans's defence is not only, as we shall see, internally inadequate, but *too late*: the invaders have been and gone, so that all that is left now are books like this one, attempting to essay some historiographical and ethical/moral aspects as part of that postmodern *retrospective* of that experiment of modernity now rapidly receding into the past – where Evans is himself mentally located.

I turn now to ideology. For the second point that Evans doesn't really register is not only that his history is not history *per se* and his practices those of *a* and not *the* historian, but that the kind of history he professes is, at best, a defence of his own style of appropriating the past and that of his friends and, at worst (as he would regard it), the way bourgeois ideology articulates itself in historical mode, and that this is what he is defending.

Thus, *vis-à-vis* the first of Evans's misrecognitions (the equating of his history with history as such), it is this that presumably allows him to entitle his book *In Defence of History* – a title that must now be seen as a glaring misnomer. Of course, this might be considered as just a slip of the pen, but Evans's assimilationist assumption (what can the benighted barbarians offer us enlightened, civilised historians?) gives good reason for thinking Evans is indeed operating with history as a rigid designator. And this view is further supported by Evans's very Whiggish first chapter (significantly entitled 'The History of History') wherein he reads the history of historiography as variously lacking until it receives the blessing of Ranke's 'three principles' (principles that he thinks still 'rightly' belong to the training of *all* historians) after which its journey eventually leads right up to Evans himself, the Hegelian terminus: the coming of history unto itself. There is no sign of the future anterior tense here. For Evans, 'proper' history, real history, just is his craft, a craft he and his fellow practitioners 'learn on the job' as they handle 'their materials and wield the tools of their trade'.[8] Meanwhile current historical method is, as noted, still based on the 'rules of verification laid down by Ranke and elaborated in various ways since his time', a method, as I've already said, Evans thinks all historians must use and which allows him, as a good Rankean, to present as illustrative of current 'good practice' his own exemplary study of Hamburg.[9]

At various places in his book, Evans bridles at his history being termed bourgeois and his profession being seen as an ideological construct to the extent that it could be said that he protests too much. For it is, after all, only a very short and very sensible step to go on from the widely accepted lower case commonplace that each generation writes/rewrites its own history, to the further step of identifying ideological positions amongst such generations and recognising that these are obviously expressive of specific interests. By which I don't mean that it thus follows that all proper historians are crude 'bourgeois lackeys' (though some are) or that they deliberately (or haplessly) write histories that directly or indirectly privilege the bourgeoisie (though many do) but rather that the point to register in this area is that it is the way in which the *nature* of the historicised past is characterised and 'personalised' (configured) in the same way as the bourgeoisie 'configure' themselves, that is important, so that the past construed 'in and for itself' has the *same* sort of self as does the bourgeoisie such that it is always amenable, given the 'proper' treatment, to bourgeois interests.

Thus, to explain what may appear to be a wild assertion, let me simply pose the question as to how a good bourgeois likes to be regarded and treated so that he or she might respond 'fully' and 'helpfully' in various situations? Well, I think such a person sees himself/herself – and here I draw most of these characteristics from Evans's text – as rational, understanding, objective, truth-seeking, open-minded, tolerant, fair and so on, before other bourgeois, the 'world' and the past: as Evans puts it at one point – adding *four* more characteristic virtues as he does so –

> I will look humbly [*sic*] at the past and say despite them all: it really happened, and we really can, if we are very scrupulous [*sic*] and careful [*sic*] and self-critical [*sic*] find out how it happened and reach some tenable though always less than final conclusions about what it all meant.[10]

This is the type of sentence that gives the game away. For what Evans is doing here, though he clearly doesn't see it (arguing not only that the past has not got a 'self' but that the bourgeoisie hasn't got one either),[11] is giving the past the *same* characteristics as he gives himself/the bourgeoisie, on the (unwitting) assumption that if he treats the past in the same way as he (and the bourgeoisie) like to be treated (humbly, scrupulously, with care . . . rationally, objectively, etc.) then the past, he and the bourgeoisie will be cooperative. Thus, to get the best out of both the past and Evans, to make it and him reveal its/his secrets, its/his meanings, its/his significance, the past just is made in the same self-image as is the bourgeoisie/Evans. It is in that sense, then, that we can talk almost literally of 'bourgeois history'; it is the general, prefigured 'nature' of history that is bourgeoisified.

And of course what applies to Evans and his backward self-projection applies to everybody else at both particular levels within ideology and generally. Thus, the characteristics given by feminist historians to their historicised past, just like the characteristics which were given by, say, Geoffrey Elton to his historicised past, mirror those of feminists and Elton. This is why feminists have no more trouble doing feminist readings of the past than Elton had doing

Eltonist ones, though curiously feminists never seem to come across Elton's past any more than Elton ever came across theirs. And obviously postmodernists characterise the past in postmodern self-images too. Thus for a postmodernist who sees himself/herself as constituted performatively so that he/she is constantly being made and re-made, read and re-read, constructed and deconstructed; who sees his or her 'self' as decentred, endlessly interpretable, positioned yet lacking any essence or foundation, intrinsic meaning or knowable purpose or teleology, and thus the possessor of a self that is ultimately sublime and radically unintelligible and only held together in a 'unity' that is clearly 'fictive', understands the past by virtue of it having all these 'selfsame' characteristics. So that, for the typical postmodernist, the past as such is sublime, relativistic in its parts, lacking any essence, endlessly readable and re-readable, demonstrably non-teleological, etc. and thus of a kind that can only be given a shape or a meaning or a style via a heuristic unity which is, again, clearly 'fictive'. Consequently, it seems that we are always able to get the kind of past we want because it's just us – back there! And because this is the case, then I think that we are now in a position to easily refute such Evansist/bourgeois notions that we are, for example, *all* striving for a 'common objectivity'. For given that the past isn't 'figured' in common, given that it varies as to what it 'objectively' is from self-image to self-image (from ideological position to ideological position), then what sort of common objectivity is he talking about? And so on and so forth.

Consequently, in the light of all this, is it really plausible to think that Evans's history is uniquely blessed so that it alone somehow escapes being as positioned a discourse as everybody else's, that his history alone is above ideological self-imaginings? Well, I think not. I think that Evans's history is just him: it's just his. Besides, if Evans really were defending historicisations of the past *per se* rather than his own ideological interest, then he should be welcoming the historical self-imaginings of others. For if he were doing this, then there is no reason why he could not relax, enjoy and intellectually luxuriate in semiotic, Lacanian, Foucauldean, New Historicist, post-structrualist, postmodern and other appropriations of the past rather than attacking them. He could celebrate and advance the cause of otherness, diversity, strangeness, newness. He could marvel at the way human beings from all manner of places and for all kinds of reasons produce identities, meanings and creative possibilities in the past or future tense. He could admire ingeniously fabricated heuristic neologisms, methodological complexity and wondrously strange perspectives. He could throw off his professional myopia and embrace historical and non-historical imaginings of hope and promise; imaginings 'which have not yet been'. He could relax and play with interminable differences; he could experiment with timing times beyond modernist linearity; he could do all this and know it would 'never have been good enough'; he could live at ease in Lyotard's future anterior. But to imagine these things himself, Evans would have to re-imagine himself too.

Can he do it? I don't know. But the omens don't look good. Of course he may think he can. He may say (as he does on occasion in his book) that he supports diversity; that he respects pluralism; that he welcomes, and does, multiple readings; that he is capable of seeing – though this doesn't come through in his book – that his history is only his and that he can conceive of any number of radically different appropriations of the past all living under a performative (non-rigid designation) of 'history'. But can he really? Let me end this first section with a short thought experiment.

Let us simply ask Evans if he could conceive of, describe in detail and subscribe to a history that really was a 'proper' history, but which has *none* of the categories and *none* of the concepts in it that he currently uses to imagine what history is. That is – to put it another way – can Evans conceive of a history that is still a history all right yet which carries with it *none* of the assumptions, *none* of the methods, *none* of the significances, *none* of the craft skills, *none* of the purposes, *none* of the meanings, etc. his history currently has? If Evans can do this then he certainly would be defending studies of the past in all their endless possibilities. And none of this would mean, of course, that he couldn't still try and discriminate between such possibilities; that he couldn't like best the one he liked best. But such a defence in these altered conditions would be altogether lighter, friendlier, ironic, playful, and thus so different in tone and temper to the narrow, possessive, privileging and ideologically sectional defence he has penned in his current book. If he could think like this, he could never have written his current book!

For what he would be *defending* in the new circumstances just described would be the right of people(s) legitimately to make of the past what they want to make of it – which might be nothing. What he would be defending would be the right for everyone to do what he currently does for himself and his friends; namely, encourage them to make histories for themselves and thence engage in that end-less, *moral* conversation – making up rules in the absence of rules – in ways that respect the conditions of the *différand* whilst (possibly) moving in loose harmony (après Ermarth) toward democracies to come (après Derrida). In his book *The Inhuman*, Lyotard argues that *being prepared to receive what thought is not prepared to think is what deserves the name of thinking*.[12] Postmodernism doesn't have a credo, but if it was ever to want one, Lyotard's open gesture must be in the running.

But, as yet, Evans seems unprepared to embrace postmodernism après Lyotard, whether cast in or out of historical mode. At the moment Evans wants us all to stay in, or at least privilege, the history club that he is a member of, a club that is resolutely opposed to postmodernism. Thus the area I now want to look at is Evans's assumption that we all ought to want to join him and that what he is doing is viable, worthwhile and worth defending. Membership of the club is open to all but the most barbaric of barbarians, but what has it really got to offer? What sort of shape is it in? What is its point? Let us investigate it for a little while.

The history club

On Evans's own account, 'proper' history is now in a number of crises – epistemological according to David Harlan, foundational according to Appleby, Hunt and Jacob, theoretical according to Lawrence Stone, and post-structural according to Diane Purkiss – all of which, singly or combined, threaten to rob the discipline of its traditional *raison d'être*.[13] Of course, in the history of history there have been, says Evans, many other periods of heart-searching and some commentators – Allan Megill, James Vernon, Nancy Partner, Patrick Joyce – apparently see the most typical response by historians to this one as disinterested complacency. And why not? For those who don't regard their discipline as theoretical, why should they care if there are theoretical problems or not? But Evans is not as sanguine. For though he is himself a practical man, he knows that no discipline/discourse is 'practical all the way down'. Consequently, Evans is of the view that postmodern critiques (of *praxis*) have indeed called into question most of the arguments put forward by Carr and Elton upon which much recent 'proper' history in its more Rankean constructionist and reconstructionist forms stands, such that many historians are understandably enough 'worried about the future of their discipline'.[14]

So, it is not a very happy or thriving club to want to join, then, and Evans spends much of his book registering some of the attacks that have been made on it, assessing the damage, and attempting any patching up he deems necessary. The list of possibly damaged areas is a long one and the responses to it generally take one of three (sometimes combined) forms. Either an attempt is made to rebut the attack, or the attacked practice is modified to incorporate any telling critiques, or it is argued that the attacks are aimed at things proper historians no longer do or believe in – if they ever did.

But arguably these tactics rarely work. Here are some brief examples, in a somewhat list-like way. Postmodern critiques of historical truth are parried by Evans with the response that no historian believes in the absolute truth of what he or she is writing but merely in its *probable* truth which, following the 'usual rules of evidence', can generally be ascertained. But this hardly meets critiques not just of absolute truth but precisely of those 'probable truths' that are actually not unproblematically ascertained by the 'usual rules of evidence' at all. I mean, what is the exact status of the 'probable' truth being gained here; at what level does it operate: the single statement, medium range inferences, synoptic accounts, etc.?

Similarly, whilst both Carr and Elton's definitions of 'objective' are 'clearly unsatisfactory as they stand', Evans says this doesn't mean that 'we' have to surrender to the hyper-relativists and admit that no kind of objective knowledge is possible in the (now much qualified but still problematic) sense of the pattern(s) of 'interconnectedness that makes it history rather than chronicle'.[15] But this sort of defence hardly meets objections of a type coming from White or Ankersmit (let alone Derrida *et al.*) that at the level of 'history' epistemology (and thus notions of objectivity and truth) no longer runs, etc.

Again, Evans agrees that Elton was 'completely wrong' to think that there is only one legitimate way to read a document; for there are many 'equally valid' ways (theoretically at least) of doing so. But Evans then goes on to say that, whilst there is 'nothing wrong with this', with a 'little academic tolerance', historical knowledge can still 'surely be generated both by the discovery of new documents and the imaginative reinterpretation of old ones', a defence that doesn't begin to recognise or engage with the devastating critiques of documentarism by La Capra, or McLennan's critique of 'documentary fetishism' and the crazy reductions of the complexities of historical production (after de Certeau) to the 'technicist fallacy', etc.[16]

Similarly, in a long discussion on causality, and having failed to understand postmodern arguments as to the necessity of reversing cause–effect temporal relationships for effect–cause ones (or better still effect–effect ones) for analytical purposes, Evans can only comment, *vis-à-vis* the difficulties of actually delineating causation etc., that of course events are 'frequently overdetermined'. Yet, all this notwithstanding, historians still see it 'as their duty to establish a *hierarchy* of causes and to explain if relevant [and when is it not?] the relationship of one cause to another'.[17] But again this doesn't even begin to answer the problematical nature of causation. For example, what counts as necessary and sufficient causes for, say, the Industrial Revolution? How many variables are involved here (hundreds, thousands, millions)? Where do you draw the lines? How do you combine the variables/factors (select them, relate them, distribute them, give significance to them, etc.) such that a hierarchy is established? How far back and how far afield do you go to establish a relationship? And what form does it, could it, take? How do you know which factors go into which category (social, economic, political, cultural, ideological, etc.) and how do such categories stay defined and agreed upon over time to become hierarchised? These questions are interminable. Moreover, these are questions ostensibly dealt with at the research phase of the historicisation of the past. How such 'resolutions' to them travel securely through the stages of argumentation, emplotment, narrative aesthetics and tropology so to get into the shape of the final narrative discourse, Evans doesn't tell us. But this is what he would have to do if he were to defend in detail the sorts of practices he refers to as the historian's 'historical duty' against those sceptical of their success.

Now one could go on adding to this list almost forever, but the point can perhaps be made at this juncture that as a defence of his discipline Evans's text is thoroughly unconvincing. Peppered with *ad hominem* asides, his evasions, misunderstandings and misreadings (of White and Ankersmit for example) are often mind-boggling. Not only that. For, in putting up his defence, Evans has had to make so many concessions to postmodern criticisms, has had to edge in his 'discipline' with so many qualifications (all those climb-downs from strong to weak definitions etc., which are so defensive and 'leaky') that it is not at all obvious what, in the end, there is left to defend. And it is this point – the 'what is there in the end left to defend' – that I want to look at now. For in fact, at the end of the day, Evans is defending a set of core assumptions which he presumably thinks can withstand the accidents that have happened to its 'accidental features'; namely, an updated Rankeanism. But, in fact, that isn't secure either.

On Ranke and other things

Once you start defending a discourse from critique – once you start tinkering around with it and adjusting it because it does indeed need to provide some answers – then any defence really has to be good. For if it isn't, then opening it up for inept navel-gazing serves only to expose any inadequacies further. And I think that this is what Evans's text has inadvertently done. Of course, one can see in the changing circumstances that embody the shift from modernity to postmodernity the reasons why modernists feel they have to update their discourse so that it still has relevance, but the problem inherent in such updating is how to make sure that both any concessions being made and any new aspects being adopted only strengthen the *essence* of the discourse at the expense of any expendable 'accidents' so to ensure (hegemonic) continuity. Accordingly, in the light of Evans's text, the question that has to be asked is whether the essence of his discourse is in better shape after his efforts than before he began.

Now, this entails our having to identify in some detail such an essence, but in this case Evans has conveniently done it for us. Qualifications and previous/current updating and upgrading fully accepted, the yardstick by which to measure whether Evans's discourse still has credibility lies in whether or not its Rankean three principles ('the basis for much historical research and teaching today' and which still provides 'the *basic* training for history Ph.D. students') are still tenable. So they need to be examined carefully, for if you want to join the history club these are the rules you are being asked to accept, and there is no reason to take them on trust.

It makes initial sense to think that each of the three principles need to be looked at separately, but this is easier said than done. For although it is possible to discriminate between them analytically, in fact they run together for both Ranke and Evans, and me. So my approach will be to treat them separately or together as appropriate, my general verdict on them – to skip ahead a little – being that, singly or together, the three principles are 'empty mechanisms' and are thus, as principles that carry 'in their discourse' narrative points of substance which are *not* entailed, to be found wanting on their own terms: these are principles that cannot remotely guarantee that history 'comes out the right way' – the point of the whole exercise.

It is ironic that Evans's insistence as a Germanist that Ranke's first principle – *Wie es eigentlich gewesen* (which helped 'establish history as a separate discipline independent of philosophy or literature') –

should not be translated as it typically and incorrectly is (to show 'what actually happened') but rather as 'how it essentially was', for this immediately makes the principle very precisely *philosophical*. For the idea of getting 'beneath' or 'inside' the past phenomenal world – even assuming one could get the phenomenal together in a synoptic form (totality) so to find its essence (which one cannot) – is obviously not only a metaphysical gesture (i.e. one has to infer from phenomenal contingency an inner 'life force' so as to divine 'how it essentially was'), but also an empty one: logically one can imagine *any* contingency as expressive of *any* posited essence. And, of course, Evans seems to be completely unaware of Arthur Danto's old (1962) but devastating critique of Ranke's first principle, in that the only conceivable representation of the past as it essentially was would be that of the 'ideal chronicler'; that is, a person able to give a total account of all events as they occurred but without any knowledge of the future, a position that would, as Danto pointed out, 'put the historian out of business'. For, for a history to *be* a history, it necessarily involves a 'looking back' which, by introducing hindsight as a necessary (formal) component of history *per se* by definition, means that ironically Ranke's first historical principle not only cannot be realised by any historian but ought not to be attempted either. In this construction, the whole point of history is *not to know* about actions and events of the past as a witness might but as historians do, while a consequence of Danto's further argument – that 'there are no events except under some description' – is, as Richard Vann puts it, 'a fatal objection to theories which founded history [like Ranke's did] on unit-events susceptible to a definitively accurate description', for this opens the door to radical uncertainty as to 'how many truthful descriptions [at the level of the statement] might be made at the same time'.[18] But maybe even Evans dimly senses this as he moves hurriedly on to Ranke's second principle; namely, that because 'every epoch is immediate to God' and thus the same in His eyes, then the past *should* not be judged (Evans writes *could* not be judged, but this doesn't convey the full force of Ranke's normative imperative) by other standards and particularly 'the standards of the present'. The past has to be seen in its own terms and for its own sake and not ours. Accordingly, Evans's rapid move from the first to the second principle now allows him to go back to the first principle and construct it not in philosophical terms but in terms of objectivity. Thus, Evans argues that Ranke's first principle distanced him from the Prussian school of German historians and from Nationalists like Treitschke who criticised him, for by not privileging Prussia, Ranke's impartiality gave him a reputation for 'being objective'. But obviously this doesn't work. For though Ranke's ultimate referent may be timeless, i.e. God, and although his quest for a stable/conservative essence on its own terms and for its own sake may seem beyond the interest of his own day, this way of construing the historicisation of the past is no more or less 'objective', and no more or less 'presentist', than Treitschke's: I mean, what lies behind someone wanting to study anything 'on its own (impossible) terms' and not ours? And why should the name history be conferred on the first formulation and not the second? Where does the legitimacy of this 'should' come from? No, one is being equally presentist (and 'interested') whether one advocates or rejects own-sakism, both positions stem from the present and because both can be read 'as you like' ('either way') they are also just empty mechanisms. Hence, being empty, the second principle is impotent *vis-à-vis* what we *ought* to do, and thus useless as a principle allowing discriminations between 'proper' and 'improper' histories.

Obviously Evans needs something a little more principle-like than principles one and two if he is to come away with something usable, and so it is that Ranke's third principle – regarded by Evans as 'the most important' – seems to fit the bill. The test-bed by which to ascertain how the past essentially was is to go back to the traces of the past and interrogate them using techniques developed by nineteenth-century philology.

Now, there is no doubt that there is an epistemological, cognitive element in history insofar as it is held not to be technically idealist; that is, insofar as it doesn't regard the way the world is and was as being *dependent* for its own actual existence on our current mental states. Consequently, because postmodernists don't think this, then they have no problem in admitting to the actualities of things 'out there'. Thus, though cognitive knowledge is much more difficult to establish 'beyond reasonable doubt' than many empiricists (and empiricist historians especially) allow, such establishments are just a fact of everyday life at the level of the (true) statement. But whilst this is the case, the main thrust of postmodern critiques is not concentrated at the level of the single, cognitive statement (at what might be called the *syntactical* arrangements of the past) but at the processes of inferential passage from the singular statement to the narrative discourse: from syntax to *semantics*. And as George Steiner has pointed out, such a passage is an impossible one:

it is this progression . . . when such approaches [as empiricism] seek to formulate meaning; when they proceed upward from the syntactical to the semantic . . . which no analytic-linguistic technique . . . has ever taken convincingly.[19]

Thus it is this that allows people such as Richard Rorty and David Roberts to agree that what has been glimpsed from the eighteenth century until now, when it ripples right across our culture, is that *anything* can be made to look good or bad, right or wrong, useful or useless, by being *re-described*, and that, shorn of metaphysical foundations, of non-terrestrial sky-hooks, we are now left with a world where there is 'nothing but history' (contingency), and where the 'past' we are left with – and the 'history' that we use to try and make sense of what we are left with – are both interminably re-describable. They agree that the apparently firmest principles are, at best, useful fictions – principles like all three imagined by Ranke.

There is every reason to think, then, that Evans is going to have insurmountable problems using Rankean principles to infer all the way up from syntax to semantics: *he would be absolutely unique if he didn't*. But that's the point. Historical 'truth' is not much in dispute at the lower level of the syntactical; the question of objectivity and truth is raised in the middle and upper ranges of historicisations of the past – which is where White and Ankersmit come in and Evans drops away. But I would like to tighten up these sometimes fairly general remarks by simply outlining an anti-Rankean/anti-empiricist argument and posing against it the question of how would, how does, Evans get around the problems the argument seems to throw up, and to do this in a way that the movement from syntax to semantics might be 'more or less' achieved. It is a position on which Evans's whole text is premised; that is, he is defending a practice that, it is implied, can achieve ('more or less') the impossible.

In his article 'Postmodern versus the Standpoint of Action'[20] Geoffrey Roberts summarised a critique I had made of empiricism which he went on to argue did *not* apply to Geoffrey Elton – one which I thought did apply. This is a detailed argument that need not be re-opened here, but I mention it because Roberts's summary of my critique is so lucidly formulated that I reproduce it, for if it doesn't apply to Elton I think it applies to Evans – who is certainly no 'standpoint of action' man. Here then is Roberts's summary, the question I want to leave for Evans being simply this: how do Ranke's principles, suitably updated, deal satisfactorily with the points raised – in detail – points not satisfactorily dealt with in the existing *Defence*?

The past was a once existing objective reality but the objective status of the past as an object does not mean that it can be known objectively. Indeed, it cannot, for the past has gone . . . All that can be known are the remnants of the past's once existing reality: documents, artefacts, and maybe memories.

So far so good. . . . But the crucial moves in the Jenkins argument have yet to come. Statements about the past are statements about the evidence. Because there is so much evidence such statements are necessarily selective. The problems arising from the selection of the evidence are manifold. First, selections from the evidence refer to a real but no longer existing object (the past) which is unknowable. The relationship between the selection and the object to which it refers is problematic and unprovable. Second, making any one selection from the evidence requires interpretation. It is interpretation that endows the selection with its coherence, unity, and significance. Interpretations are derived from various sources – political, ideological, linguistic – including previous interpretation and, maybe, the pre-interpreted nature of the evidence itself. Attempts to validate an interpretation by reference to the real object are impossible by definition; attempts to validate by reference to the evidence can only be reassertions of the interpretation in comparison and competition with other interpretations. Third, while it is possible to establish some facts about the past and to make truthlike singular statements that relate to them, collectivities of such facts/statements require the invention of a background, context, totality, story or iconic representation. Such inventions are necessary to transform collections of singulars into meaningful wholes. These wholes are inventions because the referent to which they ostensibly correspond (the past) does not exist. Conclusion: we cannot know the past, we have no direct access to it, historians have no means of breaking out of the self-serving circle of evidence-selection–interpretation (or interpretation–selection–evidence, and so on). The empiricist project of seeking to know a real past in order to seek real truths which can be validated by evidence is, therefore, an illusion. Historians – even most non-traditionalists – are notorious for insisting they deal in reality and truth. How do they maintain this position in the face of these powerful anti-empiricist objections?[21]

Ending Evans

In her 'Historicity in an Age of Reality – Fictions', Nancy Partner argues that the 'central' question that haunts western culture is some version of 'how can we depend on words to connect us to reality?'[22] In postmodern terms this might be reformulated to read: how do we constitute reality (reality effects) in language in such a way that these form ultimately foundationless pragmatic imaginaries which allow us not to know definitively but to be able to cope with what we take to be reality/actuality? And because all these coping pragmatics ultimately leave the world as such – for all we know – unintelligible, then we can say that the world is always coped with metaphorically or, better still, through the trope of *catachresis*. For as David Roberts points out, Derrida insists that even the notion of metaphor is misleading in this context because it can imply an independent reality to which the metaphor knowingly refers figuratively. For when we actually work back from this gesture seeking a reassuring connection to some preceding actual world, we find no intelligible stopping point, no solid ground. Thus the founding concepts of reality/actuality are instances not of metaphor but of catachresis – 'a violent production of meaning, an abuse which refers to no anterior or proper norm'; moreover, if we insist on the literal–metaphor distinction, it too can be destabilised as 'undecidable'.[23] Consequently, it is this condition that allows Partner to wonder about how we can ever – given that all our narratives are ultimately fictional – consider history as being somehow 'non-fiction?' (we are back to de Certeau!). And to try and explain this, Partner argues for a distinction to be made between the overarching, ultimate fictionality of *all* discourses, and, within this overall fictionality, to make the point that some fictions are more fictional than others.

Her interesting argument goes like this. History, in order to be history, 'has to call on the fiction-making capacity of the mind to such an extent (to impose form on time, to locate "event", to impose plot on the seriatim of reality) that the essential question about history is how it can separate itself out from fiction at all'.[24] For all books, simply to be books, begin in fiction, and just some of these books 'assert history as a certain kind of announced authorial commitment ... between writer and reader'. Thus, the meaning of history depends on the meaning of fiction and not the other way round 'because fiction is analytically prior, the larger category'; fiction being used here by Partner in the 'inclusive sense of linguistic artefacts; verbal objects whose coherence and intelligibility are made, not found, by exploiting the grammatical, syntactical and rhetorical capacities of language'.[25] Consequently, fictional invention (the novel, poetry, etc.) is a sub-category, 'a specific application of the larger capacity called fiction'. Accordingly, Partner argues that a great deal of unnecessary confusion can be avoided if this distinction between the primary and secondary uses of 'fiction' is kept in mind; that is, the distinction between (1) the creation of form in language and (2) the invention or imaginary description of events and persons. And it is this distinction that is then applied to history. For while history is fictional as being included in the first distinction, that is, the 'primary or formal fictions which create intelligible event and narrative structure' without which history is inconceivable, it is different from fiction in the second sense in that it 'dissociates itself from fiction as a special category of verisimilar prose through a system of (implicitly) announced limitations and accepted restrictions' which never allowed history to be second order fiction at all.

Now, it is this latter distinction between the totally imagined referent (as in the novel etc.) and a referent that refers to something not (totally) imagined but somehow real/actual (courtesy of 'fiction number one') that has been held to distinguish (from Plato and Aristotle on down) fiction from history courtesy of the imagined/real status of their referents. And it is this distinction that White and Ankersmit problematicise by stressing not the distinction between (secondary) fiction from history *vis-à-vis* the status of their referents, but the fact that, whether the referent is real or imagined, both are, to be 'books', fictional in the primary sense après Partner. For (say) White, what is at issue is not at all the undoubted 'fact' that histories refer to an actuality which is not imagined by historians in any idealist sense, but rather that in order to put *both* the 'imagined' and the 'real' referents into story and narrative forms, shapes and styles when neither 'fiction as totally imaginary' nor 'history as past events' have such narrative forms *in* them, means that all histories have to have such forms (of fiction number one) imposed upon them. Events just don't have in them 'the shapes of stories', so histories that assume narrative form (and the case can be successfully made that, in the end, all histories are of this type)[26] can thus be seen as what they are; namely, 'verbal fictions, the content of which are as much invented [or imagined] as found'.[27] For White, all historical narratives presuppose figurative characterisations of the events they purport to represent and explain. And this means that historical narratives, conceived purely as verbal artefacts, can be characterised 'by the mode of figurative discourse in which they are cast'.[28] Of course, adds White, historians do not like to think of their work as the 'translation of fact into fiction', but that is the effect:

> I know that this insistence on the fictive element in *all* historical narratives is certain to arouse the ire of historians who believe that they are doing something fundamentally different from the novelist, by virtue of the fact that they deal with 'real' as opposed to the novelists' 'imagined' events. But neither the form nor the explanatory power of narrative derives from the different contents it is presumed to be able to accommodate. In point of fact, history – the real [actual] world as it evolves in time – is made sense of in the same way that the poet or novelist tries to make sense of it, i.e., by endowing what originally appears to be problematical and mysterious with the aspect of a recognisable, because it is a familiar, form. It does not matter whether the world is conceived to be real or only imagined; the manner of making sense of it is the same.[29]

Now, these references to Partner, White and Ankersmit begin to take us away from the flat-earthism of Evans and back into the intellectual space occupied by Derrida *et al.* At this point we are able to leave Evans and the genre of history he is calling history *per se* to move back into a much more generous and reflexive world, a world discussed in such a different vocabulary and register to Evans's, a world that Evans knows exists and yet refuses or is unable to comprehend. For, to make at the end of this examination of Evans a point I made at the beginning, if Evans had really wanted to 'sort out' postmodernists, this is the world he would have to have entered *in detail.* If Evans had really wanted to have undone the attackers of his history, then he would have needed to lay out, piece by piece, the component parts of the arguments of, say, Derrida, Baudrillard, Lyotard, White, Ankersmit *et al.*, and shredded them. This would have been at least an interesting spectacle, Evans trying to take apart Derrida's *Of Grammatology*, White's *Metahistory* or Ankersmit's *Narrative Logic.* But he hasn't. Thus Evans, for all his huffing and puffing, leaves White *et al.* intact; never engaged with. For Evans's 'representative' defence is as weak as it is because he is defending, at most, the empirical/cognitive/epistemological aspects of the 'proper' historians' work that postmodernists are not really interested in attacking, and leaving as exposed as ever the 'historical semantics' they are. I therefore turn now to White and Ankersmit themselves, and I do so with David Roberts's verdict of White ringing in my ears: that, *pace* Evans, White's arguments about emplotment, tropology and narrative discourse are, quite simply, 'unassailable'.

5 On Hayden White

This is not the place for a detailed exegesis of the whole of White's work. I have tried to introduce and popularise aspects of it on other occasions and most particularly in On 'What is History?' From Carr and Elton to Rorty and White.[1] Further introductions and contextualisations of White in book length form have also recently appeared in Alun Munslow's positive overview of the ways postmodernism has arguably changed 'how we study the past historiographically' (Deconstructing History) and in Alex Callinicos's equally perceptive but negative Theories and Narratives.[2] Nor is this the place for an overly scholarly dissection of White. For again, this has been essayed over the years and still continues.[3] There is no need for more work of this kind here. Rather, I will concentrate on three things relevant to my critique of the lower case (which does not completely forget Evans's defence but doesn't much bother with it either any more) and to my further argument that in the wake of the collapse of the upper and lower case histories we can now perhaps live in the imaginaries of the postmodern that have little use for either: in this context I have thus appropriated White, along with Ankersmit, as one of my two lower case 'demolition experts'.

My three tasks vis-à-vis White, then, are as follows. First, I will sketch out briefly – for those who might have come to White via Evans or some other equally misinformed route – what might be called a review of White's more basic assumptions. Second, I will summarise why White says he went to rhetoric and tropology for an understanding of why history texts get constructed and constituted as they do. And third, I will sketch out the sorts of arguments and conclusions Evans (or anyone else) would have to engage with if the lower case genre were to be at least a little plausible 'all the way up from syntax to semantics'.

White's basic assumptions

As far as I know (and despite accusations to the contrary) White has never argued that past events, persons, institutions, social processes, etc. (i.e. the past *per se*) did not exist, did not happen, and did not happen in exactly the way it did. In fact, he insists on this.[4] Nor has White ever argued that *everything* is language or discourse, or that we cannot refer to and represent extra-discursive entities; indeed, he again insists that historical discourse refers to a world outside itself. Nor has White ever argued that things in the past didn't occur in ways that allow them to be understood chronologically. Nor has he ever denied that the traces of the past are available archivally ('archives' obviously understood as themselves historical products); indeed, he simply takes it as read that such an 'archive' exists, that it is appropriable, that historians appropriate it, and that it forms part of the 'basis' (albeit 'always in discourse') for types of historical construction relative to the protocols available at any given time and to, say, one in particular, such that cognitive knowledge of a warranted kind becomes evidential. Nor has White ever denied that there is a distinction – at the level of the referent – between the totally imaginative and the 'real'/actual. Nor does he deny the pragmatic success of the techniques practised in the archive and their sometime scientific status; indeed, 'the scope for "scientific" research, for access to information about the past', he simply takes for granted.[5]

Rather – *and against all this* – what White has been concerned with in much of his 'theoretical' work is simply this: that it is *counter-intuitive* to argue that historians cannot construct from the *same* historical traces, from the *same* subject matter/material, and from the *same* well-attested phenomena that occurred in the past (phenomena simple or complex), a range of different narratives (not stories but narratives). These narratives confer on such materials/phenomena entirely different meanings, significances and thus interpretations/readings that are *not* mutually contradictory, *not* mutually exclusive, *not* logically entailed, *not* ever definitive and thus they come (as aesthetic, shaping/styling appropriations) from a different place from the phenomena that actually occurred. There is very precisely an 'inexpungeable relativity in every representation', a relativity, White adds, that is a function of the language used to describe and thereby constitute past events *not* – and this needs to be underlined repeatedly – *not* to constitute them in the sense that until so constituted such 'events' didn't actually once take place but to constitute them so that they become 'possible objects of explanation and understanding'. All this, adds White, is obvious.[6] And so it is.

Consequently, what White is primarily concerned with in his more theoretical and methodological works is the way in which the historian – whether working in the upper or lower case, whether working on, say, intellectual or economic history, or whether working at the centre or the margins of any given discourse or any given social formation – has to go through the *same* formal (structuring) processes in order to produce from the traces of the past something such traces never were and never indicated; namely, *a narrative structured, historical text as a literary artefact whose content is as much imagined as found*, a phenomenon totally in and of language. What White is interested in (as Roth has pointed out)[7] is displacing epistemological questions and concerns about objectivity in favour of inquiries into the literary and poetic structures of historical narratives and a critique of their 'masking' function. The interesting questions for White are not about the correspondence of a story with its 'once reality', but about the fact that there is no 'reality' that can be considered apart from some meaningful emplotment of it. To write a history is to construct one kind of narrative rather than another, not to represent the past 'plain', so that White's concerns centre on how historians create criteria for what would count as 'realistic' so as to give their narratives authority. Accordingly, White starts his analyses of how histories get made not from the traces of the past up to the finished text (not from the archival/research phase up) but the other way round. White starts with the finished product – the text – and with the 'real' present which (as we saw de Certeau point out at the start of this Part) is normally effaced from the production of their texts by historians, and he works back through the various stages of its production to understand how the past – which 'in itself' is not historical – gets historicised. Again, Roth is to the point:

> Crucial for White's approach to historical writing is the idea that we endow the past with meaning because 'in itself' it has none. The historical writer must form the past into a narrative because the past is formless, or at least it does not have the rhetorical forms that alone make it meaningful in communication. White does not provide metaphysical arguments about the nature of the past prior to its textualisation but instead notes that our history comes to us in ways mediated by texts and thus always formed by tropes (usually) in a narrative. His own work explicates how the mediation achieves its effects.[8]

White's analyses concern the way that history texts – whatever meaning or significance they confer upon their object of study – all have to avail themselves, then, of a mode of emplotment, a mode of argumentation and a mode of tropicalisation to achieve a narrative form, processes given direction by – and thus embodying – an ideological preference. Which means that ultimately one chooses (in ways that do not necessarily disregard the 'empirical' evidence) the histories one likes on the basis of moral/political grounds that are precisely – if they are 'real' moral *choices* – radically contingent. As White puts it:

> Placed before the alternative visions that history's interpreters offer for our consideration, and without any apodictically provided theoretical grounds for preferring one over another, we are driven back to moral and aesthetic reasons for the *choice* of one vision over another as the more 'realistic'. The aged Kant was right, in short; we are free to conceive 'history' as we please, just as we are free to make of it what we will.[9]

Despite misreadings to the opposite effect, White's arguments are clearly not designed to deny the past (an independent – albeit textual – referent) or an empirical element in historical discourse, but concentrate on the narrative form it overwhelmingly takes in our social formation. Yet this is not to say that such linguistic constitutiveness – as the above reference to Kant and moral non-apodictic choice should make clear – means that White is arguing for some kind of linguistic determinism – again as he is often accused of doing. Quite the reverse. It is White's point that although any given culture certainly tries to restrict the range of historical appropriations, within this range the choice of plot structure, mode of argumentation and figurative trope are relatively free – and this is a good thing. As White spells it out, 'narrative accounts of real historical events admit of as many equally plausible versions in their representations as there are plot structures available in a given culture for endowing stories, whether fictional or real, with meanings', and this freedom is important both politically and for raising to a reflexive consciousness the constitutive processes involved so that one 'is in control of one's own discourse'. Here is White putting these two points – about freedom and reflexivity (hardly the hallmark of a barbarian) – together:

> Finally, it may be observed that if historians were to recognise the fictive element in their narratives, this would not mean the

degradation of historiography to the status of ideology or propaganda. In fact, this recognition would serve as a potent antidote to the tendency of historians to become captive of ideological preconceptions which they do not recognise as such [Evans note] but honour as the 'correct' perception of 'the way things really are'. By drawing historiography nearer to its origins in literary sensibility, we should be able to identify the ideological, because it is the fictive element in our own discourse. We are always able to see the fictive element in those historians with whose interpretation of a given set of events we disagree; we seldom perceive that element in our own prose. So, too, if we recognised the literary or fictive element in every historical account, we should be able to move the teaching of historiography onto a higher level of self-consciousness . . . By drawing historiography back once more to an intimate connection with its literary basis, we should not only be putting ourselves on guard against *merely* ideological distortions, we should be by way of arriving at that 'theory' of history without which it cannot pass . . . at all.[10]

To summarise: it is clearly not White's intention to deny the actuality of the past, or that the technical work in the archive produces cognitive statements, or that it is perfectly correct to assess the veracity of historical discourses in terms of their *truth value* at the level of the statement or at the slightly more problematical level of the chronicle, for otherwise, says White, history could not justify its claims to represent once 'real events'. But all that said, beyond these cognitive elements, the 'truth' doesn't enter into it; historiography just isn't – as historiography – an epistemology. David Roberts has put this well and I conclude with his comment that

it is one thing to apprehend some set of events; it is something altogether different to emplot them, to make up a coherent narrative out of them. And for White, truth is no longer at issue once we move from the archive and the chronicle into the narrative telling. So even though the mode of narrative emplotment affects the very content of the historical account, there is no scope [Evans note] for assessing modes of emplotment and narration in terms of the truth/fiction dichotomy. The scope for assessing the truth value of historical accounts is confined to the lower, pre-narrative [epistemological] level . . . [Thus] White's own priority was to show not how truth becomes possible but 'how historical discourse produces its characteristic knowledge effects.'

In the last analysis, _all_ stories for White are fictions and can only be true in a metaphorical sense. Thus his insistence that 'stories are not true or false, but rather more or less intelligible, coherent, consistent and persuasive, and so on. And this is true of historical, no less than fictional stories.' Conversely, arguments about the meaning of events are as much about the plot structure as the events themselves, so neither can they be true or false. Rather, they constitute second-order fictions.[11]

White on rhetoric and tropology

It should now be clear that for White it is just a highly desirable fact that the same subject matter is always capable of providing the basis for potentially equally plausible narratives thus (potentially) invoking highly reflexive choices and moral/political freedom and emancipation. And also, that whatever meanings and significations actually are conferred, _all_ historians inevitably construct their narratives using the same rhetorical strategies that imaginative writers use, strategies that are – and here I begin to develop this point – more tropological and aesthetic than logical in nature. For something happens between the so-called 'research phase' and the 'writing up phase' that seemed odd – and still seems odd – to White. 'I found', he comments, 'that if we start not with this kind of information [the research phase] but look at the [finished] text itself, you can see that a lot of times . . . [historians] have said things . . . that can't be justified on the basis of their reports about the research. The composition of the historian's text, just on the basis of compositional considerations themselves, transforms the materials that they have worked up from the archives.'[12]

This comment by White as he reflects back on the writing of _Metahistory_ is taken from an interview he gave to Ewa Domanska which appeared in _Diacritics_ in 1994,[13] an interview that I now want to draw on closely. For in it he answers the highly relevant question here of how and why he used a theory of tropes to help understand how historical texts are the way they are; of what the muse consists of. The gist of White's position can be put thus.

White recalls that when he came to write _Metahistory_ in the early 1960s – it was a work that took nearly ten years to write and came out in 1973 – he knew nothing about rhetoric. He had been taught that rhetoric was 'a bad thing'; that it wasn't interested in truth, that it was concerned only in persuasion and that historians should avoid it. Historians then, like now, just do not like rhetoric 'because they think that, in what they are doing, there isn't any rhetoric. They always resist. They resist anyone who tries to tell them something about what they are doing.'[14] But in order to write the book he wanted to write – a book on nineteenth-century historical writing – he felt he needed some principles 'for organizing and characterizing the different ways the nineteenth century did history, wrote about history'. What White wanted to escape from was the way most studies of historical research and production looked at what historians said they did when they were at work rather than engage with what they wrote. For White spotted some huge discrepancies between the two:

> It seemed to me that the way most people had written the history of history writing was to listen to what the historians had said they did, rather than analyzing what they actually wrote. Ranke, for example, pointed out: we go to the archives, we study this, we study that, we come out, we arrange things, then we write it up. There is the research phase, and there is the writing phase. I found that if we start not with that kind of information but look at the text itself, you can see a lot of times they have said things . . . that can't be justified on the basis of their reports about the research. The composition of the historian's text, just on the basis of compositional considerations themselves, trans-forms the materials that they have worked up from the archives. So I needed a way of characterizing different styles of representa-tion. That's why [as a historian trained as a medievalist and who wrote a thesis based on work in the Vatican archives] I started studying literary theory . . . and thus rhetoric.[15]

Of course, this is not to say that because compositional considerations transform the materials worked up from the archive that extrinsic moral/political factors don't count, because they do. For a historian who has always regarded himself as 'a Marxist basically',[16] what I think White liked about compositional rhetoric was the fact that it was so thoroughly political:

> the inventors of rhetoric, Gorgias and Protagoras and all the people [sophists] who were attacked by both Plato and Aristotle, really were philosophers of language. [For] . . . rhetoric is philoso-phy; it's a materialist philosophy and presumes an entire ontology. What the Sophists taught is that metaphysics is impossible . . . [while] rhetoric is conceived as a theory of how meaning is pro-duced, of how meaning is constructed, not how meaning is found.[17]

'A theory of how meaning is produced and not found.' This is what White wanted to help him understand political stylisation and the way formal structures worked the 'content'; a theory of language, of meaning production, and a materialist, political and sceptical philosophy. Reading the Sophists, Vico, Hegel, Mill, and literary theorists like Northrop Frye, Kenneth Burke, Lukács, Jacobson, Jameson and others, White's application of them – in *Metahistory* – was devastating.

What White got from rhetoric as a theory of language he recounts as follows. Narrative writing is *not* informed by logic. There is no narrative that *ever* displays the consistency of logical deduction. Syllogistic logic only tells you about propositions. But although narratives contain propositions, narrative is not an extended set of propositions. Again, there are extrapropositional components in narrative, and these have to do with syntax. But it's not a grammatical syntax; it's a syntax of language use beyond the sentence. Consequently, given these limitations, what White thought he required was a 'logic' of narrative composition. And this is what he found in rhetoric, though not in ancient rhetoric (he found the politics there) but in modern rhetoric. For modern rhetoric enabled him to catch the rhythms and contradictions of both 'life' and the 'writing up' of life. As White puts it:

> I believed that Hegel's dialectic . . . is an attempt to formalize practical thinking. When people relate to one another in politics or in love, they don't relate syllogistically. It is not a syllogism . . . It's an enthymeme. And most compositions – most everyday speech – are enthymemic. They do not follow rules of logical deduction . . . So, as both Hegel and J. S. Mill realized, you need another kind of logic to talk about practical affairs, a logic of praxis. The logic of praxis cannot follow the logic of identity and non-contradiction. . . . Society creates situations in which you must act in contradiction. So you need a theory of the representation of life lived in contradiction. That would allow you to account for the syntax of real lives. In the study of narrative, people who try to provide a logic of narrative fail . . . Because the point and fact is that a narrative is not a large sentence. And grammar can only tell you about sentences, not about discourses.[18]

Consequently, if such sentences are not linked together by logic, but if they somehow have to make sense, this can only be done by tropology:

because you need a theory of *swerve*, of systematic deviation from logical explanation. That's what is fascinating about narrative. It can't be governed by strict rules of logical deduction. So I turned to rhetorical theories, because I believed that rhetoric provides the theory of improvisational discourse.[19]

This is why White went to tropology. Not to confuse, not to distract attention from the archive, not to call into question referentiality, but to try and explain how, in even our most 'plain-speaking' discourse, it is rhetorical tropes (of metaphor, metonymy, synecdoche and irony) that join sentences together semantically to form meanings in narrative structures. And, because rhetoric also drew attention to philosophical scepticism and relativism, this allowed White to link tropology to both his humanist/materialist and his relativistic political position. For what Sophist rhetoricians taught is that metaphysics is impossible; that existence, the past, the world remain, even after our best efforts to constrain them, unintelligible, sublime. Rhetoric is thus based on an understanding of human finiteness and catachresis: it is sceptical; it is morally relativist; it is anti-logic 'writ analytical'. As White puts it, Gorgias and Protagoras realised that

> there is no such thing as one correct way of speaking and representing the world, because language is arbitrary in its relation to the world that it speaks about. And what was proper speech [and history], correct or truthful speech [and history], depended on who had the power to determine it. So rhetoric is the theory of the politics of discourse . . . It says that discourse is worked out in conflicts between people. Those who determine who will have the right, the power, the authority to say what correct speech is, and those who attempt to name correct speech . . . to legislate it, are always authoritarian, from Plato on.[20]

Consequently, what the rhetorician knows is this: that meaning, significance, purpose, truth, is always produced through the machinations of *regimes of truth*. Which is why a rhetorical conception of any form of discourse – like history – that can't be formalised provides some kind of equivalent to what poetics tries to do with its analyses of poetic diction and speech.

History, then, has an irreducible poetic element which means that it can never be fully logical or true or scientific or an epistemology:

History has a double face. A scientific one and an artistic one. That's what makes it interesting. You're always facing in two directions. But the historians don't know that, because since the nineteenth century they have been taught that they must keep literary and poetic effects out of their writing . . . You do your research as a scientist, but then, when it comes to writing, its okay, make it . . . so people can read it easily, but your writing does not add anything except cosmetics to your truth . . . And that's *wrong*. Any modern linguist knows that the form of the representation is a part of the content itself. That's why I call my most recent book *The Content of the Form* . . . To choose the form is already to choose a semantic domain.[21]

Thus the interesting question about the practices of the historian which White has been pondering on since the 1960s is formulated by him precisely as a question: 'if the old nineteenth century easy distinction between fact and fiction can no longer be maintained, and if instead we see them as a continuum in discourse', then, says White, I would ask 'what is the fictional function in nonfictional discourse, or in discourse which tries to be nonfictional?' Because anyone who writes a narrative is fictionalising.

All this being the case, then, White's 'non-barbaric' intentions and his genuine desire not to destroy history but to understand it as an ambivalent discourse is essayed in the final comments of his interview. White's views on history *resemble* those of Derrida and Lyotard. A series of statements from him, then, to bring this section to a close. Thus, 'there are many ways of studying history . . . there is no possibility of legislating one orthodoxy about the way history is to be studied'. Again 'One can improvise different techniques of representation for the past, and that's why the writing of history has a different kind of history from the study of physics.' Again 'we have only to look at the history of historical writing to recognise that there are different stylistic variations. And what is really naive about historians is that they always think that the current way of doing history is finally the best.' Again 'It is impossible to legislate the way people are going to relate to the past because the past is a place of fantasy. It doesn't exist any more . . . so [its people] can't be studied empirically. They can be studied by other, nonempirical kinds of methods, but there is no way of finally determining what is the best theory for studying and guiding research in history. But you can have a theory of historical writing.' Like *Metahistory*. Like White's works. And these works are offered by White in the same spirit as Collingwood offered his. Collingwood used to say, concludes White, that he didn't bother to reply to criticism too much. I just do my best, he used to say, and if people can use what I do then fine; if not, then they are free to do it better. And this is White's view too. There is none of the tightness, the retentiveness and petulant hurtfulness of Evans's text in White's laid-back, generous and humanist, emancipatory position which, for me, makes him such an attractive intellectual. 'I don't mind what anyone calls me', he writes. 'I don't think labels are important. My view is this: don't worry about labels or schools. Here is a book. Read it. If it helps you in your own work – good; if it doesn't – forget it.'[22]

Engaging with White

Insofar as we are interested in history continuing I don't think we ought to choose to forget *Metahistory* (or, for that matter, White's other texts). Maybe White himself (as he sometimes says) can. Maybe White has moved on so that, for him, some aspects of *Metahistory* are now passé.[23] But most of us are so theoretically backward, most of us still have such a lot of catching up to do, that for us *Metahistory* is still *a book for the future*. But of course the point here, in the context of *this* book, is that White is also useful for those who may be thinking that history is coming to – and ought to be coming to – an end. That White is useful not for what he can help us become as historians (reflexive; able to see history can never be an epistemology; that all narrative histories – in whatever case – are by their form, meta-histories, etc.) but for the help he can give to undercut not just existing upper and lower case genres but maybe history *per se*. For what White's works do is to confront lower case historians (like Evans) with a way of historicising the past that is so unlike theirs that were it to become a new norm then history 'as we have known it' – and maybe history as such – would disappear.

It is for this reason that I said earlier that if Evans had really wanted to defend his genre then he would have had to 'take apart' postmodern exponents in detail at the level of their texts. This he does not do. Consequently, the question that still remains for Evans and fellow defenders is whether, say, White's argument on the nature of history can be rebutted. I don't think it can, and so I will now briefly outline the methodological thread of arguably White's still most powerful text – *Metahistory* – and leave it as a challenge for Evans *et al.* in the same way as the more nuts and bolts critique of empiricism was posited at the end of the third section of Chapter 4 (p. 110).

Metahistory is a big book. But in his Preface, Introduction and Conclusion, White outlines its general thesis and methodology, and gives a list of seven conclusions he reaches about the 'nature of history'. What follows is an analysis of White's methodological position and the listing of the seven conclusions which are then left as they stand: what, I wonder, is there left of the lower case, Evans style, after White?

White says at the start of the text that he treats 'the historical work for what it most manifestly is: a verbal structure in the form of a narrative prose discourse' adding, later, 'the content of which is as much invented/imagined as found'.[24] Histories, it is well recognised, *all* combine a certain amount of evidence/data, categories and concepts for explaining such material, and a narrative structure for their presentation as an icon 'of sets of events presumed to have occurred in the past'. This is straightforward stuff. It admits of the past, of traces of it, of archival work, of 'hard' evidence, of evidential facts of an empirical type yielding – at the level of the statement particularly – knowledge. Of course. But then White goes on to claim that, 'in addition, I maintain, they contain a deep structural content which is generally poetic, and specifically linguistic, in nature, and which serves as the precritically accepted paradigm of what a distinctively "historical" explanation should be. This paradigm functions as the "metahistorical" element in all historical works.'[25]

Such a precritically accepted paradigm is not, says White, to be confused with the theoretical concepts (of causality, consequence, context, etc.) *overtly* used by 'proper' historians to give histories 'the aspect of an explanation', for these are precisely on the surface of the text, often referred to, and identified easily. Rather (and remember this is a text of a 'structural moment') White is after those (metaphorical) 'deep structures' that constitute, whether they are recognised or not, the formal strategies that always enter into the text-to-be-produced:

> I distinguish among three kinds of strategy that can be used by historians to gain different kinds of 'explanatory affect'. I call these . . . explanation by formal argument, explanation by emplotment, and explanation by ideological implication. *Within* each of these . . . I identify four possible modes of articulation by which the historian can gain an explanatory affect of a specific kind. For arguments these are the modes of Formism, Organicism, Mechanism and Contextualism; for emplotments there are the archetypes of Romance, Comedy, Tragedy, and Satire; and for ideological implication there are the tactics of Anarchism,

Conservatism, Radicalism and Liberalism. A specific combination of modes comprises what I call the historiographical 'style' of a particular historian or philosopher of history.[26]

In addition, goes on White, there is also a fourth strategy by which the components of the other three are held together in a particular style of configuration. These are White's tropes, tropes that prefigure the historical field and constitute it as a domain upon which to bring to bear the specific theories the historian will use to explain 'what really happened in it'. 'I call these types of prefiguration', says White, 'by the names of the four tropes of poetic language: Metaphor, Metonymy, Synecdoche, and Irony.'[27]

Now, in his Introduction and throughout his text, White adds enormous detail to these categories, but for my purposes here, further explanation of them can be left, save for adding one thing, as White does in his Preface. It is that he postulates 'four principle modes of historical consciousness on the basis of the prefigurative (tropological) strategy which informs each of them'. Each of them provides the basis for a 'distinctive linguistic protocol by which to prefigure the historical field and on the basis of which specific categories of historical interpretation can be employed for "explaining" it . . . it is my view that the dominant tropological mode and its attendant linguistic protocol comprise the irreducibly "metahistorical" basis of every historical work'. Consequently, concludes White, 'in any field of study not yet reduced (or elevated) to the status of a genuine science, thought remains captive of the linguistic mode in which it seeks to grasp the outline of objects inhabiting its field of perception'.[28]

It is White's hope that the understanding derived from this method will enable historians to become self-consciously aware of how their discourse – a narrative prose discourse – works, and thus be in control of it rather than it being in control of them. Rather than White being an obscurantist, he actually sits in the middle of the Enlightenment tradition which values rational understanding of the sometimes apparently 'irrational' or 'illogical' or 'mythical' parts of historians' practices, and this is brought out very clearly in White's self-conscious desire to live in a post-ironic but rational/reflexive world. His argument to this end builds up in the following way.

White thinks that his method allows him to penetrate the metahistorical basis upon which both speculative philosophies of history (metanarratives like Marxism) and 'proper' history rest, so that their alleged differences come down to a matter of emphasis. That is to say, in 'proper' history 'the element of construct is displaced to the interior of the narrative, while the elements of "found" data are permitted to occupy the position of prominence in the story line itself'. Conversely, in philosophies of history, the 'element of conceptual construct is brought to the fore, explicitly set forth, and systematically defended, with the data being used primarily for purposes of illustration'. White thus concludes that every history contains within it the elements of a full-blown philosophy of history';[29] and that history is irreducibly theoretical.

But it's not just that. For White thinks – and why not (though this reverses the way 'proper' historians normally consider things) – that 'speculative' philosophers of history operate at a higher level of methodological consciousness than 'proper' historians in that they seek 'not only to understand what happened in history but also to specify the criteria by which [they] can know when [they have] successfully grasped its meaning or significance', such a history being an analysis not only of the historical past but of the practices by which 'a given encoding of the historical field can be permitted to claim the status of knowledge'.[30] In that sense 'speculative' historians are far better historians than 'proper' ones in that the latter, being unconcerned with theorising their practices in reflexive ways – indeed making a point of not doing so – are pale, benighted second-raters. And hence the theoretical mess most 'proper' historians get into when they try to think non-philosophically about the metaphysics, ontology, epistemology and methodology of historical discourse, for these are philosophical areas that cannot begin to be broached from the level of practice – nor reduced to it. For besides,

> no given *theory of history* [and all historians are 'theorists'] is convincing or compelling to a given public solely on the basis of its adequacy as an 'explanation' of the 'data' contained in its narrative, because, in history, as in the social sciences in general, there is no way of pre-establishing what will count as a . . . 'theory' by which to 'explain' what the data 'mean'. In turn, there is no agreement over what will count as a specifically 'historical' datum. The resolution of this problem requires a metatheory, which will establish on metahistorical grounds the distinctions between merely 'natural' phenomena and specifically 'historical' phenomena.[31]

Of course. But (and this is a big but) because such metatheories are themselves ultimately arbitrary, disputes over meaning (both *within* any metatheory at the level of the detailed significance and *between* them) are, short of any transcendental/infinite fix, interminable:

scepticism about ultimate and indeed contingent meanings are thus inexpungeable (to recall – 'there is an inexpungeable relativity in every representation of historical phenomena') and now we can easily see why. We can now also see why White has to be a historical sceptic about representations of the past *and* about the methods making them up – as we all do.

But this isn't all either. For it is the recognition of this inexpungeable scepticism and relativism that actually helps explain, for White, the nineteenth-century historical imagination and, more than that, those of the eighteenth and twentieth centuries too. White's argument isn't difficult to understand and it casts Evans's chapter on 'The History of History' into another, paler world. White argues thus.

The eighteenth-century historical imagination was ironic. 'It' knew that the past could be read in innumerable ways; that what appeared to be done up in one instance could be undone in another; that numerous reversals, unintended consequences and umpteen ironies could never be straightened out. But the 'classic age' of historical thought – broadly speaking the nineteenth century – thought that they could. Thus, for White, historical thought from Hegel to Croce 'represented an effort to constitute history as the ground for a "realistic" science of man, society, and culture', a realism to be founded on a consciousness that had freed itself from the scepticism and pessimism of the 'late Enlightenment irony on the one hand and the cognitively irresponsible faith of the early Romantic movement on the other'.[32] But – and this is another big but – this realist optimism was only a temporary blip. For what nineteenth-century Europe succeeded in producing was a host of conflicting 'realisms' each of which was 'endowed with a theoretical apparatus and buttressed by an erudition that made it impossible for one to deny its claim to at least provisional acceptance'.[33] Thus it was impossible to prove that, say, Michelet was 'refuted' by the more scientific or empirical Ranke, or that Ranke was nullified by the even more scientific or realistic de Tocqueville, or that all three were surpassed by the 'realism' of Burkhardt, or that Marx was more 'scientific' than Hegel, etc. For what was at issue throughout the nineteenth century in history (and other discourses) was precisely the form that a 'realistic representation of historical reality' ought to take. Accordingly, this matter being unsettled, the so-called 'crisis of historicism' entered into in the last decades of the nineteenth century and the first of the twentieth, was little more than the 'perception of the impossibility of choosing' on an adequate ground (for what would count as that?) mutually exclusive ways of viewing the past historically. This perception has continued in the twentieth century right up until today, so that ours is just a sceptical, relativistic, *ironic* century.

On the basis of this position, White is then able to locate present-day historiography as a specific manifestation of a specific phase of 'the history of historical consciousness in general'. Though much of the finest historical reflection in the later twentieth century has been concerned to overcome sceptical and relativistic irony, it has clearly and inevitably failed. Late twentieth-century historical writing, in both the upper and lower cases, thus is permeated by irony – perhaps the defining trope of postmodernism. Nobody believes in those upper case teleologies any more, whilst the lower case – in its attempts to still be 'realistic' (i.e. true, objective, unbiased, disinterested, serious ...) is warrened by sceptical/relativistic awareness that these things will never be unequivocally achieved; that *différance* is inevitable. And thus is provoked the fear – it grips Evans like a vice – that if it is held that 'anything' is permitted to have a claim to be 'history', worse, if it is held that there is no such thing as 'history' to lay claim to but only ever practices having at least a nominal interest in the past which all lay claim to legitimacy, then 'anything goes'. And I think that, in the final analysis, this is what White – and everybody else – either accepts or 'has to accept'. And I think White is also wonderfully perceptive in seeing how attempts to head off this unavoidable conclusion manifest themselves in 'proper' history. For White, proper history attacks irony in two basic ways. First, it seeks to overcome the scepticism of history by valorising scholarly caution and empiricism and, second, it valorises objectivity and ideological neutrality in order to offset moral undecidability. Accordingly, one can now see why Evans *et al.* should so privilege those qualities of scholarship, of empirical facts and own-sakist, non-presentist 'neutralities', and we can now see – again – why postmodern irony is such a threat.

But for White such irony isn't so much a threat but something happily to accept and, maybe, go beyond. For here one can be a Sophist again; can live with scepticism and relativism as being the best *solutions* to the problematics of existence. And White thinks one can even turn this irony into post-irony. The irony White welcomes (much like the irony Richard Rorty welcomes) is one that allows people to live with a radical contingency which recognises that everything can be redescribed. It recognises people 'who know what they know can be (and probably will be) redescribed in another vocabulary, and that there is no useful way of trying to see which vocabulary is more authentic or more realistic.'[34] And just as Rorty

has shown that the so-called 'problems of philosophy' have been
shaped by particular historical circumstances so that today such
problems are 'no longer worth pursuing' (that the traditional role of
philosophy as a tribunal of reason has gone bankrupt so that it
might now become just another conversation), so White thinks that,
in today's altered circumstances, the irony that makes the choices
one makes always radically undecidable also provides that reflexivity
necessary for taking responsibility for those choices in highly self-
conscious (and thus, in a way, post-ironic) ways. I have already quoted
part of White's last paragraph of *Metahistory* but I do so again here
and add to it the bulk of it. For this 'bulk' summarises so much that
is White, so much that is attractive in his generous, humanist position:

> The late R. G. Collingwood was fond of saying that the kind of
> history one wrote, or the way one thought about history, was
> ultimately a function of the kind of man one was. But the
> reverse is *also* the case. Placed before the alternative visions that
> history's interpreters offer for our consideration, and without
> any apodictically provided theoretical grounds for preferring one
> vision over another, we are drawn back to moral and aesthetic
> reasons for the choice of one version over another as the more
> 'realistic'. The aged Kant was right, in short; we are free to con-
> ceive 'history' as we please, just as we are free to make of it
> what we will. And if we wish to transcend the agnosticism
> [of] an Ironic perspective on history passing as the sole possible
> 'realism' . . . we have only to reject this Ironic perspective and to
> will to view history from another, anti-Ironic perspective. [For] I
> maintain that the recognition of this Ironic perspective provides
> the grounds for a transcendence of it. If it can be shown that
> Irony is only one of a *number* of possible perspectives on history,
> each of which has its own good reasons for existence on a poetic
> and moral level of awareness, historians and philosophers of
> history will then be freed to conceptualize history, to perceive its
> contents, and to construct narrative accounts of its process in
> whatever modality of consciousness is most consistent with their
> own moral and aesthetic aspirations.[35]

A post/anti-irony consciously accepts difference, alterity and the
différend, it builds on a relativism and scepticism that are
inexpungeable. This is the conclusion that White reaches and that is
embodied in the seven 'methodological' points he thinks his arguments
demonstrate. They are arguments that will have to be refuted by Evans

et al. if they want to privilege a history they have not so far delineated at all precisely. Here are White's seven general conclusions:

> (1) there can be no 'proper history' which is not at the same time 'philosophy of history'; (2) the possible modes of historiography are the same as the possible modes of speculative philosophy of history; (3) these modes, in turn, are in reality *formalizations* of poetic insights that analytically precede them and that sanction the particular theories used to give historical accounts the aspect of an 'explanation'; (4) there are no apodictically certain theoretical grounds on which one can legitimately claim an authority for any one of the modes over the others as being more 'realistic'; (5) as a consequence of this, we are indentured to a choice among contending interpretative strategies . . . (6) as a corollary of this, the best grounds for choosing one perspective rather than another are ultimately aesthetic or moral rather than epistemological; and finally, (7) the demand for the scientization of history represents only the statement of a preference for a specific modality of historical conceptualization, the grounds of which are either moral or aesthetic, but the epistemological justification of which still remains to be established.[36]

All this needs to be said and White says it brilliantly. But there still remains a question he doesn't really address 'seriously'. As Michael Roth points out in his *The Ironist's Cage*, while White wants us to go beyond irony by making a choice from 'among different strategies of figuration', in, as I have said, an emancipatory way, all this raises the question of why choose to go to history at all. What do 'we want from the past, and what [should] we do with our history once we understand that it can no longer function as a court of appeal?'[37] This leads, for me, to the question of why not now forget history and live in imaginaries without it? This will be the question considered by Ermarth and Harlan, but first I want to turn to the second 'demolition expert of the lower case', Frank Ankersmit.

6   On Frank Ankersmit

Frank Ankersmit is currently Professor of Intellectual History and Historical Theory at the University of Groningen, the Netherlands. Apart from several books in Dutch he is the author, in English, of _Narrative Logic: A Semantic Analysis of the Historian's Language_ (1983) (perhaps Ankersmit's seminal text) and many essays, some of the most important being collected in his _History and Tropology: The Rise and Fall of Metaphor_ (1994); he has also co-edited, with Hans Kellner, _A New Philosophy of History_ (1995). Ankersmit is one of the few historians who have openly come out in favour of postmodernism (his manifesto-like 'Historiography and Postmodernism' appeared in _History and Theory_ in 1989) and he is identified by Evans (and dismissed without engagement) as one of the most barbaric of invaders and slighted as a second- or third-rate theorist.[1]

But he is neither of these things. Ankersmit's historical research and philosophical understanding have given him a range of reference and a sophistication that affords his writings a lucidity, breadth and power I cannot follow here in the detail deserved. In particular I cannot follow him when, in the last three chapters of _History and Tropology_, he begins to explore in detail the possibilities of a 'post postmodern' non-Kantian, non-metaphorical form of historical writing and consciousness. For my purpose in using Ankersmit here is different from his own way of using himself. Above all I want to examine his argument that we have come to 'the Autumn of history', as he puts it, under the critical impact of postmodernism. It is an argument that he construes as perhaps heralding that new, spring-like opportunity of the non-Kantian, non-metaphorical history he essays, but which for me – whilst not simply ruling out Ankersmit's vision – suggests a way of doing without history, Kantian or non-Kantian, metaphorical or non-metaphorical. It suggests to me that we might be entering a period when history, and associated ethics, does not survive the ensuing winter: that his particular historiographical spring may never come.

My reading of Ankersmit to eventually reach this conclusion is in two sections. In the first, 'From statement to text, from modernism to postmodernism', I introduce and outline what I take to be possibly the main critique he levels at 'proper' history; namely, that the failure to make the distinction between the historical *statement* and the whole historical *text* (a failure that is perfectly explicable given what it conceals) is, when exposed, enough to undercut the viability of the lower case as overwhelmingly practised. In the second section, 'Autumn has come', I examine what Ankersmit sees as some of the fatal implications of the above-mentioned exposé – the end of 'proper' history – and link his critique to my own argument about the end of history *per se*.

From statement to text, from modernism to postmodernism

Twentieth-century philosophy, says Ankersmit in the opening paragraph of *History and Tropology*, has been dominated by the 'phenomenon of language' in ways that have *not* helped historians' self-understanding. Early on in the century Bertrand Russell and the logical positivists saw formalised language as the logical matrix through which was gained all our worldly knowledge, arguing that by reducing language through formal analysis to its 'logical core' we could see how all reliable (scientific) knowledge is composed of its atomic constituents. It was on this reductive basis that Carnap argued that speculative western metaphysics was an enormous philosophical mistake which originated in, and continued because of, ignorance about the syntactical rules for ascertaining the 'logical composition of the world'. He saw his task as driving home the point that because metaphysics went beyond the senses it was literally non-sense (nonsense). Then, in the work of Wittgenstein, Ryle, Austin and Strawson *et al.*, language, though still living within the influence of logical positivism, became construed not so much as a logical calculus but as a social practice; a way of coping with the world rather than really understanding it. But for Ankersmit, what these intellectual expressions had in common – despite much diversity and disagreement – was the assumption that language is the vehicle of all verifiable knowledge and meaningful thinking, an assumption he sees as living on in two ways in contemporary philosophy, both of which have negatively affected the knowledge status of historiography. First, there is the methodological assumption (harking back well beyond the twentieth century to Descartes's and Hobbes's *resolute-compositional* position) which, connected up to arguments from the philosophy of language, holds that complex problems always have to be broken down into their simplest components. And second – and building on the first – the problem of how language might account for a complex 'reality' in terms of texts rather than individual propositions ('the professional concern of the historian') is regarded as a *non-problem*. That is, Ankersmit sees a general unwillingness to expect problems in this area that could *not* be reduced to the 'kinds of problems encountered in the analysis of propositions and their parts'.[2] Accordingly, this allows Ankersmit to argue that most of 'the misfortunes of contemporary philosophy of history can be explained from this perspective'. Thus, in the 1950s and 1960s, philosophers of history concentrated on singular statements about historical description and explanation, about causality and consequences, such that 'the historical text as a whole was rarely, if ever, the topic of philosophical investigation'.[3] And what is obviously unfortunate in this, is that whatever problems there may have been held to be in the production of historical knowledge, they are seen to lie in its parts and not where they *actually* lie, at the level of the text. Thus, 'only a philosophy of history concentrating on the historical text as a whole could contribute importantly to contemporary philosophy of history and go beyond a mere application of what had already been discovered elsewhere';[4] a philosophy exposing the limits of the *resolute-compositional* method. And although Ankersmit sees (and charts) the increased attention given to the text since about 1970, he correctly argues that most philosophers of history – and certainly most of the thinking by practising historians of an empiricist/realist type – have resisted the challenge to think textually. And so, concludes Ankersmit, 'if philosophy of history presently is in such poor shape that one might well ask if it still exists at all, this has much to do with the unwillingness of philosophers of history to explore the philosophical gold mine [textuality] that is their exclusive possession'.[5]

For this resistance to think textually has drastically affected historians' thinking about the nature and status of their discourse in two important, negative ways. First, the crucial distinction between historical research ('the results of which are typically expressed in terms of individual statements about the past') and historical writing ('which has integrated the results of historical research within the whole of the historical text') has been both massively down-played and, when noticed, has unfortunately privileged the former so that most philosophy of history has only been 'a philosophy of historical research'. And this is disastrous because it can be easily shown that texts differ logically from individual propositions/statements and that, consequently, historical writing (on a par with the historian's text) can never be completely reduced to (the results of) historical research (on a par with individual propositions about historical states of affairs) such that 'something essential' has now been lost as we 'reduce the historical text as a whole to its constituent parts'.[6] And second, since the philosophy of language as adapted by philosophers of history didn't provide insights into the status of the historical account (historiography) as such, then those interested in this turned (like White) to literary theory. But here as well, the opposition to White on the part of entrenched philosophers of history and those 'practising historians' who thought about such things (and for whom toying with literary theory opened the door to all kinds of 'imaginative' factors) has meant, says Ankersmit, that open-minded thinking about the textuality of history 'all the way down' has remained enormously underdeveloped.

Now, Ankersmit broadly accepts the bulk of White's position and those few philosophers of history like Louis Mink, Hans Kellner and Michel de Certeau who have a similar disposition. He writes in *History and Tropology* that as 'will be clear from the foregoing, the greatest debt I owe is to Hayden White [whose] . . . capacity for identifying what really demands attention at each phase of the intellectual debate on historical writing is, in my opinion, the most formidable asset in the possession of contemporary philosophy of history'.[7] But this is not to say Ankersmit merely replicates White. For Ankersmit is original and complex in his own right and particularly in his work on the concept of *narrative substances*, work that shifts attention from the research phase to the production of the whole text.

Ankersmit details the ideas behind and about narrative substances in enormous detail in his *Narrative Logic* (ideas that he summarises in his *Six Theses on Narrativist Philosophy of History*, which is reproduced in its entirety as an appendix at the end of this section) but the gist of his argument can perhaps best be approached by way of his much more accessible article 'Reply to Professor Zagorin', which appeared in *History and Theory* in 1990. Ankersmit's argument there – which I follow closely here for a few pages – opens with the ringing statement that 'At the start of our line of march from modernism to postmodernism we find the (historical) text', a line of march that can be put thus.

We can say about the text two things. First, the historical text consists of many individual statements most of which are deemed to give an accurate or true description of some state of affairs that occurred in the past. These evidential statements are based on the traces of the past 'found' in the historical, generic archive, and have about them – when suitably 'contextualised' and corroborated – the aura of facticity. This is straightforward, though we might note in passing that this research phase, coming to the surface of the text replete with all the scholarly apparatus of 'proper' history (footnote piles etc.) lends to such facts the deceptive aura of the real ('reality effects') that in turn tends to suggest that what is being assessed and interrogated here is the past as such (for though 'the fact can only have a linguistic existence, as a term in a discourse . . . it is exactly as if this existence were merely a "copy" . . . of another existence situated in the extra-structural domain of the "real"'). But since Barthes's *Discourse of History* (from which the above quote comes) nobody really takes the view – 'now surely archaic' – of history as a discourse committed to the recovery of the past in some kind of pre-discursive state.[8] For as Tony Bennett has commented – complementing Ankersmit and Barthes – all that has ever been and can ever be of issue in historical discourse is what can be drawn from the historical record as archive, it being this (itself discursive construct) that functions as the historians' referent in that it is this that constitutes the 'last court of appeal' for the *veracity* of historical statements; the point at which, so to speak, they hit base – but 'a base within discourse'.[9] But it is Ankersmit's point that whilst this court of appeal exists (albeit in a far from unproblematic way) at the level of the singular statement (and sometimes simple sets of statements establishing 'some sort' of chronicle) it *does not* exist where it most matters – at the level of the text – which means that the discourse of history *per se* never has been and never will be an epistemology; that objectivity and truth (epistemological/cognitive criteria) are therefore not finally at issue – and cannot ever be at issue – at the level of the 'historicised past as discursive text'.

Thus Ankersmit's second point is that, with the possible exception of archaeology and some areas of 'history' with almost non-existent traces, the evidential traces and thus the (evidential) true statements available to most historians allow them to write many *more* true statements about the historical past than are actually found in their texts. It is sometimes argued – it is a typical seminar topic – that there are no such things as historical facts, and this is 'true' in the sense that facts always have to be established and given that status by, often, a lot of interpretative investigation. But that investigation done, the result is not that there are then no '<u>facts</u>' but that there are <u>millions of them</u>. Consequently the situation facing most historians is not one of non-existence or scarcity, but of <u>plenitude</u>. Thus the problem then becomes that of the <u>selection and distribut</u>ion; the weighing up and the giving of significance to always *some* of the facts in always problematical combinations relative to a whole range of interests. Thus, as <u>Ankersmit</u> says,

> Out of all the statements historians could possibly have made about the relevant part of the past [relevant, that is, to the way they have been put under a description] they carefully select *qua* descriptive content and *qua* formulation the statements they will ultimately decide to mention in their books or articles – one might [thus] say that the writing of the historical text requires of <u>historians</u> a *politics* with regard to the statement, and the text is the result of this politics.[10]

And the reason why historians are relatively careful about *their* statements (but never 'the past's' statements or 'history's' statements) is that, as Ankersmit explains, '<u>these statements</u>, when considered together, determine the "<u>picture</u>" of <u>part of the pas</u>t they wish to present to their readers and for historians this "<u>picture</u>" is no less important than the <u>statemen</u>ts that make it up'.[11]

Thus, one can immediately see the problems in trying to verify as 'objective' or 'true' any resultant picture so produced, for such synoptic (generally narrativised) pictures are of a different *kind* – not different *degree* but different *kind* – from singular statements such that their 'proving' is ultimately impossible. For whilst it is generally the case that individual statements of a cognitive kind can indeed be checked against a discrete source to see if they 'correspond', 'pictures of the past' can never be so checked simply because the statements combined to form such a picture do not have a picture of their own prior to this assembly/combinatory for this assembly/combinatory to be checked against. And since what is most crucial in the writings of historians is not to be found at the level of individual statements but at the level of the iconic representation/appropriation (in that it is these representations/appropriations that, say, stimulate historiographical debate and thus determine 'over time' the ways we *imagine* the past) then we have to concur with Ankersmit's (and White's) point that <u>historiogra</u>phy is as much in<u>vented/imagin</u>ed (the pictures, the <u>appropriations</u>) as <u>found (the facts</u>) and <u>that the resultant</u>

historicisations are always, when thus combined/interpreted, 'inexpungeably relativistic'.

Thus Ankersmit is able to draw two conclusions and several
'implications' from the two points he has made about the text and
their statements. That (1) the text's statements 'refer to and describe
part of the past and can be either true or false' and (2) they define/
individuate the 'picture of the past' historians wish to convey to
readers who themselves, as readers, bring to the resultant text their
own multi-level and multifarious 'reading and working' habits such
that, again, interminable, interpretative intertextuality is the result,
with the implication that objectivity and truth become casualties.
For as Ankersmit explains, it is very hard, indeed ultimately impossible, to tell from the finished *text* what the set of statements to individuate the particular 'pictures' of the past consist of, and what
statements have been omitted and why. Because a text is the way it
is because of the way it is not (by virtue of what has been left out as
much as what has been put in), what has been left out is crucial to
know. But most historians are not methodologically/positionally
explicit about the way they have constituted their texts (their emplotments, argumentative strategies, tropological configurations, ideological positionings) so such *knowledge* remains generally unavailable.
Consequently, Ankersmit is able to say in conclusion that saying *true*
things about the past's traces at the level of the statement is easy – 'anybody can do that' – but saying true things about the past's traces at the
level of the text is categorically impossible – 'nobody can do that'. For
texts are not, sadly, cognitive, empirical, epistemological entities, but
speculative, imagined 'imaginaries', it being their status as imaginaries
that *guarantees* difference and the *différand*: at the combined levels of
the statements and texts we thus have the phenomenon of interminable
redescription and interpretative flux (freedom); of always (potential
and actual) incommensurable, discursive regimes.

It is now clear that what most interests Ankersmit (like White) is not
at all what happens at the research phase *vis-à-vis* the establishment of
statements – for this is easily described in the many primers that exist
(give or take emphases and the riding of hobby-horses) – but what
can be said about the textual appropriations of the 'always already
historicised past'. Accordingly, one of Ankersmit's most original
contributions/formulations to an understanding of 'the nature of
history' and the status of knowledge in 'proper' history style (though
his insight applies everywhere it is particularly relevant to the lower
case) is via his concept of *narrative substances*. For him this concept

definitely shifts attention from statements to texts and from, as he puts it, 'modernism to postmodernism'. As he says:

> If we take seriously the text and its narrative substances we will become postmodernists; if we see only the statement we will remain modernist. Or, to put it in a slogan, the statement is modernist, the (historical) text is postmodernist.[12]

So, what are narrative substances and what are the implications of them for 'modern' historiography especially of the lower case genre?

Narrative substances, Ankersmit points out, do not often get names of their own. Normally they operate as organising categories, heuristic collating devices (collective nouns). But sometimes they do get accorded names – the Renaissance, the Industrial Revolution, the Eighteenth Century, the Seventeenth-century Crisis. What, then, is the relationship between such substances and the 'actual/historicised past'?

Ankersmit argues that modernists (Walsh and Mink are mentioned as examples) would try to find something to correspond with such a substance and credit it with *describing* part of the past. But Ankersmit's postmodern reading is that such notions as the Industrial Revolution

> should be seen as the *names* of narrative substances and, therefore, as far as reference or correspondence is concerned, these names must be denied the capacity to refer to anything outside the text: they refer to narrative substances (that is, a set of statements contained by and within the text).[13]

This is not to say these notions are completely unrelated to the 'external' past, for in the set of statements the name the narrative substance refers to (the Industrial Revolution), reference *is* made to the past. As Ankersmit puts it:

> The narrative substance is a linguistic object we can refer to, either in statements using its name [e.g. the Industrial Revolution] . . . or in statements expressing the narrative meaning of the historical text, but that never refers to anything other than or outside itself.[14]

That is to say, what prevents the narrative substance from itself referring to something outside itself is that the Industrial Revolution didn't exist *as such* to refer to. The Industrial Revolution is a concept produced by 'colligating' the text's *internal statements* and thus has nothing outside of them to refer to: therefore, it can only be self referencing. This means that narrative substances are only ever *analytically* true about the text's internal statements and never *contingently* true externally because there is no Industrial Revolution 'out there' to correspond to *before* the narrative substance *creates* it as a collective noun/name for 'its' set of statements. What it is that is responsible for the way terms like the 'Industrial Revolution' can be held to refer to a past actuality is that a narrative substance sometimes gets to be widely accepted by historians; it then looks as if there was an Industrial Revolution 'out there' and that it has been 'discovered'. But the Industrial Revolution is, as a narrative substance, a concept, so actually what is going on here in the widespread acceptance of such a substance is that 'a new convention has been produced in language for relating words to things'. But, as Ankersmit goes on, as long as such universal agreement has not been reached, which is rare (think of all the 'debates' over the 'Industrial Revolution', the 'Cold War', the 'Seventeenth-century Crisis') then we can only say that a 'semantic convention was *proposed* by the historian'. Thus we are lead to think of such narrative substances as hypotheses, as *proposals* for thinking about ways of carving up the historicised past textually. And thus Ankersmit reaches some important findings about this way of thinking about historical knowledge; just *three* of these are discussed below.

First, and to reiterate slightly, narrative substances are imaginary, organising notions that make heuristic sense of statements in texts, which individually, as statements, refer outside of themselves but which, as narrative substances, do not do so. And yet, it is these narrative substances that are essentially the semantic units that, together or singly, organise our 'pictures of the past'. And such representations can never be true to the past *per se* in any correspondence sense.

Second, because there is no past given to us plain against which we could compare two or more combinations of statements and narrative substances (i.e. interpretations) to find which one corresponded to the past *per se*, then the past *per se* has no role to play in historical discourse. From the point of view of historical practice, concludes Ankersmit, 'this referential [non-existent] past' is a useless notion. Texts are all we have and we can only compare texts with texts.'[15] This doesn't mean to say – again to reiterate slightly – that there are not things 'out there' to have beliefs about, that cause us to have beliefs (about, say, a phenomenon we might propose to name as the

Industrial Revolution). But the causal independence of the once actuality that is named the Industrial Revolution doesn't mean that the historian can (as Richard Rorty puts it) perform the impossible feat of stripping this 'object' of all the ways we have used to refer to it, see it somehow as it was 'in itself', and *then* see how our various interpretations measure up to it and decide which one is true or the best. Again, this doesn't mean to say that, in the 'middle range', if we are looking for the most plausible interpretation for something we think we have good reason for thinking occurred, then we can't 'ask ourselves in which of these texts [interpretations] available historical evidence has been most successfully used'. But, and it's another big but, 'we can never test our conclusions by comparing the elected text with "the past" itself'. Here is Ankersmit's final spin on this point:

> One might put it as follows. When we speak about reality in simple constative statements like 'the cat lies on the mat', there are a number of semantic conventions that decide about the meaning, the truth and the reference of such statements. How these conventions – meaning, truth, and reference – hang together is an immensely complicated problem ... But such semantic conventions are conspicuously absent when we use the kind of historical notions we are now investigating; hence, at this stage, we cannot properly speak of truth, falsity, reference, or of a failure to refer ... that at the level of the historical text and of historical interpretation, we cannot appropriately use the words truth and falsity ... we can say a lot of things about proposals, for example, that they are fruitful, well-considered, intelligent ... and so on [we do not have to leave entirely 'empty handed'] ... but not that they are true or false.[16]

Third, for Ankersmit this radical undecidability is an integral part of political freedom. That is to say, for freedom to exist there must be choices. If there was only one interpretation then it would no longer be an interpretation but the (ostensible) truth. And this would have to be accepted save by those happy to be dissenters and prepared to be treated accordingly; here truth begets closures of all kinds. Thus the good thing about the impossibility of 'interpretative truth' (an oxymoron anyway: you can have a true truth or an interpretative interpretation but not the two together) is that it raises to consciousness the problematical nature of such claims – and claimers. Thus, says Ankersmit, at the level of 'historical debate' views of the past we reject are an integral part of realising the status of those we accept. Politically, then, it is not the sceptic or the relativist, the laid-back interpreter whom one *ought* to fear, but people, or institutions, or states, who claim to know the truth of things at the actually irreducible level of interpretation. For Ankersmit such relativism is not seen as a licence for anything goes – any more than it is for White, Derrida, Baudrillard, Lyotard and, as we shall see, Ermarth or Harlan (though logically 'everything is permitted') – but, with an (arbitrary) informing humanistic, emancipatory desire, it is the precondition of freedom, alterity, otherness, variety and vitality. This is the bottom line. Relativism has no foundations. But that doesn't make it weak. For nothing has foundations in this sense. Thus, it is that the ultimate arbitrariness of *all* decision, of the *aporia*, leads to a politics of hegemony (after Laclau . . . as we shall see below, p. 182).

Now, many of the above points from Ankersmit have been put skeletally and just some of their implications considered curtly; there is no substitute for going to Ankersmit for the details. And it just happens, in the 'context' provided here, that Ankersmit has recently 'written up' the conclusions he reached about 'history' in his *Narrative Logic* in the form of 'Six Theses on Narrativist Philosophy of History'. Taking up fewer than a dozen pages, these theses seem so lucidly compressed that to reduce them further by selective commentary would be too much. But they are important to study. Thus I append them here, to this first section, for possible 'introductory discussion' and engagement, after which I go on to the second section, 'Autumn has come'. Here is Ankersmit's 'Summary' of his *Narrative Logic* taken from his *History and Tropology* (Berkeley, University of California Press, 1994).

ANKERSMIT'S 'SIX THESES ON NARRATIVIST PHILOSOPHY OF HISTORY'

1.   Historical narratives are interpretations of the past.
1.1.   The terms *historical narrative* and *interpretation* provide better clues for an understanding of historiography than the terms *description* and *explanation*.
1.2.   We interpret not when we have too little data but when we have too much (see 4.3). Description and explanation require the 'right' amount of data.

1.2.1.   Scientific theories are underdetermined since an infinite number of theories may account for the known data; interpretations are underdetermined since only an infinite number of interpretations could account for all the known data.

1.3.   Interpretation is not translation. The past is not a text that has to be *translated* into narrative historiography; it has to be *interpreted*.

1.4.   Narrative interpretations are not necessarily of a sequential nature; historical narratives are only contingently stories with a beginning, a middle, and an end.

1.4.1.   Historical time is a relatively recent and highly artificial invention of Western civilization. It is a cultural, not a philosophical notion. Hence, founding narrativism on the concept of time is building on quicksand.

1.4.2.   Narrativism can explain time and is not explained by it (see 2.1.3 and 4.7.5).

1.5.   Twenty years ago philosophy of history was scientistic; one ought to avoid the opposite extreme of seeing historiography as a form of literature. Historism is the *juste milieu* between the two: historism retains what is right in both the scientistic and the literary approaches to history and avoids what is hyperbolic in both.

1.5.1.   Historiography *develops* narrative interpretations of sociohistorical reality; literature *applies* them.

1.6.   There is no precise line of demarcation between historiography and narrativist philosophy of history (see 4.7.5 and 4.7.7).

2.   Narrativism accepts the past as it is. In the form of tautology: it accepts what is unproblematic about the past. What is unproblematic is a historical fact. Both senses of the latter statement are true (see 3.4.1 and 3.4.2).

2.1.   It is necessary to distinguish between historical research (a question of facts) and historical writing (a question of interpretation). The distinction is similar, though by no means identical, to the distinction in philosophy of science between observation statement and theory.

2.1.1.   The results of historical research are expressed in statements; narrative interpretations are sets of statements.

2.1.2.   The interesting distinction is not that between the singular and the general statement but between the general statement and historical narrative. The singular statement may serve both masters.

2.1.3. Temporal determinations are expressed *in* statements and not *by* statements and are therefore not of particular interest to narrativist philosophy of history. Narrativist philosophy of history deals with statements and not with their parts (like temporal indications).

2.2. There is an affinity between philosophy of historical research and the components (statements) of a historical narrative. Philosophy of historical writing and the historical narrative in its totality are similarly related.

2.2.1. With a few exceptions (W.H. Walsh, H.V. White, L.O. Mink), current philosophy of history is interested exclusively in historical research.

2.2.2. Its distrust of (narrativist) holism prevents current philosophy from understanding historical narrative.

2.3. The most crucial and most interesting intellectual challenges facing the historian are found on the level of historical writing (selection, interpretation, how to see the past). The historian is essentially more than Collingwood's detective looking for the murderer of John Doe.

2.4. Since it deals only with the components of historical narrative, philosophy of action can never further our insight into historical narrative.

2.4.1. Philosophy of action can never speak the language of the unintended consequences of human action. As a philosophy of history, philosophy of action is only suited to prehistorist historiography. Being unable to transcend the limitations of methodological individualism, it is historiographically naive.

2.4.2. Von Wright's and Ricoeur's attempts to solve this problem for philosophy of action are unsuccessful. Historical meaning is different from the agent's intention.

2.4.3. The language of the unintended consequences is the language of interpretation (there ordinarily is a difference between the historian's perspective and that of the historical agent).

2.4.4. The *logical connection argument* is a special case of narrativism (in that it provides a logical scheme in which knowledge of the past is organized).

3. Narrativism is the modern heir of historism (not to be confused with Popper's histori*ci*sm): both recognize that the historian's task is essentially interpretative (i.e., to find unity in diversity).

3.1. Interpretations strive for the unity that is characteristic of things (see 4.4).

3.1.2. Historists attempted to discover the essence, or, as they called it, the *historische Idee*, which they assumed was present in the historical phenomena themselves. Narrativism, on the contrary, recognized that a historical interpretation *projects* a structure on to the past and does not *discover* it as if this structure existed in the past itself.

3.1.3. Historism is an unexceptionable theory of history if it is translated from a theory about historical phenomena into a theory about our speaking about the past (that which was metaphysical must become linguistic).

3.1.4. Insofar as the notion of plot or intrigue is suggestive of a structure or story present in the past itself, this notion is an unwarranted concession to historist, or narrativist, realism.

3.2. Historical narratives are not projections (on to the past) or reflections of the past, tied to it by translation rules which have their origin either in our daily experiences of the social world, in the social sciences, or in speculative philosophies of history.

3.2.1. Narrative interpretations are theses, not hypotheses.

3.3. Narrative interpretations *apply* to the past, but do not *correspond* or *refer* to it (as [parts of] statements do).

3.3.1. Much of current philosophy of historical narrative is bewitched by the picture of the statement.

3.3.2. Narrative language is autonomous with regard to the past itself. A philosophy of narrative makes sense if, and only if, this autonomy is recognized (see 4.5).

3.3.3. Since narrative interpretations only apply and do not refer (cf. the point of view from which a painter paints a landscape), there is no fixity in the relation between them and the past. The requirement that there should be such a relationship results from a category mistake (i.e., demanding for historical narrative what can only be given to the statement).

3.3.4. Narrative interpretations 'pull you out of historical reality' and do not 'send you back to it' (as the statement does).

3.4. In narrative language the relation between language and reality is systematically 'destabilized' (see 5.1.2).

3.4.1. Epistemology is of relevance to philosophy of historical research, but of no importance to philosophy of historical writing or philosophy of narrative interpretation.

3.4.2. Epistemology, studying the relation between language and reality insofar as this relation is fixed and stable, disregards all the real problems of science and of historiography which only arise after that which bothers epistemology has been accepted as unproblematic. *Foundationalism* is interested in what is fundamentally uninteresting.

3.4.3. The philosophical investigation of 'what justifies historical descriptions' is an implicit denial and denigration of the historian's intellectual achievements.

4. Narrative language is not object language.

4.1. Narrative language *shows* the past in terms of what does not *refer* or *correspond* to parts or aspects of the past. Narrative interpretations in this regard resemble the models used by fashion designers for showing the qualities of their gowns and dresses. Language is used for showing what belongs to a world different from it.

4.1.1. Narrativism is a constructivism not of what the past might have been like, but of narrative interpretations of the past.

4.1.2. Narrative interpretations are *Gestalts*.

4.2. Logically, narrative interpretations are of the nature of proposals (to see the past from a certain point of view).

4.2.1. Proposals may be useful, fruitful, or not, but cannot be either true or false; the same can therefore be said of historical narratives.

4.2.2. There is no intrinsic difference between speculative systems and history proper; they are *used* in different ways. Speculative systems are used as *master-narratives* to which other narratives should conform.

4.2.3. The writing of history shares with metaphysics the effort of defining the essence of (part of) reality, but differs from metaphysics because of its nominalism (see 4.7.1).

4.3. Narrative interpretations are not knowledge but *organizations* of knowledge. Our age, with its excess of information – and confronted with the problem of the organization of knowledge and information, rather than of how knowledge is gained – has every reason to be interested in the results of narrativism.

4.3.1. Cognitivism, with regard to narrative interpretations, is the source of all realist misconceptions of historical narrative.

4.4.　　　Logically, narrative proposals are of the nature of things (not of concepts); like things they can be spoken about without ever being part of the language in which they are *mentioned*. Language is used here with the purpose of constructing a narrative interpretation which itself lies outside the domain of language, though the interpretation is 'made out of' language (similarly, the meaning of the word *chair* cannot be reduced to the letters in the word).

4.4.1.　　Narrative interpretations cross the familiar border between the domain of things and the domain of language – as does metaphor.

4.5.　　　A historical discussion about the crisis of the seventeenth century, for example, is not a debate about the actual past but about narrative interpretations of the past.

4.5.1.　　Our speaking about the past is covered by a thick crust not related to the past itself but to historical interpretation and the debate about rival historical interpretations. Narrative language has no transparency and is unlike the glass paperweight through which we gain an unobstructed view of the past itself.

4.6.　　　The autonomy of narrative language with regard to the past itself does not in the least imply that narrative interpretations should be arbitrary (see 5.3, 5.6).

4.6.1.　　Facts about the past may be arguments in favor of or against narrative interpretations but can never determine these interpretations (facts only [dis]prove statements about the past) (see 1.2.1). Only interpretations can (dis)prove interpretations.

4.7.　　　Narrative interpretations may have proper names (like the General Crisis of the Seventeenth Century, the Cold War, Mannerism, or the Industrial Revolution). Mostly, however, this is not the case.

4.7.1.　　Narrative logic is strictly nominalist.

4.7.2.　　Names like 'Mannerism' refer to historical interpretations and not to past reality itself ('What Mannerism do you have in mind?' 'Pevsner's Mannerism.').

4.7.3.　　This does not imply that these names are floating in a domain unrelated to historical reality itself (example: the name 'Mannerism' refers to the statements of a narrative interpretation, and in these statements, reference is made to historical reality itself).

4.7.4. Narrative interpretations have no existential implications (for example: the Industrial Revolution is not a vast impersonal force in historical reality, unnoticed and undiscovered until 1884 when Arnold Toynbee wrote *The Industrial Revolution in England*, but an interpretative instrument for understanding the past).

4.7.5. Nevertheless, if a narrative interpretation goes unquestioned for a long time, is accepted by everybody, and becomes part of ordinary language (thereby losing its historiographical nature), it may turn into the notion of a (type of) thing. A *narrative thing* (see 4.4) has become a *thing in reality*. This is how our concepts of (types of) things originate. Typification procedures decide what is still merely interpretative and what is real; there is nothing fixed and absolute about the demarcation between what is interpretation and what belongs to the inventory of reality.

4.7.6. Concepts of (types of) things (like 'dog' or 'tree') are logically more complicated than narrative interpretations, since they presuppose a typification procedure still absent in the case of the latter. Interpretation logically precedes our (notions of) types of things. Ontology is a systematization of interpretation.

4.7.7. Metaphor and narrative interpretation form the basis of our language.

4.7.8. Without a theory of types, narrativism is impossible. Without it, we inevitably look in the wrong direction. (Types of) things are then more fundamental than narrative interpretations.

4.7.9. To require fixed meanings for words like 'the Cold War' or 'Mannerism' would amount to requiring that historical debate should stop. Historical writing does not presuppose, but results in definitions.

4.7.10. Notions like 'the Cold War', being sets of statements, are logically distinct from theoretical concepts.

4.8. Causal explanation – for instance, along the lines of the *covering law model* (CLM) – has its function exclusively on the level of historical research (and on that of the components of historical narrative): we should not ask for the cause of the Cold War since what this term refers to is a narrative interpretation. It makes no sense to ask for the cause of a historical interpretation. Anyone who asks for the cause of the Cold War is really asking for a vigorous interpretation

| | of events between 1944 and the early 1990s and not for a causal tie between two separate sets of events. |

5.   The statements of a historical narrative always have a *double* function: 1) to describe the past; and 2) to define or individuate a specific narrative interpretation of the past.

5.1.   Logically, both historical narratives and metaphor consist of two operations only: 1) description; and 2) the individuation of a (metaphorical) point of view. Historical narrative is a sustained metaphor.

5.1.1. Metaphor shows what the metaphorical utterance is about in terms of something else (e.g., 'John is a pig'); similarly, historical narrative shows the past in terms of what is not the past (i.e., a narrative interpretation) (see 4.1).

5.1.2. Thanks to its autonomy with regard to historical reality – in historical narrative the relation between language and reality is constantly destabilized – historical narrative, like metaphor, is the birthplace of new meaning. Accepted, literal meaning requires a fixed relation between language and reality.

5.2.   The discrepancy between the (literal) meaning of the individual statements of a historical narrative – if taken separately – and the (metaphorical) meaning of historical narrative – if taken in its totality – is the *scope* of historical narrative. This shows the difference between the chronicle (corresponding to the separate statement) and historical narrative (corresponding to the totality of a narrative's statements). A set of statements arbitrarily jumbled together has no scope.

5.2.1. A historical narrative is a historical narrative only insofar as the (metaphorical) meaning of the historical narrative in its totality transcends the (literal) meaning of the sum of its individual statements. Being a historical narrative, therefore, is a matter of degree.

5.2.2. The historical narrative resembles a belvedere: after having climbed the staircase of its individual statements, one surveys an area exceeding by far the area on which the staircase was built.

5.2.3. The historian's capacity to develop (metaphorical) narrative scope is the most formidable asset in his intellectual arsenal.

5.3.   The best historical narrative is the most metaphorical historical narrative, the historical narrative with the largest scope. It is also the most 'risky' or the most 'courageous' historical narrative. In contrast, the non-narrativist has to prefer an unmeaning historical narrative without internal organization.

5.3.1. The narrative scope of a historical narrative cannot be established by considering only *that* historical narrative. Narrative scope only comes into being when one compares narrative interpretations with rival interpretations. If we have only *one* narrative interpretation of some historical topic, we have *no* interpretation.

5.3.2. Historical insight, therefore, is only born in the space *between* rival narrative interpretations and cannot be identified with any specific (set of) interpretations.

5.3.3. *Cognitive knowledge* is to be identified with the linguistic means used for expressing it (singular statements, general statements, theories, etc.); *historical insight* lies in the empty narrative space between the narrative interpretations (it is stereoscopic, so to speak).

5.3.4. Historical insight is constituted in and by historiographical controversy and not by the individual phases of historiographical controversy, hence not by individual narrative interpretations in isolation from others.

5.3.5. Historiographical debate, ultimately, does not aim for agreement but for the proliferation of interpretative theses. The purpose of historiography is *not* the transformation of narrative things into real things (or their type concepts) (see 4.7.5). On the contrary, it attempts to bring about the dissolution of what seems known and unproblematic. Its goal is not the reduction of the unknown to the known, but the estrangement of what seems so familiar.

5.3.6. This emphasis on disagreement and historiographical controversy requires us to reject the notion of a Cartesian or Kantian, interchangeable, transcendental knowing subject. The Aristotelian view is to be preferred. For Aristotle, experience and knowledge *are* the interaction between us and the world and not an abstraction from it determined by a transcendentalist, formal scheme. Similarly, historic interpretation arises from the interaction of interpretations and should not be attributed to either a concrete individual or to a transhistorical, transcendental subject.

5.4. Narrative scope is logically independent of the realm of values; therefore, historical narrative need not be value-free in order to have a large scope – that is, in order to be objective (for example, the notion of the totalitarian state proposed by K. Popper, J.L. Talmon, H. Arendt, and others was not value-free but had a very large scope).

5.4.1.   The historian is the professional 'outsider': the gap between himself and historical reality, which he is always attempting to bridge, is identical to the gap between the individual and society, which ethics and political philosophy attempt to bridge. The ethical dimension must therefore be ubiquitous in historiography. Modern historiography is based on a political decision.

5.4.2.   Metaphor and narrative are the *trait d'union* between the *is* and the *ought* – the *is* of the constative statements of a historical interpretation may suggest what *ought* to be done.

5.5.   Leibniz's predicate in notion principle is the crucial theorem of the logic of historical interpretation. All statements about a historical narrative are *analytically* either true or false.

5.5.1.   The fashionable view that the variables of quantification will take the place of the subject term in statements (Russell, Quine) is incorrect for narrative statements (i.e., statements about historical narratives). The subject term in narrative statements is unvoiceable, precisely because it merely 'collects' the statements contained by a historical narrative.

5.5.2.   Narrative interpretations have explanatory force since the description of historical states of affairs can be analytically derived from them.

5.6.   There is no room for historical skepticism. We can see the rationality of why historians in a certain phase of historical debate preferred one view of the past to another. Skepticism only results if one is not content with the rationality of historical debate and absolute *foundations* are required. But, in practice, this requirement can never be more than an exhortation to historians to do their job carefully and conscientiously.

6.   The roots of historicity go deeper than is suggested by either modern historiography or current philosophy (of history).

6.1.   The notion of the self is a historical, narrative interpretation – the narrative interpretation that is presupposed by *all* other historical interpretations. This is the kernel of truth in Anglo-Saxon hermeneutics.

6.1.1.   Consequently, the fact that narrative interpretations already play a role on the level of the life of the human individual can never be an argument in favor of a certain variant of narrative realism (i.e., the view that historical knowing should be modelled on our experiences of daily reality). It is the reverse: interpretative narrativism has already invaded our daily reality.

6.1.2. The concepts of (types of) individual things are logically dependent upon narrative interpretations (identity). Thus: identity precedes individuality, not the reverse, as positivism suggests.

Autumn has come

In his 'Historiography and Postmodernism', published first in *History and Theory* in 1989 and reproduced in *History and Tropology* (my page references refer to this reprint), Ankersmit says that, 'for various reasons, we can presume that Autumn has come to Western historiography'.[17] In his *In Defence of History*, Evans refers to this statement, not to explicate why Ankersmit is of this view and to discuss it, but to locate him as one of the main barbarians loitering at the disciplinary gates with hostile intent: '"Autumn", declared the Dutch postmodernist Frank Ankersmit triumphantly in 1990 [actually 1989] "has come to Western historiography"'.[18] Well, yes it has, and we have already seen why Evans is afraid of this, but what we haven't yet seen is the far from triumphalist reasoning behind Ankersmit's verdict. But this reasoning is important here in this examination of the possible 'end of "proper" history' under the impact of the postmodern, and so I turn to a reading of it now.

Ankersmit starts out – in the midst of a discussion about history as an aesthetic discourse – from certain remarks by Arthur Danto that the 'intentional nature of statements and texts is nowhere clearer than in literature, including history as a literary artefact'.[19] We might see this element, says Ankersmit's Danto, 'perhaps nowhere more clearly than in those literary texts, where in addition to whatever facts the author means to state, he or she *chooses the words* with which they are stated', and where the intentions of the writer 'would fail if other words were used instead'.[20] Consequently, because of its intentional nature, the literary text, including the history text, has 'a certain opacity' and thus a certain capacity to draw attention to itself instead of just to – or only to – the fictitious or historical referent. Thus, concludes Ankersmit at this point, 'historical writing possesses the same opacity and intentional dimensions as art'.[21]

As such it can be compared to science, in that science has 'at least the pretension of being transparent'; if it 'impedes' our view of 'actuality' it will have to be refined. Of course, some historians have claimed that history is also scientific in that it too aims at transparency. But Ankersmit's point is that aiming is one thing, achieving another. For where the 'insights provided in a discipline are far more of a syntactical than semantic nature' – as is the case in the exact sciences where the ambition is to achieve truth without semantics – there is little room for intentionality. Consequently, says Ankersmit, 'if we are in agreement with the above – that is to say, with the applicability of postmodernist insight into historical writing – I would like to draw a number of conclusions'. And Ankersmit's conclusions run thus.

Unlike the postmodern historian who sees the evidence derived from the traces of the past as pointing not towards the past *per se* but to other intertextual interpretations, the modernist (more 'scientific') historian construes evidence as, essentially, 'the evidence that something happened in the past', following a line of reasoning moving from the evidential traces 'back' to an actuality 'behind' the sources. Ankersmit expresses this difference by way of the following imagery: 'for the modernist the evidence is a tile which he picks up to see what is underneath; for the postmodernist . . . it is a tile which he steps on in order to move to other tiles: horizontality instead of verticality'. And it is this essentialist, vertical way of thinking that he sees postmodernists leaving behind:

> What we are witnessing could perhaps be nothing less than the definitive farewell, for the time being, of all the essential aspirations which have actually dominated historical writing as long as it has existed. Historians have always searched for something they could label as the essence of the past – the principle that held everything together in the past (or in part of it) and on the basis of which, consequently, everything could be understood. In the course of the centuries, this essentialism . . . has manifested itself in countless different ways.[22]

This sense of an ending, this closing down of an essentialist tradition, has manifested itself in many different ways too. Postmodernism is all about endings: about the end of the Western Tradition, the overthrowing of the upper case, the historicisation of the a priori, the acceptance of anti-foundationalism, the welcoming of catachresis; it's all about surface, horizontality, intertextuality, difference, the *différand*, deferment, alterity. Postmodernism is thus the arguable 'breaking point' of modernity, the intellectual equivalent of the straw that broke the camel's back; a movement in consciousness that, historically speaking, Ankersmit explicates through the following seasonal, autumnal, analogy.

Compare, says Ankersmit, history to a tree. Here, the metanarrative tradition of Western historiography focused on the trunk, using it to define, as it were, the essence of it. Historicism and modernist scientific writing of the 'more lower case' and the lower case variety (with their attention to what 'the past essentially was') were situated more on the branches of the tree but, from this position, still remained focused on what held the branches together, the 'actuality of the trunk':

> Just like their speculative predecessors, both the historists and the protagonists of so-called scientific historical writing still had the hope . . . of ultimately being able to say something about the trunk after all . . . whether it was formulated in ontological, epistemological, or methodological terminology, historical writing since historism has always aimed at the reconstruction of the essentialist line running [objectively] through the past or parts of it.[23]

And this is what postmodernism has changed. And what it has changed is the direction and the object of the modernist's gaze. It has changed it away from the trunk and the branches (and one might add the twigs and the stems) to the *leaves*. Within the postmodern view of history, the aim is no longer integration, or synthesis, or totality, or objectivity, or truth. In the anti-essentialist, anti-foundational, nominalist perspectivism of the postmodern, *if* we want to privilege anything, then we privilege the *leaves*.

This brings Ankersmit to his main point. For it is a characteristic of leaves that they are relatively loosely attached to trees and that, when autumn comes, they are blown off and away by the wind. Thus:

> For various reasons, we can presume that Autumn has come to Western historiography. In the first place there is, of course, the postmodernist nature of our own time. Our anti-essentialism . . . has lessened our commitment to science and traditional historiography. The changed position of Europe in the world since 1945 is a second important consideration . . . The trunk of the tree of Western history now strikes us as merely being part of a whole forest. The *meta-récits* we would like to tell ourselves about our history, the triumph of Reason, the glorious struggle

for emancipation of the nineteenth century workers' proletariat, are only of local importance and for that reason can no longer be suitable metanarratives. The chilly wind, which . . . rose around 1900 simultaneously in both the West and the East, finally blew the leaves off our historical tree as well in the second half of this century.[24]

There is, *pace* Evans, nothing triumphalist about this sober assessment of the coming of our postmodern condition. Indeed, Ankersmit's tone is so careful and moderate ('I am referring here to trends and not to radical breaks', he writes, 'to avoid any pathos or exaggeration')[25] that it might be useful to add a little to his tree analogy/metaphor. For I think that we now know that there never has been anything but the leaves. It's not so much that they've blown off the tree. There never was a tree. There never was a trunk. Nor branches. Nor twigs. Nor stems. All there has ever been are leaves. And we have no idea where they have come from, or what they mean, or why they exist(ed). They're just, as it were, 'lying around', being blown hither and thither. Without any knowable point. Coming and going. And from their phenomenal existence we have inferred back on the basis of causal logic (behind every deed a doer; behind every effect a cause ...) *fantastic* essences, meanings, teleologies, objectivities and truths to explain what we have apparently been and are – and will be – both at the level of the parts and such putative wholes as we have been able to imagine. We have, in our raking together of the leaves, in the various piles we have tried to put them in, read into them, much like the leaves in our teacups, all manner of fortunes. And now as we dissolve all of this into contingency, and aleatory and the ludic, into the relativism that just *is* the human, moral condition, we are left, as Baudrillard sees clearly, with the only radical illusion there is: the radical illusion of 'the world'. This is, going back to George Steiner, Nietzsche's challenge: to accept this as our lot (*amor fati*) with joy, and to give to this apparent meaningless of existence an *urgency* which can still – even after the failure of the experiment of modernity to build human rights communities – animate us after 'the end of history', modernist – or postmodernist – style.

Now, there is something of this 'end of history' argument in Ankersmit, but, in many ways, he is still 'a historian'. He still wants a past (albeit of the leaves) in non-Kantian, non-metaphorical ways. As I said at the start of this chapter on Ankersmit, although I cannot follow him as he explains what sort of future history he would like after the end of modernist histories, a few concluding points can be briefly made to this reading of him.

Ankersmit, then, still wants a history. What remains now, he says, is to gather together the leaves to study them (why?). What is important now, he argues, is not to try and find the place the leaves had on the tree, but the patterns we can make of them *now*; for us; for our sakes. For today, the getting of the right 'historical context' has lost its traditional importances (this will be David Harlan's point), not because one wants to take up an 'a' or 'anti' historical position, but because we have 'let go of' the historical context.[26] Today, everything arrives unannounced, and in this radical contingency lies our hopes for the future.

Ankersmit is not talking barbarism here, nor new forms of solipsistic subjectivity. Nor does he want to impose contemporary desires on the past ('legitimating anything at all is best left to the modernists').[27] No, the 'ironic essence' of postmodernism for Ankersmit, after the *end* of metanarratives and the statemented horizons of the lower case, is 'precisely that we should avoid pointing out essentialist patterns in the past'. For if this is avoided then history could be transformed. Its role would no longer be the 'reconstruction of what has happened to us in the various phases of our lives, but a continuous playing with the memory of this'. 'Remembrance', Ankersmit writes, has to 'have priority over what is remembered.' And something similar *ought* to now characterise historiography, postmodern style:

> The wild, greedy, and uncontrolled digging into the past, inspired by the desire to discover a past reality and reconstruct it scientifically, is no longer the historian's unquestioned task. We would do better to examine the result of a hundred and fifty years' digging more attentively and ask ourselves more often what it all adds up to. The time has come for us to *think* about the past, rather than *investigate* it.[28]

A new phase in historical writing has thus perhaps begun, Ankersmit adds finally, in which meaning is more important than reconstruction, and where theorising and thinking about the past and the present and the future is more to the point than traditional historiography:

> In the postmodernist view, the focus is [for Ankersmit] no longer on the past itself, but on the incongruity between present and past, between the language we presently use for speaking about the past

and the past itself. There is no longer 'one line running through history' to neutralise this incongruity . . . Postmodernism does not reject scientific historical writing, but only draws our attention to the modernists' vicious circle which would have us believe that nothing exists outside it. However, outside it is the whole domain of historical purpose and meaning.[29]

I dissent perhaps only from Ankersmit's last two sentences, above. But I do agree with: 'The time has come for us to *think* about the past, rather than investigate it.' But because I also agree that the modernist vicious circle still exists – albeit in a moribund state – I see some good reasons for thinking that that magic circle of historiography might be expendable, and that, rather than propping it up, no matter how indirectly, postmodernists should just let it wither away – helped along by arguments, like Ankersmit's, that draw attention to what lies *beyond* it.

Now, I've already said several times that thinking about the future in temporal, moral ways *without history and ethics* can be gleaned from an increasing number of 'postist' theorists, from whom I have chosen to look at just two in Part III: Elizabeth Deeds Ermarth and David Harlan. But before I turn to them I will end this Part, on Evans, White and Ankersmit and the possible end of proper history, with a resumé that again draws on Derrida and which, in a slightly different way, makes the point that 'difference' and 'deconstruction' (for both the lower as much as the upper case) pretty much says it all.

In Derrida it is possible to identify what he and some commentators have called 'three types of violence', the first two of which are important here theoretically, the third (everyday violence – war, murder, rape, etc.) being marginal to this particular argument.

First, there is an originary violence. Here the argument is that the initial rupture between the transcendental gesture and its empirical inscription is a violent act, an act that marks the impossibility of thinking the ideality or the purity of a term (be it Law, Justice, History, Ethics ...) on any other level than that of the empirical, yet which is, as an act, a necessary and irreducible condition for all meaning and representation: 'all determined relations presuppose this original violence of the Proper name', the Proper name signifying here the logic of the idealised (quasi-) transcendental gesture.

Second, Derrida sees what he calls secondary violence; namely, the attempt (violently) to *conceal* the fact that the ideality of a term will never be realised and that we shall never overcome the original act of violence by attaining full presence. Primary violence just is the way that language works (wholes to parts, genus to species, ideality to empirical inscription); it is the necessary condition for its performance and thus, to recall, the 'fact' that makes *différance* (the tension of the quasi transcendental between the transcendental gesture and the empirical) irreducible and thus deconstruction inescapable. But secondary violence is not 'necessary' in the same way. For it is possible to live reflexively without this concealment, to live knowing all our meanings are ultimately arbitrary impositions (catachretic). And it is the covering up of this fact – so essential for discourses of a realist/empiricist type – that postmodernism exposes. For insofar as any dominant discourse of a realist/empiricist kind exists, then it is in its interests to pass off its settlement of the first act of originary violence in the second as not violent at all but natural; it is a naturalness that deconstruction deconstructs.

Now, my argument here is that Evans lives a highly unreflexive intellectual life in the realm of secondary violence. I have two reasons for saying so. First Evans is radically unreflexive (and thus violent) because, despite occasional reservations, he still tries to achieve 'real' objectivity, 'real' truth, 'real' historical knowledge, as if such 'reality' wasn't always a radical impossibility. And second, Evans does not see (and ideologically couldn't admit) that a thinking of secondary violence opens up all of our categories and concepts to contingency, to interminable redescription (for instance what is the Law, Justice, the Ethical, the Historical, *really*?).

Unlike Evans, White and Ankersmit recognise all this. They recognise that idealised gestures – the condition for all empirical inscriptions – are 'empty mechanisms'. That anything – or nothing – can, with ingenuity and a bit of luck (normally spelt *power*) be made into any substantial content. Thus White and Ankersmit, and I think also Derrida are well aware that we have come to the end of what are imagined to be 'real' transcendentals. Accordingly, the possibility opened up by postmodern theorising is not just that of exposing (and bringing up to speed) those who live at the level of secondary violence in a non-reflexive state, but also of dropping history and ethics as categories to be reflexive about. For in the condition of postmodernity, no imaginaries are sacred; all have pragmatically to 'earn their keep'. Consequently, this text could be seen as considering the possibility of, as it were, standing on, then going beyond, White and Ankersmit: to query if we still need, in a future that might see the end of unreflexive second-level violence, history and ethics modernist-style. It is on that basis that I now move to two people who have, I think, also been effectively thinking about these kinds of things: Elizabeth Deeds Ermarth and David Harlan – and in ways which affect third-level violence too.

Part III

Beyond histories and ethics

The positions taken by Elizabeth Deeds Ermarth and David Harlan are not, I believe, the most extreme or revolutionary or abnormal around. Nor do I think that they have finally got things right.[1] They are the subjects of this final Part because I use the arguments of their books (Ermarth's *Sequel to History: Postmodernism and the Crisis of Representational Time* and Harlan's *The Degradation of American History*) to help us consider certain possibilities.

Imagine a culture where it has become the norm to argue, rather as Ermarth and Harlan do (or can be read as doing), for a way of timing time or of appropriating the past in non-historicising ways. Then consider which elements of what currently passes for history (in both the upper and lower cases) would still be of any use in this new construction. More pointedly with regard to what currently passes for history for the representative Evans, in the intellectual, postmodern worlds of Ermarth and Harlan, would anything Evans had to say be remotely to the point? Or put it another way. We can easily imagine that the new situation would be one wherein, whilst Evans(ists) cannot conceive of a way of timing time without still using the old historicising vocabulary and methodological habits, Ermarth and Harlan cannot conceive of timing time whilst doing so: here we have entered a new paradigm. And then consider that this same culture drops the concept of ethical systems in favour of new types of morality appropriate for living in this new intellectual landscape; it is in order to help us imagine this too that Ermarth and Harlan are being appropriated here.

Although Ermarth and Harlan are the heroes of this last Part, the point needs to be made that they are imperfect heroes. To me both seem to have an unnecessary nostalgia for, say, ethics (Ermarth) and history (Harlan). But as postmodern proponents, together they can be read to help us along the post-historical/post-ethical road that I think we should be going down, uncluttered pretty much by previous baggage. Indeed, that we might be so lightly packed that we can happily be Cronopios and rhythmics (Ermarth) and Rorty-like bricoleurs (Harlan) without giving our modernist preoccupations much thought. So I shall use a reading of Ermarth and Harlan that will, I hope, give us some ideas about how to live in time and morality as construed in postmodern ways; I claim no more than this – to help us conceive what living in some of their imaginaries could be like.

Given the nature of my appropriation of Ermarth and Harlan, I should say briefly what will be taken from their respective texts. My argument will be that Ermarth's is a brilliant, suggestive book wherein she successfully critiques modern linear histories out of plausible existence through her notion of rhythmic time. But arguably, she fails to embrace an easy acceptance of moral relativism. Nevertheless, Ermarth does open up, I think, the ethical space to locate a Derridean-type of morality (of the 'madness of the decision').

From Harlan's evocative text, I take particularly his Rorty-inspired suggestion that we might simply lift texts out of their historical context in order to weld together an eclectic, anti-foundational imaginary of, for Rorty, a pragmatic, and for me, a relativist morality.[2] But I don't think we should do this in order to restore – which seems to be Harlan's reason for doing it – a moral dimension *to* history, a moral dimension he thinks it once had and should have again. For I think that if *his* Rorty is applied to 'history', so little has it to do with history as currently or (arguably, *pace* Harlan) as previously understood, that the term 'history' might as well be dropped. And I think that, in fact, this is what Harlan's own arguments propel him towards. For what he is arguing against in his text is the insistence by 'proper' historians that texts etc. should only be studied in *their* contexts, whereas Harlan is arguing that they should only be studied in *ours* – overtly. He says that the only point of studying the past is for what it can mean for us today (just like Ankersmit) and that ripping texts out of context to suit us to live moral lives *is* the point of studying such texts. This is fine, except that it seems to me that this so undercuts all that the 'proper' historian holds sacred, that we might as well call this something else – 'temporal studies' or 'appropriative studies' perhaps – so to escape the connotations history still has clustered around it. In fact, I think we might profitably link together the timings of Ermarth and the moral combinatories of Harlan without nostalgia, drawing on the strengths of each to think 'beyond histories and ethics'.

7   On Elizabeth Deeds Ermarth

Ermarth's book is not easy to read or summarise. For although her text on postmodernism is written at times in the language of representation – 'it produces meaning, assumes a consensus community, engages in historical generalisation and footnotes' – Ermarth also notes that the postmodernism she is considering exerts

> a kind of gravitational pull that is bound to influence any writing 'about' it. The reflexive qualities of my writing (e.g. the rhythm sections punctuating the macro-sequence, the paralogical pulse of particular sentences, the repetition of key quotations, phrases and points) may cause problems for die-hard representationalists, dualists, and dialecticians who will want to factor them out as 'noise'.[1]

Now, I do not want to be thought of as any of those, but given Ermarth's is indeed a noisy and repetitive text, an element of quietening down and straightening out is perhaps necessary to give a reading of a two-hundred-page book in about twenty. My reading thus has the following, three-part shape.

First, I want to unpack some of the thinking lying behind Ermarth's thesis that she herself gives as follows:

> My thesis in brief is this: postmodern narrative language undermines historical time and substitutes for it a new construction of temporality that I call rhythmic time. This rhythmic time either radically modifies or abandons altogether the dialectics, the teleology, the transcendence, and the putative neutrality of historical time; and it replaces the Cartesian *cogito* with a different subjectivity whose manifesto might be Cortázar's 'I swing, therefore I am'.[2]

CHRONOS (LINEAR)   KAIROS (NON-LINEAR)
            TIME

Second, and against this unpacked thesis, I argue that Ermarth's text is composed of a series of densely elaborated arguments which, somewhat ironically, have much of the form of an old binary opposition. Despite seepages, Ermarth's text is basically organised around the attempt to show (a) what is *wrong* with modern, linear history and what are some of its more serious failings and (b) what is *right* about rhythmic temporality and what are some of its particular strengths.

Third, I shall argue that, whilst Ermarth's essaying of the rhythmic possibilities *after the end of history* seem exhilarating (if nothing else her optimism displaces those more common mournful musings on the loss of one of the West's most enduring mythologisations – history – articulated by those who have the most to lose), the relativistic thrust of her text is one that she arguably (and I stress 'arguably') resists. It may, of course, appear churlish at this stage of the game to level against Ermarth some concluding criticisms after all that by then she will have done, thereby remaining trapped within the ritualistic convention of the expositor turning critic as he or she – having lived parasitically off the text – has the 'correct' last word. But I intend any criticism to be slight and constructive. It seems to me that Ermarth succeeds brilliantly in her critiques of modernity's ways of organising temporality in overwhelmingly linear, historical forms, in that it is indeed possible to conceive of a life without them. It is possible to live outside of history and in new rhythmic timings that signal the end of the modernists' way of conceptualising the past. But – and this is a small but – it will be clear by now that I think it is possible to live outside ethics in the type of morality suggested by Derrida's notion of the 'undecidability of the decision'. I thus question Ermarth's occasional reluctance to appear to be a 'happy relativist' via a critique of how and why she wants to cling to some form of ('real'?) constraint. I conclude that she has few reasons for thinking in this way, thus opening up a space for a reading of the (more) relativistic Harlan.

So, to the first item: what are some of the arguments Ermarth uses to establish her general thesis as just outlined? It is in her Prologue and in the first section of Part One that her general position seems to be established, especially by the following (type of) remarks.

Ermarth's general assumption is that the term 'modern' designates a period and a discourse that had pre-eminence between the Renaissance and the turn of the twentieth century, and that what succeeds that modern culture is simply postmodern; postmodernism is thus both a 'chronological indication' and a 'mark of general awareness that something, indeed, is happening to discourse in the post-Renaissance, post-Reformation, and post-Enlightenment West'. For across

> a broad range of cultural manifestations a massive re-examination of Western discourse is underway: its obsession with power and knowledge, its constraint of language to primarily symbolic function, its ethic of winning, its categorical and dualistic modes of definition, its belief in the quantitative and objective, its linear time and individual subject, and above all its common media of exchange (time, space, money) which guarantee certain political and social systems.[3]

The postmodern phenomenon that most interests Ermarth is its subversion of time and the individual subject. Time, she argues, is often omitted from discussions of postmodernism which 'cycle through endlessly reflexive and spatial and static modes without ever revealing the disappearance of history and the practical reformation this implies', portraying a view of historical time that is, ironically, ahistorical.[4] The belief in a temporal medium that is natural, neutral, linear and homogeneous, argues Ermarth, thus underwrites those mutually informative measurements between one historical moment and another in order to support most forms of knowledge still circulating in the West. Unproblematicised historical time (the most 'commanding metanarrative in western discourse') informs the bulk of what we tell ourselves about individual and collective life so that the critique of historical time involves a critique of everything *in* it:

> not just anthromorphism, not just the metaphysics of presence, transcendence and depth, not just the structure of the human sciences, not just the definition of subjectivity as 'individuality'. The postmodern subversion of historical time threatens other things still broadly taken for granted in universities and constitutional governments: the idea of 'natural' or 'human' or 'inalienable' rights, the definition of disciplines and fields of research . . . the possibility of 'representation' in political as well as aesthetic terms, the nonceremonial (ie., informational) functions of language. There are some who fear that postmodernism, by depreciating traditional causalities, portends an end to morality [ethics] itself, and the fear is not unfounded so far as traditional morality [ethics] is concerned. After all, how *do* we deal with each other . . . when we can't be certain who or where each other is? And who, for that matter, is 'we'? . . . We are surrounded

by a world that operates on the principles of quantum theory; we are living in mental worlds that operate on the principles of Newton.[5]

For the constant in postmodern 'ways of telling', the controlling factor that makes possible all other definitions relative to each other, is no longer

the time of history, the time of project, the time of Newton and Kant, the time of clocks and capital. Narrative no longer inscribes the time that makes possible the perception of invariant identities like 'subject' or 'object'; instead it concentrates phenomenologically on the reader-events that collapse the distances between object and subject, inside and outside . . . By focusing on a phenomenal 'event' in which subjectivity and objectivity cannot be distinguished, phenomenology anticipates the always-embedded and in-process subjectivity . . . In postmodern narrative . . . we experience temporality as an imaginary ambiance containing tension, fields, tectonics, values . . . Time, in other words, is not neutral and absolute but a function of position . . . [Consequently] once we begin to see our mental manoeuvres as inventions they become not 'neutral' or 'natural' ways of behaving but instead modes of exercising responsibility and freedom . . .

Implicit in this shift . . . with the shift in postmodern narratives from one time to another, from the linear track of historical time to the conjugating rhythms that Cortázar describes . . . are new definitions of subjectivity. Because the individual subject is largely a construct of historical conventions, the replacement of the Cartesian *cogito ergo sum* with a new formulation, 'I swing therefore I am' . . . subverts the metaphysic that posits essences like stable, self-identical, nondiscursive identities and the transcendental 'laws' that operate 'in' them. Such a metaphysic simply becomes inadequate in the discourse where essence or identity is multiplied because it is always *situated*, and where the situation is always discursive, which is to say always constructed by signs whose function is differential.[6]

Thus summarised, the changes Ermarth sees signalled by postmodernism constitute an epochal, cultural deformation and critique, a critique that she feels 'cannot be deterred by any amount of dismissal'. For postmodernism makes us face up to problematics in the 'history of consciousness' that are 'inescapable' now that the discourse that has constituted linear historicity turns out to be just another imaginary like our other habits and beliefs. Accordingly, on the basis of the 'end of history' and that 'famous subject', Ermarth attends to new questions and opportunities opened up in theory/practice, the oblique in the theory/practice couplet indicating that, of course, to say that the 'real' is invented in language ('to live in reality is to live in a language; to live in language is to live in reality') is not to deny the extra-discursive actuality 'out there', nor the material effects of language itself, but to emphasise that the notion of 'the real is imaginary and the imaginary is real' is a radical, political gesture. And it is a gesture Ermarth pulls together and summarises (in these – her and my – 'preliminary remarks') in opposition to the characteristics of modernity:

> Discarding the terms of modernist discourse, while not easy, is a necessary discipline to postmodernism. The discourse of historicism and representation . . . will not help us appreciate post-modernism. The discourse of modernism extends its media (space, time, consciousness, money, humanity) to infinity and encourages us to forget finitude and to distribute energy toward an infinite horizon. The discourse of postmodernism finds time and space warped and bounded by finite and newly defined subjective systems. Modernist discourse respects primarily the constraints of an 'objective reality' that, from a postmodern context, appears to be the mediated construct of a founding subjectivity. In post-modern discourses the primary constraint is absolute and un-mediatable finitude, a recognition that inspires reflexiveness because activity no longer can be referred to unchanging external absolutes . . . I call it 'improvisation' . . . the operative constraint in postmodern writing [living] is not any transcendent 'reality' beyond language but language itself: its substitutions are the events of rhythmic temporality and its figures are the unique poetry of individual life. The collapse in postmodern writing [and living] of dualisms that sustain representational distance and enables its mediations, opens an unfamiliar and surprising situation where both time and consciousness belong to the linguistic figure.[7]

Ermarth thus seems to be of the opinion that postmodernism has just about got all the imaginaries needed to end linear time and the modernist subject and begin to live in rhythmic time and multi-levelled consciousness – and she's glad. For whereas modernist discourse has got used to its timings of time so to regard it as 'really real time', postmodernism urges us to remember that every such construct is actually the 'mediated construct of a founding subject'. For Ermarth, objects – including phenomenal timings and historicisations – are not really 'objectively there' but are the 'subject objectified' or, better still, are products of the subject-in-process performatively objectifying from specific enunciative locations interminably. This construction dismantles the Cartesian ego/subject in favour of the iterable subject, playfully constituting and deconstructing fictive, temporary shelters as pragmatically necessary. Such performative changes open up, for Ermarth, erotic possibilities. These possibilities – not already existing in the restricted economy of linear histories (or elsewhere) – will thus effectively draw on the metaphysical/imaginary *excess*, it being the (counter) penetration of the excess (imagined by Ermarth as feminist-friendly rhythmic time) into the phallo-logocentric, productivist, 'historical' economy that destabilises it. And it is this that then explains the opposition, fear, and indeed the sometime hatred postmodernism often engenders amongst modernist historians. For as we have seen, postmodern, rhythmic criticisms carry within them the promise of undermining everything held 'dear' within the productivist economy of modernity.

Such then, seems to be something like Ermarth's general estimation of the profound changes postmodernism is working in our contemporary social formation, changes that make both 'cases of history' look so passé that it hardly seems to Ermarth to be worth bothering very much about going into detailed arguments as to their end. Instead, Ermarth just lets history slip away – *who knows or cares what it means anymore?* – without so much as a longing, backward glance. For so many 'irreversible events have rendered historical thinking problematic', she writes, that she doesn't see herself as having to 'lobby for postmodernism at the expense of history'. Rather, she is concerned to explore some of the implications of the 'major discursive shift' postmodernism is inflicting upon previous understandings of temporality, casually dismissing those who still wish to defend history with the argument that anything which is deemed to be 'self-evident' can no longer be defended or maintained.[8] Again, Ermarth writes that whether or not it is meaningful to speak of postmodernism inaugurating some sort of 'new history' is still an open question, but it's not one that she is much bothered to pursue, not least because 'the term "history" has become so saturated with dialectical value that it may no longer be very buoyant'.[9] Accordingly, Ermarth clarifies that her emphasis on the 'disappearance of historical thinking' does not mean 'that I advocate either overthrowing "history" or rallying to its defence', it just means that its ending is taken for granted so that she can attend to things 'more complex and interesting', things of the future.

For what Ermarth seems primarily to want is not in the least past-orientated; it is present- and future-orientated. And this is important to stress. For unlike many postmodernists who see themselves as post-modern historians – and thus postmodernism as beginning a new type of history (post-colonial, post-feminist, etc.) – and who feel (incidentally) that they have to respond to modernist historians' requests to say 'what a postmodern history would look like', Ermarth seems not in the slightest way to be interested in interpreting the past in, say, rhythmic ways. It is not at all that she wishes, for example, to re-interpret the later medieval period, or say something new about the condition of nineteenth-century working-class women. Rather she wants to forget the historical past for future-orientated adventures. To be sure, adds Ermarth as something of a codicil, in demonstrating the power of rhythmic temporality she doesn't mean that 'history' doesn't still exist ('although a non-trivial case can be made for this view'), nor is she wanting simply to 'trash history'. It is just that, at best, the old 'conventions of history' will be incorporated into rhythmic time as just 'one game, one set of rules among many'. Confined to a mere 'rhythmic sequence', she concludes, history will become just one more 'thematic formulation, like any other, and no longer a commanding (determining) premise': modernist history ends here out of neglect and irrelevance.[10]

It is this position that allowed me to say in my introductory remarks to Ermarth that, once having 'set up' her general position, her text is structured around the attempt to show (to recall) (a) what is wrong – and what is so irrelevant – about modernist, linear history especially and (b) what is right about rhythmic temporality. Thus, having 'established' what can count as Ermarth's general position, it is to the first of these two other aspects that I now turn.

Ermarth's accusations against modernity's histories add up to a catalogue of faults that is heavy indeed, the main target for her critique being the peculiar construction of the timing of time which emerged roughly contemporaneously with – and analogously – to single-point visual perspective (in Piero della Francesca for example) and which produced the broad parameters for the modern 'idea of history'. This is a view of time as a neutral, objective, homogeneous medium to which (as in single point perspective) informative measurements could be made. From any viewpoint available in a common horizon 'a spectator could grasp an invariant logic of relationships (a 'world') that remained the same regardless of his or her position and that extended to infinity, thus having the value of universal truth';[11] a timing of time where 'consciousness is rationalised by a narrative time that extends from here to eternity, perhaps encountering many disturbing warps but no disturbing fractures'. In this rendition of historical time, this genre, all temporal perspectives, no matter how widely dispersed, in the end 'agree' in the sense that they don't contradict, so that 'in this powerful sense they achieve a consensus tantamount to the creation of a common horizon in time and hence of the power to think historically'.[12]

Within this type of history, then, Ermarth points out that we are living within a concept of time construed in such an objective and potentially truth-full way, that it 'almost naturally' gives rise to the construction of the mythical figure of the 'omniscient narrator', that sleight of hand and mind that produces the idea of the 'history narrator as nobody', the illusion in historical narrative that it is quite naturally 'history speaking'. It is a way of letting the past ostensibly articulate itself as the actual narrator attempts to go so native, so as to erase himself/herself from the text. The narrative thus disembodies this actual narrator, so making the resultant version seem indistinguishable from the way the past would, if only it could, express itself. As Ermarth puts much of this:

> Such 'Nobody' narrators literally *constitute* historical time by threading together into one system and one act of attention a whole series of moments and perspectives. Thus the continuums of time and of consciousness literally appear inseparable, functioning together as the medium of events even though this particular mutuality is rarely explicitly mentioned because to do so would be to compromise the whole effect . . . and locate a vulnerability grasped by postmodern writers.[13]

For while it may still appear to be common sense to think that a homogeneous notion of time (and space) is natural, the opposite is obviously the case. What postmodernism has thus exposed for Ermarth is the utter foundationlessness of this curious way of historicising time:

> The formal achievement that I call the realistic 'consensus' has itself *created* the media of space and time in which we [then] proceed to make our mutually informative measurements, arrive at

our hypothesis, formulate our laws, and produce our experiments, our capital, and our knowledge . . . There is nothing 'natural' about it.[14]

Thus we are reminded of what we have often learned to forget: 'that in a culture nothing cultural is natural'. Fabricated, positioned, far from neutral and far from objective, historical time is to be overcome if the 'differences' bottled up inside it are to be released. For this kind of history has done its best to snuff out otherness:

By emphasising what is linear, developmental, and mediate [such] historical thinking . . . modernity's thinking . . . by definition involves transcendence of a kind that trivialises the specific detail and the finite moment. In [this] mobile culture every moment *has* to be partial so that we can pursue development, so that we can seek a completion that, by definition . . . we will never actually find but that has emblems along the way: more information, more clarity, more money, more prestige, more of the constituents of heaven.[15]

This is a modern history that is (allegedly) going somewhere, so that 'it doesn't pay' to hang around. This is a heavily productivist, developmental imaginary that, western and male-driven, has excluded as the main beneficiaries just about nine-tenths of the world, including most women. Consequently, it is this sort of 'fact' that helps Ermarth's discarding of that sort of history, an act that feels not only comfortable, but absolutely necessary. For

one thing . . . seems certain: no effort to come to terms with social agendas will succeed without the recognition that history itself is a representational construction of the first order, and that new social construction cannot take place until history is denaturalised. [Consequently] . . . the effort of this book is to forward that possibility by imagining . . . what an alternative temporality, a postmodern temporality, might be like, and what its implications might be for a now questionable subject-in-process, and in a context where the operative dualisms [binary oppositions] . . . are collapsed.[16]

What Ermarth is thus seeking is a way of getting rid of history as an *alibi*; a way of getting *out* of a history that forces 'us' to live in such a way that one's immediate present is effectively nullified by a linear/teleological/dialectical imaginary that is going somewhere else and which thus seems somehow bigger, better and more commanding than our own, personal histories, and to which we are to be subservient. What Ermarth thus wants is a way of timing time that will not subvert the *now* of one's own finite existence.

To develop this idea – as a critique of modernity's dominant historical imaginary – Ermarth therefore invokes Heidegger's stress on the necessity to place death (and thus the finitude of *this* life) at the centre of the agenda. *'Fleeing in the face of death'* is, for Heidegger, the very basis of historical thinking, a way of thinking he calls 'inauthentic temporality' because, as Emarth reads him, it 'exists in order to cover up the fact that existential time ends, and that end *is not mediated*'.[17] She dedicates her book to 'Cronopios Everywhere' (Cortázar's Cronopios, as Ermarth explains, is a term that Cortázar 'sometimes applies to his most postmodern personae', who, better humoured than Heidegger himself, embody the rejection of 'transcendence and dialectics', reject the living of a life 'on a linear track'). Ermarth's invocation of death is no dalliance with morbidity, but a way of putting finitude back into the frame in a positive manner. For

> if death remains perpetually outside the frame of my picture – that is, if my own inevitable finitude is not part of the discourse in which I make my *choices* and my commitments – then questions of value can be infinitely deferred. However, if I remain aware of my own inevitable finitude, questions of value become urgent.[18]

Accordingly, it is this *urgent* insistence on value and choice that has made, as Ermarth puts it 'feminist theory such a powerful extension of other postmodern theory based on linguistics, anthropology, and phenomenology'.[19] Drawing at this point on Julia Kristeva's *Women's Time* to complement and 'extend' Heidegger, Ermarth goes along with her insistence that we should work for the end of a history that has articulated 'time as project, teleology, linear and prospective unfolding; time as departure, progression and arrival'; in other words, that we should work for the end of a history that is supportive of 'the values and exclusions of patriarchy'. The ending of such an imaginary is rich in new possibilities, opening up a space that is 'presentist' and 'futurist' and that values the disposition to 'play, multiply and diversify', and to concentrate not on that universalising sweep of history (which is 'totalitarian' towards what it excludes as 'nonessential or even nonexistent'),[20] but on the most intimate, the most practical and the most apparently innocent of the rhythms of daily life and the phenomenological appropriation of time. Here the end of history is to be welcomed joyously:

> The postmodern idea that time and space are themselves defined, limited, discontinuous, is so contrary to habit that it may seem almost unthinkable. Yet this is precisely what postmodern narratives establish – an alternative temporality . . . to think what seems unthinkable . . . As postmodern narrative breaks down the convention of historical time, it reveals the arbitrariness of its historical 'neutrality' and this opening forces us to focus on precisely those questions of value . . . that historical thinking defers.[21]

It is at this point that, history now behind her, Ermarth's own project begins to take shape and moves into the space opened up by the collapse of a history beyond its time limits. To be sure, to think the present and the future *in* time but *outside* history – to end one's 'tenure as an implied spectator or neutral historian' and accept a position within the frame of postmodernism in general and feminism in particular – is not easy, involving as it does the seeing of every method ('including my own', every value 'including my own', and every language game 'including my own') as radically historicist, as radically contingent. This recognition, concludes Ermarth, certainly *ought* to unsettle old habits, it being exactly this problematic at the heart of postmodernism that really does seem to disturb 'the complacent reader-writer-citizen and that partly accounts for the reaction against it'.[22] Thus as Ermarth draws down the curtain on history and expectantly prepares the stage for a performance of *Time as Rhythm* we can take 'time out' for those final bits of stage setting. Here is the first bit:

> The best definition of postmodern narrative might be precisely that it resolutely does *not* operate according to any form of historical time, and in many cases directly parodies or disputes that time . . . Such subversions necessarily precede [as here] those experiments with new forms of time that postmodern narrative makes possible . . . For postmodernism, historical time is a thing of the past in more than one sense. History now is not just the convention that uses the past to hold the present in a controlled pattern of meaning: history now takes up the interesting position of confronting its own historicity . . . [and finitude].[23]

Of course, there may well be those who lack the energy for such uncertain postmodern adventures in a new intellectual landscape; many who are not well prepared for the next act of the 'performance': 'Happy were those who lived and slept in history',[24] Ermarth is willing to acknowledge, but happier still could be those now fully awake to the invitation 'to swing'. Here is the second bit of stage setting:

> 'I swing therefore I am.' In this conjugating rhythm, *each move forward is also digressive*, also a sideways move. A postmodern narrative . . . at every juncture keeps alive . . . an awareness of multiple pathways and constantly crossing themes . . . Narratives where time is rhythm give readers an opportunity to take up a new kind of residency in time, a way of staying in the narrative present . . . [Thus] rhythm's time . . . destroys the historical unity of the world by destroying its temporal common denominator . . . Gone are the linear co-ordinates that made possible a stable, objective world. . . .
>
> A postmodernist would [therefore] never speak of 'historical reality': not just because 'reality' doesn't exist except as defined locally but also because history doesn't exist either, except as defined locally . . . The dissolution of neutral space and time and with them the bracketing of empiricist and historical thinking as just . . . one more thematic . . . puts emphasis in quite different places than it has been for at least several centuries.
>
> The challenge, and the excitement of postmodernism . . . comes in learning to manage this power of self-reflexiveness and to perform its particular . . . experiments.[25]

And third, and finally, this means that such experimentation and improvisation affects everything, including 'theory':

> The postmodern idea of theory as a guerrilla tactic – if you haven't got one make one up – flies in the face of [older] discursive habit[s]. The practice of postmodern theory [thus] . . . requires a fine sense of play and a total willingness to live without discursive sleep.[26]

This is my reading of what Ermarth thinks is wrong with the 'over-arching construct' of modernist, linear, dialectical, objectivist, neutral/natural history, the negative part of her binary opposition; the prologue, the getting-history-out-of-the-way-bit before the coming of rhythmic time. For by comparison with the heavy seriousness of history, Ermarth's vision of postmodern timings of time is altogether lighter. Accordingly, the bulk of her text is taken up with making residence in the postmodern attractive, especially for women. The benefits seem enormous, and I follow her as she first of all extols the positive value of rhythmic time in general terms (i.e. what the general characteristics of rhythmic time are) before going on to look at just a few details. So, what does playing theoretical guerrilla with Ermarth turn out like?

As we have seen, rhythmic time is her favourite trope. As opposed to modernist linear time, rhythmic time has no essence, no universals, no meaning, no point. Rather, rhythmic time depends on local arrangements whose 'amplifications' are unpredictable. Rhythmic sequences fork and re-fork, exfoliating, proliferating thematic threads which come to arbitrary ends, a chaotic coming together of details patterned paratactically, which is to say, asyntactically, which is to say meaninglessly; details are unexpectedly complex and rich without ever becoming 'knowledge'; this way of reading the world is essential equipment for a postmodern at ease with herself. Ermarth elaborates:

> The . . . paratactic moves forward by moving sideways. Emphasising what is parallel and synchronically patterned rather than what is linear and progressive . . . Paratactic narrative [and lives] move . . . in several directions at once.[27]

Such stylistic self-fashioning offers new discursive possibilities, multi-level thinking which makes available multiple beginnings and endings. It pluralises perspectives, mixes and remixes those interpretative frames that subjects-in-process live through so as to make the past – including those causal powers that have blindly impressed thus far 'her' behavings bear in future 'her' impress. To be free of the burden of history is the aim, to be a happy Cronopios, to refuse histories of infinity and dialectics and to face with joy the finite tomorrow. Postmodern time is thus Cronopios time: it's performative, it's improvisation, it's jazz, it's bricolage, it's individual and it's collective.

Drawing on the 'semiotic' potentialities of language (after Kristeva) and coupling it with Derrida's notion of the endlessly ludic character of language (and thus life – for to have residence in a language is to have residence in a reality), Ermarth extols the possibilities of that play which, in its endless deferments, prevents systems ever becoming definitively closed:

to the extent that a structure limits play in the interest of closure, precision or 'perfection' it becomes 'ruined' . . . no new experiments or adventures are possible. By contrast, the incompleteness of living systems guarantees . . . play remains open . . . systems that seek to exclude play are also seeking death.[28]

Ermarth is seeking life. Drawing on the figure (*figura*), Ermarth hints at a future of interminable play where meanings always remain open: events may be congruent but they don't necessarily connect; may be adjacent but not related; may be sequenced but lack direction. Things just don't add up. No sign of dialectics is ever found – because nobody looks. Postmodern figures – temporary arrangements/ meanings in a chaos that makes such meanings self-referentially meaningful – make unequivocal 'truths' and purposes non-permanent:

This disorientation for its own sake is very unlike the effect of the medieval *figura* which makes truth only temporarily inaccessible . . . Postmodern *figura* make univocal truth permanently inaccessible. On the 'other side' *of* a medieval figure is a clarifiable structure and stable, cosmic meaning. On the 'other side' of postmodern figures is the marvellous mystery consisting of the fact that these figures *are* the tangible world, and that the tangible world is discourse, is language, is figure . . . *Rhythmic's time and its multilevel consciousness ARE this process of anthematic substitution in which readers maintain simultaneously various different figures.*[29]

It is this play of meaningful meaninglessness – being on the edge of every semantic abyss yet not regarding this as abysmal – that arouses eroticism. Not, Ermarth hastens to add, eroticism in the 'narrow, shabby sense', but in the sense of having the capacity to surprise – forever. This is subversive. In a productive culture that lives in the linear, the purposeful, playing unpredictably and without a necessary end conjures up notions of waste: of wasting time, of time mis-spent. Digressive, paratactic play, however, confers for Ermarth 'an exquisite pleasure by relieving the mind of its already recognisable meanings . . . [It restores] to language its electricity . . . its power to shock, to derail it from a track of conventional formulas.' But this won't happen easily. For it involves the kinds of play unprivileged in the cultural formation in which we presently 'operate our universities, watch our markets, and pursue our careers'. But such play can be – and ought to be – done.

This challenge to history, to the closure of all systems, including ethical ones of course, this living a life rather than going through a living death – this is what makes rhythmic, ludic time, the future time Ermarth wants. For this you can forget history and ethics:

> The rhythmic conventions of time offer new starting points for discursive reformation. To expand the richness of the moment . . . is not stupidly to stop all forward motion or to suppose there is no 'after' or 'before', instead, that expansion makes available more starting points and more alternative routes . . . The result is an ineffably social achievement.[30]

Consequently, concludes Ermarth, this manoeuvre of imagination in play, in language, in a life, is an invitation to get *out* of history in ways where we take responsibility for our own discourse, to indeed live a life

> that does without history, without a millenary kingdom, without Kantian categories or vodka, without Marx, Freud, or 'all the religions dreamt up by man' . . . In their place postmodern[ism] . . . offers its precision, its erotic (chance) conjunctions, its rhythmic series: the coloured bits or elements of kaleidoscopic arrangements, and whatever patterns emerge. These are the materials for the anthematic figure, a mandala, a polychromous rose design, a rhythmic, momentary, fleeting, life-affirming arrangement. Trying to give these arrangements fixity, or to control this rhythm in advance, would be like trying to redirect the arrow after it has left the bow.[31]

As noted in my introductory remarks, this essaying of postmodern possibilities *after the end of history (and ethics)* seems exhilarating. So that it is in the spirit of complementing Ermarth's position that I now want to examine what may be some slight resistances to a moral relativism which I think her text leads her to. For in the end Ermarth's notion of rhythmic time may still have something of the ring of truth about it.

At various points in her text, Ermarth seemingly qualifies the relativism I think is inescapable. For example, whilst Ermarth knows there is nothing meaningful outside of the text such that 'nothing exceeds its practices or its play', this fact, she adds 'is quite far removed from any relativist catastrophe'.[32] The postmodern idea that the past is a function of consciousness; the idea that the past is invented historically despite the fact that it seems we know that 'things happened in this way, not that'; the postmodern subversion of 'facticity' which goes far beyond 'any mere revision or substitution of one "history" for another', indeed, the fear that we may not be just substituting a 'false history for a true one' but not bothering to substitute one at all – all these things threaten not just the historical world but 'the moral universe with total solipsism'. And whilst Ermarth cannot head this off directly, she does have some reassuring words: 'The requirement of reader complicity does not let the reader do whatever he or she likes with the writing [the history] in question; in fact, postmodern narrative is a very demanding discipline precisely because it requires new acts of attention';[33] whatever else it may be, postmodernism is no cultural or moral bonfire. Accordingly, says Ermarth, although a postmodern future 'may raise the fear of total relativism', there is, in fact, 'no such thing' as that.

No. Fears of moral catastrophe following in the wake of a 'relativistic postmodernism' have been much exaggerated. For nobody denies, Ermarth again reassures us, 'the presence of conditions external to our descriptive and linguistic systems; nobody hopes for complete solipsism of the kind that some ascribe, completely wrongheadedly, to postmodernism and that would in any case only be possible in a classical system', even though, she admits, a term like 'reality' looks increasingly unworkable and uninteresting in a situation that no longer sustains faith in universal, 'rational laws'.[34]

Why is Ermarth saying all this? Why not freely embrace relativism? I think there are two main reasons. The first is this. Ermarth feels the need for some kind of *consensus* (recall that at the start of her text she said that she had 'assumed' such a thing) amongst postmodern rhythmics: some sort of accepted constraint to ensure social cohesion. For without this, she says, 'what is there but force?'[35] But it is perhaps the second (and not disconnected) reason for qualifying moral relativism that I think is the more important; namely, Ermarth is concerned to head off the possibility of future holocausts. In the end – and this really is ironic as soon as you think about it – it is this typical *modernist* objection to postmodern relativism (that relativism leaves us unable to answer a Hitler) that seems to motivate her to try and find a 'real constraint'. Here is Ermarth worrying about future holocausts:

> Practically speaking, the debates about postmodernism come down to a discussion about what, if anything, provides a reality principle for any construct. Postmodern writers and theorists do not deny the existence of the material world . . . nor, so far

as I know, does anyone familiar with the issue seriously deny the exclusiveness of discursive languages to which we necessarily resort in order to say anything 'about' either the material or the discursive worlds . . . But if discursive rules provide untranscendable constraints, what constrains the discursive rules? This question is haunted by the specters of holocausts which, in various national forms, have already demonstrated what appears to be no restraint. If anything can be justified in some Name, is there no way to choose between justifications? If every interpretation, every system, every set of laws is a closed inertial system and if there is no longer validity for any privileged position . . . how can a person or a polis choose between . . . this or that course except by chance?[36]

Well, chance may, Ermarth allows, have much to do with it, and she will go on to consider surrealist pronouncements in favour of 'objective chance'. But leaving this aside here (as Ermarth herself does at that precise point of her text – besides, it's a totally inadequate solution) I want to concentrate, as she does, on whether there are any 'general grounds' for constraint against relativism. And her answer here seems to be *yes*, maybe there are. Here Ermarth reviews and rejects possible answers given by, variously, Nancy Fraser and Linda Nicholson, Richard Rorty and Fredric Jameson, Katherine Hayes and Barbara Herrnstein Smith, and Lyotard,[37] not least on the grounds that they don't understand the way postmodernism has changed our understanding of 'history' and 'reality', for like the concept of history, 'reality' no longer means what it used to.

For 'classically', explains Ermarth, reality implied something stable and self-identical, but physical reality (which non-idealist postmodernists do not doubt) has been redescribed in postmodern idioms by people such as Ilya Prigogine and Isabelle Stenger; their treatment of reality as 'chaos as a phase of order' means that 'reality' is in a 'constant process of fundamental redefinition, so that the term "fundamental" does not even apply'.[38] Consequently, to give up on 'classical reality' does not mean we give up on postmodern 'chaotic' notions of reality as things that actually *do* constrain us. For the chaos theory and the 'dissipative structures' described by Prigogine and Stenger introduce us to a 'new conception of order that is independent of the closures and finalities of classical dynamics and that permit us to see how *"nonequilibrium brings order out of chaos"*'.[39] Thus, for example, the element of chance in a stochastic (probabilistic) process – where an 'end' becomes the possibility of a new 'beginning' which is not controlled in the classical sense by that 'end' – opens up new sources of life, new rhythms of continuance in ever new states and modes: 'The more determinist laws appear limited, the more open the universe is to fluctuation and innovation.'[40] Without wanting, as Ermarth puts it, to draw 'facile political analogies' from Prigogine and Stenger, this is what she does indeed seem to do as the following quotation shows. In a problematic process, she argues, things must be considered in the context of the moment when individual behaviour can be decisive or ineffectual but *not* predictable:

'Even small fluctuations may grow and change the overall structure. As a result individual activity is not doomed to insignificance. On the other hand, this is also a threat since in our universe the security of stable, permanent ruler seems gone forever.' What social (that is moral) implications this may have remains to be seen, but it is not clear that there is any greater threat of moral catastrophe in probabilistic social descriptions than has already been shown in logocentric ones.[41]

Consequently, Ermarth's postmodernism acknowledges not single but multiple constraints; postmodern time and space are warped and finite through 'the play of chance and necessity in the processes of life themselves ... "Reality" ... never stays "the same", it is not inert but interactive ... This awareness of finitude, of limit, is the basis of an entirely new aesthetic and' (and *I* want to underline this) '*provides the main restraint on construction that postmodernism respects*'.[42]

Now, I have to say that this seems an unconvincing argument if it is meant by Ermarth to be an answer to relativism. One can see why she is running it; probabilistic/chaos theory seems to be, as she comments, another way of talking about rhythmic time. But it is difficult to see how, even if this is the nearest we can get to the way the world is, it can be any kind of constraint on moral choice. For we postmodernists have given up trying to draw any sort of entailed *ought* from any *is*, stable or unstable. Let us suppose that the actual world is like Ermarth's rhythmic description of it après Prigogine and Stenger. And let's say everyone accepts this – liberals, Marxists, feminists, Fascists – everyone. What difference would it make? Do we seriously think that a political/moral 'constrained' consensus between Ermarth and Fascists is going to be arrived at because of the way an (indifferent) world is under the description of physics? Well, I don't think so; their moral differences remain incommensurable because they're 'moral all the way down'. Whilst views of the world après physics may contingently affect politics, of course, it is difficult to see how they can determine them in any is–ought way that involves moral entailment. Besides, Ermarth has herself admitted as much in the last sentence of the last extracted quote (above) where she says that it isn't clear if there is or isn't any greater threat of moral catastrophe in probabilistic social descriptions than has been already shown in logocentric ones – in other words the effect of either can go either (or any) way. Thus, it seems that Prigogine and Stenger cannot provide the actual constraint to moral discourse Ermarth seems to think they can. But not to worry – nobody and nothing can . . .

There is another point here too with regard to closure. For it looks as if Ermarth, in following Prigogine and Stenger, could just be saying that chaos theory/rhythmic time are somehow *closer* to the way 'reality' actually is than are other 'metaphoric' correspondences. But surely she cannot be saying *that*. Because if she is, then her notion of rhythmic time as being nearer to 'actuality' and therefore the best (truest) basis for a life (better than modernist, historical life) is just as much a universal/transcendental closure – albeit of a different substantive content – as the historical was. But if Ermarth is being faithful to her own creative theorising, presumably she ought not to *care* if anybody chooses to live non-rhythmically. Or is she suggesting that we (all) ought to be rhythmic because linear time (admittedly still available as 'another thematic') is somehow *intrinsically* rather than just *contingently* repressive; that rhythmic time is somehow *intrinsically* liberating and not just *contingently* liberating and that these 'characteristics' cannot be reversed/redescribed . . . that rhythmic time just cannot be repressive in its experimentations and improvisations; as if from the activity of postmodern play it is somehow guaranteed we can't play neo-Fascist? But what could stop this? Something *intrinsic* to play? But surely Ermarth can't think *that* either, anymore than Derrida could think – which he doesn't – that the irreducibility of deconstructive play means it isn't available to the political right as well as to the left. For postmodernism has – in its radical historicity (a point Ermarth brilliantly demonstrates) – emptied everything intrinsic out. Yet there is just a hint that Ermarth may still be somehow substituting one closure (linear history/logocentrism) with another (probabilistic/rhythmic time) which we *ought* to be constrained to follow because it is nearer to actuality and thus, presumably, a help to the realisation of emancipation.

To be sure, Ermarth seems also to be saying that she isn't doing this. As she writes at the end of her text (repeating earlier, similar disclaimers) the 'multi-level play described in this book belongs to an effort to renew social codes by restoring powers that have been repressed . . . not . . . to enforce another repression'.[43] Of course. But maybe she can only say this because she somehow *knows* what it is that has been repressed (something more than another vocabulary/imaginary?) and that, unrepressed, it will liberate us. But how could she possibly *know* this? No. I think the best Ermarth could do here is to be happy with her own preferences, tell some nice stories about them to attract other people, admit they're just hers and forget 'real' groundings and 'real' constraints – not least as expressed by chaos *theory* – *if* this is something she seriously entertains. And if she doesn't entertain it, why bother telling us about it?

And my reasons for saying this are that I think that relativism (the relativistic *différend* of moral discourse) really does seem to be the only plausible postmodern position, that in the end relativism is 'the only game in town' and that, at the end of the (indeed unfortunate) day, 'might' (as Stanley Fish also reluctantly accepts) 'is right'. As a consequence, political *hegemony* is also the only game we just have to play. As ever.

Ernesto Laclau has seen this more clearly than most, and here he is to help bring this discussion of Ermarth towards a close, his own preferences intruding, as they must, into his text at the end of the extract:

> The metaphysical discourse of the West is coming to an end, and philosophy in its twilight has performed . . . a last service for us: the deconstruction of its own terrain and the creation [like history] of the conditions for its own impossibility. Let us think, for instance, of Derrida's undecidibles. Once undecidability has reached the ground itself – once the organisation of a certain camp is governed by a hegemonic decision – hegemonic because it is not objectively determined, because different decisions were also possible – the realm of philosophy comes to an end and the realm of politics begins. This realm will be inhabited by a different type of discourse, by discourses such as Rorty's 'narratives', which tend to construct the world on the grounds of a radical undecidability. But I do not like the name ironist – which invokes all kind of playful images – for this political strong poet.[44]

It is at this point – because Laclau's invocation will be repeated by Harlan – that we can move towards David Harlan. For on my reading, Harlan accepts relativism with a positiveness that makes objectivity look more and more unnecessary. As Harlan puts it: 'It is not so much that the arguments against historical objectivity seem convincing (though there is that); it is that we do not *need* a theory of historical objectivity – and that all our efforts to come up with one have only obscured issues far more pressing and important'. This is a position he finds support for in Peter Novick's argument that, 'just as in matters of religion, non-believers feel that they can get along without a god [and do] so we who are called historical relativists believe that we can get along without objectivity . . . To say of a work of history that it is or is not objective is to make [après Ankersmit *et al.*] an *empty* observation, to say something neither interesting nor useful.'[45]

These references to Harlan *et al.* signal the end of this reading of Ermarth. I think Ermarth's critique of linear history has a profundity and a detail I have only been able to hint at here and that the imaginary of rhythmic time and all it might imply and suggest means we can think positively about living beyond history in new modes of temporality without anxiety. We can also think about living without an ethics stronger than that of the undecidability of the moral decision – Laclau's point here. Yet if in respect to this last point, Ermarth still seems to be in 'the grip of the tradition' insofar as relativism appears to be 'a *problem* still to be solved' and not the best *solution* we can come up with, nevertheless her text enables us easily to conceive of a Cronopios social formation wherein we live in time but outside history, and in morality and outside ethics. And why not? For, to repeat what has been said before, *if only we had known it, this is the way we have always had to live our lives – and always will.* In this respect – and it is in this respect that postmodern reflexivity is so useful – we might thus just as well relax and say – with Baudrillard – '"Nothing" hasn't changed.'

Who Do You Say That . . . . I AM ?

8 On David Harlan

If John Patrick Diggins is right in his characterisation of David Harlan as a 'postmodernist intellect with a pre-modern conscience' – and I think he is right – then one can immediately see both why Harlan feels so out of step with contemporary American historiography (and most of history *per se* as he reads it) and what he wants to replace it by. In the Introduction and Epilogue of his *Degradation of American History* the way Harlan sees things and what he wants to do about it are 'contextualised' (an irony given his anti-contextualist stance) by the following argument which serves to establish his position. I take his general position to be as follows.

Not so long ago, history in America was one of the prime forms of moral reflection. In holding up 'a mirror to our common past' historians like Perry Miller, Alfred Kazin, Arthur Schlesinger Jr. and others taught 'us' to speak in the first person plural, writing about the past but with present and future agendas which served to remind us 'this is what we value and want, and don't yet have. This is how we mean to live and do not yet live.'[1] But things have changed since the 1950s. Today, such a history would be seen as moralistic, patronising, elitist and altogether too cosy; historians don't write in the first person plural today.

Why not? Harlan offers a short 1950s–1990s résumé. In the 1950s, history students almost universally first encountered history through a 'History of Civilisation' course, an extended 'moral debate' carried on across the centuries from Plato on down. It was these courses that were attacked by the left in the 1960s and by postmodernists in the 1970s and 1980s. For the left, such courses were seen as elitist and 'ethnic', as ignoring women and minorities, and underplaying racial diversity; the 'solution' was to have courses that exposed the 'real' socio-economic and ideological forces driving American history and which replaced moral reflection by types of 'cultural unmasking'.[2]

Then, in the 1970s, postmodernism began to impact on history just as it was being refocused. It was generally unwelcome. Opposed by the right for the usual knee-jerk reasons (it undermined truth, encouraged cultural and moral relativism, 'invited' nihilism ...) it was resisted by the left for its 'dead-end scepticism' and its critiques of objectivity. (How convenient when, just as the left was beginning to get into a position to tell its 'true stories', truth and narrative were 'undercut'.) For though many historians were and are cultural relativists, they were and are not generally epistemological sceptics; besides, one needed objectivity to critique ideological mystifications and 'really' expose those 'underlying structures of power'. Yet, says Harlan, by the end of the 1980s most historians – of whatever stripe – had just about given up on objectivity, not necessarily because of postmodern theory ('theory does not come easy to historians; they like to keep their noses close to the ground, like hunting dogs')[3] but because of the all-pervasive power of a capitalism whose cultural logic generally was very precisely 'postmodern'. For even anti-worldly historians found it difficult to ignore the implications of a consumer-driven economic system and mass culture characterised by 'the ceaseless appropriation, recombination, and global dissemination of local styles and forms of expression'. Historical homogeneity – the assurance of a dominant discourse – gave way to an array of disconnected ways of making sense of 'ourselves', our world and the past. A commodification and repackaging of the past exploded as the number of its appropriations and consumers grew, multiplying historical objects of enquiry, subjects, perspectives and styles, such that the historian's 'one basic atomic unit', that guarantor of 'stable, reliable, objective interpretations' – the historical *fact* – now jumped its reassuring 'context' and went into 'representational free-fall'. No 'objective historian' was ever going to be able to put that Humpty Dumpty together again. Here, objectivity, 'that dull-witted monarch who despotically ruled the discipline of history since the late nineteenth century, lies dethroned'.[4]

Consequently, by the mid/late 1970s, says Harlan, a group of younger historians 'repelled by the predictability of their colleagues on the left – and alarmed by the rise of postmodernism' – turned to the social sciences for a way out of uncertainty, seduced by what the social sciences had always offered: redemption through methodology. Here the holy grail of objective knowledge still beckoned; if *the* truth couldn't 'be gotten' at least 'warranted assertability' could. And for Harlan, such methodologically informed professionals – neo-pragmatists – have, by now, taken over the running, establishing the 'new' constructionist *doxa*, in the 'most powerful and broadly influential attempt yet to cope with history's declining status'.[5] Yet it is an attempt, Harlan complains, that is fatally unable (given that methodology is, of course, an 'empty mechanism') to say anything definitive about the substantive issues a synoptic historiography is so 'obviously concerned with'; that is, it is unable to move from fact to value. Consequently, Harlan sees such approaches as inadequate precisely on the question of meaning and value that he thinks historians *ought* to be addressing:

> Will historians have anything left to teach us if they no longer insist on the redemptive power of the past – on the importance of learning how to think with our predecessors' thoughts, how to create our own vocabulary of moral deliberation by fiddling around with theirs? Or does this whole attempt to save us from the pit of postmodern theory miss something important?[6]

From the rhetorical phrasing it is clear that his answer is yes. So what is missing? According to Harlan it has everything to do with what he takes to be 'the way things really are'. That is to say, it is to do with the moral implications of recognising the sublime nature of existence. It is to do with the fact that 'we will always be unfinished persons, as mysterious and inaccessible to ourselves as we are to others', a view that allows him to rescue Derrida from accusations of irresponsible nihilism and rehabilitate him as a theorist asking us rationally to consider how to live a life that contains neither truths nor foundations.[7] In Derrida's writing Harlan detects 'a deep and welling sadness . . . a pervasive melancholy that reminds us of Pascal'. Linking Derrida to those for whom full presence is unavailable to underwrite metaphysics (in his Introduction referring variously to Holbein, Henry James, Faulkner and Nietzsche especially) Harlan reads the existential past in ways that, in *this* book, we should now be familiar with. For him the past is unintelligible, sublime and unpresentable in its 'whole', and interminably relativistic in terms of the appropriations of its parts; neither history nor ethics should deprive us of this meaninglessness nor conceal the lack of any foundations for *choosing* what we want to be. (For me, if not necessarily for Harlan, this is a positive sublime for which a historical consciousness is not required other than the one that allows me to write and understand *this* sentence: a theoretical consciousness.) Referring to Henry Adams, the nineteenth-century American littérateur and philosopher, Harlan describes how, under the pressure to gain more and more historical (empiricist) knowledge, Adams recounts the accelerating spiral of doubt as the seemingly solid ground of historical truth collapsed into a multitude of purely personal perspectives so that, in the end

> one sought no absolute truth . . . One sought only a spool on which to wind the thread of history without breaking it. Among indefinite possible orbits, one sought the orbit which would satisfy the observed movement of the runaway star Groombridge, 1838, commonly called Henry Adams.[8]

Now, professional historians may find all of this totally irrelevant to their job, says Harlan. After all, what has this to do with professional history, with modern research methods, scholarly apparatus, refereed journals and the writing of research proposals? What has this got to do with that neopragmatism exemplified in *Telling The Truth About History* by Appleby *et al.*?[9] Here, instead of fretting about the real knowledge we can never have, Appleby *et al.* ask us to consider as 'good enough' the practical, down to earth 'knowledge' we can: 'the reality of *this document*, the garden of *this world*, the love of *this woman*.'[10] Yet this is exactly what Harlan rejects about current historiography; what is missing is what he calls the obstinate and intractable nature of spiritual hunger:

> To imagine that we can lay aside our longing for the absolute . . . the longing for presence that seeps from the very marrow of our bones – is to imagine we can somehow escape our own humanity.[11]

Accordingly, and taking this longing as an axiom, what Harlan wants 'history' to do is to meet this need. At which point he becomes pre-scriptive: there are *three* basic approaches to the past which will give him what he wants. First, we must be happy sceptics (and relativists). We must get to:

> the point where we no longer feel that if we cannot refute contem-porary scepticism [and we cannot] then all is lost, history will slide into fiction, Holocaust deniers will rise up everywhere and we shall have to fight the Second World War all over again.[12]

Thus we ought to forget such notions as historical objectivity because the quest for it is (a) unnecessary ('it has not gotten us anywhere in our long, twisted past, and is not going to get us anywhere in the crooked future') and (b) passé; we should just drop 'the whole shop-worn subject'.[13]

Second, we must forget what historians consider as their *raison d'être*; the idea that 'we' should put the things that happened in the past into *their* 'historical context' unalloyed, if possible, by *our* current concerns. For this is to get things the wrong way around:

> E. P. Thompson . . . used to say that our primary responsibility is to the people of the past, for they lived through those times and we did not. [But] we can *not* fulfil that responsibility by insisting that [say] the books they wrote be returned forthwith to their 'proper historical contexts' as if they were no better than apprehended fugitives . . . The only way we, as historians, can fulfil our responsibility to the dead is by making sure their works do not get lost in the past . . . by raising them up from . . . dead contexts and helping them take up new lives among the living.[14]

Third, and interconnectedly, Harlan argues that we must thus *appropriate* the past for *our* sakes – to rip events and texts out of the past and, forgetting their contexts, insert them into ours. Referring to Walt Whitman's *Song of Myself*, Harlan argues that the value of Whitman's poem is what we value it for now, not the context in which it was written. Thus

> It is *Song of Myself* that moves us, that nurtures . . . our best hopes for democracy in America, not the personal life of the purportedly racist and bigoted little man who is reputed to have written the great poem. If we are told – as the historian David Reynolds recently told us – that 'the real Walt Whitman' did not, in fact, live up to the vision of America he gave us . . . all we can do is shrug our shoulders and say, 'Too bad for the real Walt Whitman'. The only Whitman that matters to us is the Whitman who emerges from his poems.[15]

Accordingly, it is only in trying to make Whitman's hopes our own – 'transforming them from something that merely existed in the past into something we have made ours' – that history is justified in the only way it can be, 'as a mode of moral reflection, a way of curing up life into meaning'. For by this process of *appropriation* we can reflect comparatively on our own lives, relativise and thus unsettle our own prejudices and myopic preoccupations, and so turn our 'impoverishing certitudes' into 'humanising doubts':

> Trying to figure out what all these *chosen* predecessors may or may not have in common, trying to perceive affinities and attractions between them, trying to arrange them in chronological order so that you can think of yourself as the latest in a long line of such thinkers – this is pretty much what people *used* to mean when they talked about acquiring 'a sense of the past'.[16]

And so it should be again, says Harlan. Of course, it won't be easy. There is now no single historicised past commonly to draw on. If we wish to establish connections with the dead we will have to forge them ourselves, populating our own imaginaries with people and ideas that can help us say: 'This is how we mean to live, but do not yet live.' This is what a historical consciousness ought to be used for argues Harlan, and neither the hubris of the social sciences nor the horror stories of postmodern 'subversions' should change it. Harlan's 'postmodern intellect' and his 'premodernist conscience' do indeed come together here. Like everything else in the past and in the present, postmodernism will be used if and when it energises moral thinking, history as moral reflection.

Now, in his text, Harlan has a range of chapters (on the linguistic turn, left and feminist histories, the return of the moral imagination, and so on, populated by such 'theorists' as Quentin Skinner, Elaine Showalter and Henry Louis Gates), but it is in his chapter on Richard Rorty (fittingly entitled 'A Choice of Inheritance') that Harlan's appropriative, anti-contextualist, anti-objectivist, pro-moralistic (and thus 'anti-lower case') approach is best exemplified, and which arguably renders the name 'history' for what Harlan is there advocating obsolete. For I think that it is in his chapter on Rorty – whom Harlan approves of for using postmodern theories and methods to get him what *he* wants – that we see how Harlan might get the history *he* wants, and the kind of postmodern practices I myself advocate. Thus Harlan writes:

> If we want to know what written history would look like once we dropped our current obsession with historical context and objective truth – and more important, if we want to know how history might reoccupy its former office as one of our primary forms of moral deliberation – we have only to look at the sort of history Richard Rorty has been writing these past several years.[17]

So far so good, then, but before I briefly follow Harlan's own *appropriation* of Rorty, I just want to comment briefly on the idea of *appropriation* and the arguably polemical way he is using it. For in this usage I think there is an important change in the way we might think of going beyond the idea of interpretation and the notion of providing (putative) neutral and objective readings and representations, etc. of the past (or anything else).

For I think Harlan's move from interpretation to appropriation, and from description and contextualisation to 'polemic' is important to note; it is an important postmodern usage I myself have tried to employ in this text throughout. In mainstream historiography, the past (events, people, texts, etc.) are there to be 'interpreted' or, slightly differently in, say, some of Ankersmit's arguments, 'represented', so that the historian is essentially passive and subordinate. The historian is slavishly to serve the past, at best letting it overwhelm him or her, imposing its own contexts on any presentist preoccupations/contexts. But appropriation not only blows that construction away – we only ever appropriate the past for presentist concerns especially when we cannot recognise that that is what we are doing – but draws attention to what appropriation is like; that is, an active seizing, gutting, cutting, carving and shaping of the past in ways reminiscent of Foucault's 'effective' history. This also means that such appropriations must inevitably be polemical and thus not instrumental in producing a consensus – the single-point perspective of linearity Ermarth critiques. For construed as a site and occasion for polemic, the past isn't something that one can any longer disinterestedly describe or understand 'objectively' (and where disputes/controversies arise only over the details such that 'the facts' might 'settle things'); rather, a past that is explicitly appropriated throws down a challenge. It is staking a claim. Whilst in matters interpretative the aim is ideally to be able to dispense with interpretation once it has led to the truth, appropriation is playing no such game, so that here we move into the realm of stubborn, incommensurable genres of discourse and phrase regimes; into the realm of the *différend* that not only, after Lyotard, registers difference, but valorises it as the mechanism for moral undecidability and non-totalitarian politics. Consequently, being overtly presentist in both origins and destinations, appropriation privileges current theorising and casts doubt – for me if not necessarily for Harlan – on why the journey 'imaginatively' back into the past is necessary in any sense we might normally name 'historical'. For we might live in time (Ermarth) and in moral choice (Harlan) without the past entering into it. I shall return in the Conclusion to this point – the point pretty much of this text of course – but, in order (polemically) to advance its feasibility, I now turn back to Harlan's use of Rorty 'as a lesson for us all'.

Harlan sees it as his first task to sketch in (to contextualise – ironically) Rorty's general background. This is lucidly explained and, for those interested in Rorty 'the man', to the point. But we can dispense with it here, picking up Harlan's argument at that stage where he is depicting Rorty's mature position as that of a liberal ironist with a 'voluntarist' and 'progressive' view of history. For Harlan, Rorty's liberal assumptions are easy to summarise: 'that human beings are inherently outgoing and creative; that they have the capacity to continually expand their range of emotional identifications; that they are capable of mastering their own history; that with a modicum of luck they just might create a more free and equitable society'.[18] Rorty's liberal humanism is evident in this description, as it is in his own (borrowed) definition of liberals as being people who think that 'cruelty is the worst thing we do'. But Rorty's liberalism is also, of course, without foundations. Rorty is an *ironic liberal* in that, like the heroine of his *Contingency, Irony, and Solidarity*, he is the sort of person who 'faces up to the contingency of his or her own most central beliefs and desires – someone sufficiently historicist and nominalist to have abandoned the idea that those central beliefs and desires refer back to something beyond the reach of time and chance'.[19]

Consequently, Harlan sees this as leading towards a view of the past (and present/future) as nothing more than the 'rattle and hum' of contingency to which have been drawn an endless proliferation of appropriations which, though they may invoke notions of meanings, essences, teleologies and so on, do so in vain. Rorty insists that we must abandon any hope of learning the reasons for our tangled and clotted existence; as Harlan summarises him:

> We will not be delivered from the seething coils of language, we will not be released from the gravitational pull of an infinite regress, we will never touch bottom. And we most certainly will not experience a manifestation of historical truth . . . that our history will always be what it always has been: the unrecorded and unrecordable hum of discontinuous coincidence.[20]

Rorty's view of history is thus relativistic and endlessly capable of appropriation; here anything can be made to look good or bad by being redescribed. Yet this position, says Harlan, far from casting Rorty into gloom, is the contingency that forms the 'basis' for a positive, optimistic, *voluntarist* attitude towards making up any pragmatically required narrative. As Harlan explains, Rorty's hope is that as creative 'strong poets' we might escape the determinations of the past and, unburdened by them, create newness:

> the hope of such a poet is that what the past tried to do to her she will succeed in doing to the past: to make the past itself, including those very causal processes which blindly impressed all her own behavings, bear *her* impress. Success in that enterprise – the enterprise of saying 'Thus I willed it' to the past – is success in what Bloom calls 'giving birth to oneself'.[21]

Accordingly, on the basis of such a position, Harlan sees Rorty accepting a type of postmodernism that can give rise to a humanism where contingency and irony is precisely not how you spell 'barbarian', a position where, stoically and with dignity, we can perhaps allow 'chance to be worthy of determining our fate'.

So much for Rorty's general, humanistic, ironic, liberal position, but what, asks Harlan, 'has all this to do with us hobbit-like historians? What can we find here that might be useful to us? Does Rorty really have anything important to tell us about the nature of written history in a postmodern world that no longer accepts the historian's claims to objective truth?'[22] Harlan thinks he does, basing this estimation on *three* areas: on Rorty's pragmatic reading of texts, upon his ideas of objectivity and the self, and, finally, the exemplary and detailed application of these things to his general view of history as just outlined. It is to these three areas that Harlan attends in turn.

For Harlan, Rorty's reading of texts is a brilliant example of how to appropriate past ideas (and thus by extension past events/situations etc.) for current, moral purposes. Locating himself in a genealogy of pragmatism that privileges William James and John Dewey, the question Rorty asks of texts (and other things) is not whether they are true or false, or where they come from, or how and why they were generated 'in and for themselves' (antiquarian questions) but how useful they are for the creation of a polity of Rorties, of liberal ironists. As Harlan says, Rorty's approach was and is to

> read German 'philosophers of being' like Nietzsche and Heidegger, French poststructuralists like Foucault and Derrida, and American antirepresentationalists like Wilfred Sellars, W. V. O. Quine and Donald Davidson as if they had all been talking to one another in a single unbroken conversation.[23]

In other words, says Harlan – and this is central to what Rorty has to offer historians – 'Rorty simply arranged his favourite thinkers in such a way that they seemed to constitute a distinctive and continuous intellectual tradition.'

It is this appropriation for moral purposes that Harlan calls post-modern history and which he juxtaposes against the idea of traditional, 'proper' history; that is, the discourse of objective own-sakism etc. And, of course, Harlan is right to do this; we can indeed call what Rorty is doing 'history'. Except that, given that it is so unlike such 'proper' history, we might as well call it something else. In which case, if Rorty is 'all we need', such 'other' history is something we don't need. In that sense, I therefore think that Harlan might just as well forget the genre of history altogether and take the opportunity offered by Rorty's further undercutting of objectivity and the self simply to abandon it.

Moving on, Rorty's critique of objectivity presupposes the general recognition that he is no idealist. The world (as an object) is 'out there' all right, but objectivity and truth are not because objectivity and truth are produced in sentences, and sentences are not 'out there'. The world is out there but descriptions of it are not. Only descriptions of the world can be true or false; the world on its own – unaided by the describing power of human beings, cannot. Truth, then, is a particular way of making descriptions of the world to the satisfaction, via the criteria they hold, of the describers ('Truth is that which is best by way of belief for good, assignable reasons', Rorty says) and is thus, in that sense, a function of language and enunciative positions. This doesn't mean, says Rorty (undercutting the usual objections that come forth at this point from realists), that the actuality of the world doesn't stubbornly affect the way it is put 'under description', nor that all the ways of putting it under description are equally good ways of getting things done particularly well. Rorty is a pragmatist after all. Neither does it mean that once under description we don't regularly let the world decide (especially at operationally low-level singular events/statements . . . it is far less easy and ultimately impossible at aesthetic/moral levels) the competition between alternative sentences (e.g. 'the butler did it' or 'the doctor did it'). But the fact that this is the case shouldn't allow us to then run together the 'fact' that the world contains the causes of our being justified in holding a belief with the claim that some non-linguistic state of affairs in the world is, in and of itself, the embodiment of truth, or that some condition 'makes a belief true' by corresponding to it.[24] Truth – and objectivity – are thus never statements about the actuality of 'the world' or parts of that world 'gotten plain', but, to say it again, the function of our (subject-ive) language: the object is thus always the contingent, performative projection of subjects-in-process and thus, because the subject is 'iterable', so is the world. Accordingly, Rorty's view of objectivity is thus a radically contingent, historicist, nominalist, pragmatic (and hence Darwinian) one: truth and objectivity are useful tools for getting around in what is *imagined* to be 'the world'. As Harlan briefly summarises all of this:

> Rorty thinks that, if he can break down the idea that language copies nature, rather than merely *coping* with it, he will have exploded the very possibility of objectivity, and thereby all our hand-wringing about the creeping menace of moral relativism.[25]

For we humans are destined to be creatures capable of choosing without any apodictic basis upon which to do so. Thus the choices we make about the past, about our decision to historicise it or not, bother about it or not, are choices we *can* make. Take only the most obvious example, says Harlan: 'we have no objective calculus that can tell the historian what she should write about; she simply has to use her own sense of what is important and what is not'.[26] Exactly.

Given these views, there is, as expected, no such thing for Rorty as an '*objective*' *substrate/ self*; we have nothing deep down inside us that is recognisably our invariant essence. And this is crucially important for history and morality as soon as you think about it. For Rorty, before socialisation, human beings are just animals. And although the types of animals we are – we're not elephants or kangaroos – ultimately limit our actual possibilities to those of our species type, that said, socialisation then goes 'all the way down'; 'our' world is thus just 'our' world. And, because this just is our natural condition, there is nothing to be anxious about in terms of our radical subjectivity and the collapse of the old subject–object distinction so central to classical Western epistemology; we can live at ease in the knowledge that we subjects constitute objects; that, in a radical sense, this subjectivity *is* objectivity. As Elizabeth Ermarth has put it (putting it better than Harlan and maybe Rorty too), 'if the subject gets conceived ontologically as an existing *Dasein* where Being is grounded in temporality, then one must say that the world *is* subjective. But in this case, this "subjective world", as one that is temporally transcendent, is "more objective" than any possible "Object".'[27] Yet,

Why, as Robbe-Grillet asks, should this be grounds for pessimism? Is it so distressing to learn that one's own view is *only* one's view, or that every project is an invention? 'Obviously I am concerned, in any case, only with the world as *my point of view* orients it: I shall never know any other. The relative subjectivity of my sense of sight serves me precisely to define *my situation in the world*. I simply keep myself from helping to make this situation a servitude.'[28]

Far from being some form of angst-ridden solipsism then, argues Ermarth, this kind of postmodern consciousness and confidence is creative, playful and enervating, such that,

> We no longer require an 'objective' world to guarantee – like some sort of bank for intersubjective transactions – the relations between one consciousness and another, or to guarantee an identity between illusions. There is *only* subjectivity. There are *only* illusions. And every illusion, because it has no permanently objectifying frame, constitutes reality and hence is totally 'objective' for its duration. The postmodern event comes in negotiating the transitions from one moment to another.[29]

This is not to say, as Laclau has pointed out, that individuals are so radically contingent that there is a total lack of social structuration such that 'anybody can be anything at any time with absolute certainty and impunity'; rather, by talking about the radical contingency of the subject and of (moral) choice, one means that opportunities for selfness and other-ness occur 'within the limits of a partially destructed context' where the self can 'only appeal to itself as its own source' for legitimation, for 'foundations'. Consequently, there is no need here for this iterable self to dwell on or in the limitations of the past (previous failures, the 'realities' of previous experiences which encourage one to always be 'sensible' ...), or in the present, but to *raid* both the past (as the past *always* in the present) and the present, in the manner of the *bricoleur*: to knock something new into shape in the absence of shapes; to make up new rules in the deliberate 'making absent' of rules: to be a strong, moral poet.

So, armed with the tools of appropriation and a self-conscious iterable self that constitutes its objects ironically and calmly, Harlan gets directly to how Rorty sets to work historically, so that we might get history to reoccupy its former office 'as one of our primary forms of moral reflection'.

So, what is this history like? It is simply this. Rorty the bricoleur
isn't interested (any more than Ermarth is interested) in interpreting
the past for its own sake. Rather, Rorty raids the past (and the
present), or, more accurately perhaps, he raids the bookshelves for
authors he already likes or has heard of as promising new candidates
for being liked – to give him inspirational ideas. In particular, says
Harlan, he is looking for people he can 'develop an attitude towards';
thinkers who can give him a new image, metaphor; something to help
open up another angle of vision; another way of seeing/being. Rorty
couldn't care less about the blood and bone of the author himself –
say, the real personage named Friedrich Nietzsche – or about his contextualising 'life and times'. What he does care about is the character,
Nietzsche, 'who seems to haunt all those books said to have been
written by Friedrich Nietzsche'. Harlan, quoting from Rorty's
Contingency, Irony, and Solidarity underlines the point:

> We treat the names of such people [e.g. Nietzsche] as the names of
> the heroes of their own books. We do not bother to distinguish
> Swift from *saeva indignatio*, Hegel from *Geist*, Nietzsche from
> Zarathustra, Marcel Proust from Marcel the narrator, or Trilling
> from *The Liberal Imagination*. We do not care if these writers live
> up to their own self-images. *What we want to know is whether to
> adopt such images.*[30]

All of this is perfect grist for Harlan's mill; Rorty's practice *is* what
Harlan thinks we should all be doing as we choose our own inheritance:

> Rorty is talking about lifting texts out of their 'proper' historical
> context, rearranging their internal balances, then using these
> newly arranged texts to illuminate something that concerns him
> in the present. But he is also talking about recontextualising
> texts – plopping them down in new and unexpected contexts . . .
> laying one text alongside another hitherto unrelated text and
> discovering . . . 'they have interpenetrated and become warp
> and woof of a new, vividly polychrome fabric'. He thinks the
> writers he admires proceed in just this way: they recontextualize
> 'whatever memory brings back', thereby extending their own
> possibilities.[31]

In other words, argues Harlan, Rorty has learned that the best way
to enlarge his own imagination is – and this is 'the lesson to us
all' – to

recontextualize every book, every idea, every image of metaphor the past has to offer, tearing them out of their original contexts . . . thereby creating a new conceptual web.[32]

This approach is a long way from the sort of thing 'they teach in university history departments'; Harlan says that it 'will sound foppishly postmodern to most historians' (which it is). But it is history for Rorty, and why not? We know by now that history is no 'rigid designator'; that is, that it is never the case of placing an empty name on to an actually existing preconstituted object so simply describing something already meaningfully there; rather, objects such as history come *into* existence as a retroactive affect of the very process of naming – of nomination. So that Rorty is quite legitimately able to call his practice 'proper history' if he wishes, thus replacing what previously filled that adjectival space. Here is Laclau putting the implications of the subversion of rigid designation for politics:

> if the unity of the object [history] is the retroactive effect of naming itself, then naming is not just the pure nominalistic game of attributing an empty name to a preconstituted subject. It is the discursive construction of the object itself. The consequences of this argument for a theory of hegemony or politics are easy to see. If the descriptivist approach was correct, then the meaning of the name and the descriptive features of the object would be given beforehand, thus discounting the possibility of any discursive hegemonic variation that would open the space for a political construction . . . But if the process of naming the objects amounts to the very act of their constitution [is anti-descriptivist] then their descriptive features will be . . . open to all kinds of hegemonic rearticulations.[33]

Both Harlan and Rorty are anti-descriptivists on this count, and so obviously Harlan approves of the way Rorty 'creatively misreads' not just definitions of history but everything else, the relativistic conclusion being that there are as 'many possible meanings to a text (or a discourse) as there are possible contexts'. Here, fixed meanings drop out of the conversation and pragmatic use-value drops in.

In a sense there is nothing new in this. For everyone is a pragmatist whether they know it or not, not least those 'proper' historians whose contextualising, own-sakist practices just as much serve the positioned ends they desire as Rorty's anti-contextualising practices serve his.

And whilst the obviousness of this isn't a problem for Harlan, for traditional historians across the left–right spectrum it clearly is. For them the fact that both the past and the discourse that historicises it can be radically redescribed, variously evokes fears of moral relativism – and thus the associated, obsessive search for that impossible historical objectivity and truth – and their hostility to those 'mere' theorists who have taken it away. But this is not a problem for Harlan or Rorty, for not only are such things impossible to get, it's not obvious what you would do with them if you got them. Here is Harlan pulling this together:

> The irony is not simply that after two hundred years of searching we have yet to come up with the hoped-for-set of objective criteria; it is rather that we do not *need* them. The dream of possessing a formula, a procedure that would guarantee the objectivity of professional judgements is just the sort of thing that pragmatists . . . tried to talk us out of – largely because the result so often turns out to be what Rorty once called 'a string of platitudes, hooked up to look like an algorithm . . .' historians have been trying to apply 'the logic of scientific method' to historical writing ever since they heard [of it, but] they have not come up with much.[34]

To conclude Harlan on Rorty, what is Rorty's importance? Harlan suggests it is at least twofold. First, Rorty's critique of objectivity underlines the fact that once you start down the historicising, relativistic road, there is nowhere to stop. As Stanley Fish has pointed out, once you have taken the anti-formalist choice there just is no 'high level, non-local, ideologically neutral theory' of knowledge; there is no set of stable, widely-agreed-on principles that can be used to evaluate competing historical accounts objectively, prior to and free of any particular context or interpretation. And nor, second, do we need this myth of objectivity. The idea, says Harlan, that conservatives evoke – of relativism as a cultural menace – is a way of demonising theorists in general and, lately, postmodernists in particular. But this crude demonising is unnecessary:

> The response to this sort of thing is just what it has always been: that we continue to cherish our beliefs, continue to regulate our conduct by them – indeed, continue to profess our willingness to lay down our lives for them – even though we know they represent nothing more than the random products of a random historical process. Not long ago . . . Michael Sandel asked: 'If one's

convictions are only relatively valid, why stand for them unflinchingly?' But the answer had already come, years earlier . . . 'To
realise the relative validity of one's convictions and yet stand for
them unflinchingly, is what distinguishes a civilised [person] from
a barbarian'.[35]

Accordingly, to get the moral lessons needed to make moral choices
people should stop trying to formulate abstract, high level, pseudo-
scientific practices to gain objectivity, and start 'ransacking the past
for men and women whose lives exemplify the moral values desired'.
This is, of course, an empty mechanism – it leaves open the question
of what is a desirable moral desire. This is, to recall Derrida, the
risk. But it is also the chance for emancipatory discourse, a discourse
to stand for 'unflinchingly'.

Of course, says Harlan, by way of coming to conclusion,
'proper' historians don't like this kind of talk. The Labour historian
D. T. Rodgers, opines Harlan, probably spoke for most of his colleagues when he berated postmodernists for 'portraying the past "as
a vast attic of referents and motifs open to a multitude of ransackers,
not just those pledged to historical rules of sequence and context"'.[36]
And, to be sure, Rorty's rejection of historical objectivity and contextualisation may well be an attack on 'real' history. But if so,
'then too bad for real history'. For there is more at stake in life than
the hegemonic continuation of an ideologically positioned set of
guild practices reified by their professional beneficiaries into tablets
of stone. No, we bricoleurs would be better off getting rid of
contextual, objectivist history in favour of what it (arguably) used to
be and might become yet again – overt, positioned, reflexive, moral
reflection:

> We historians do not talk about this very much, but it is just here,
> in this always complicated and often impenetrable business of
> arguing with our adopted ancestors, that history comes into its
> own as an essential and indispensable form of moral deliberation.
> What is at issue . . . is not our ability to know the past but our
> ability to find the predecessors we need.[37]

I think we might be better off to translate 'the predecessors we need'
into 'the imaginaries we need'. And, *pace* Harlan, we may not need
to go to history to get these. Certainly we needn't go to 'proper'
history, for Harlan is right, this is not what 'proper' historians
provide – nor see it as their job to provide. So again Harlan is right:

'too bad for proper history/historians'. But my point is, as expected, that given this vast gap between Harlan's desires and those of 'proper' historians, he might best forget to call what he is doing 'history', and maybe forget the past too. Of course he can continue to call what he wants to do 'history' if he wishes, but the term 'history' is still – though no rigid designator – so radioactive with upper and lower case connotations that, despite its fatal meltdown by the postmodern, it does perhaps give but a further lease of life to something our lives might be better without. And maybe that goes for the past as such, so cloying is it in its 'realism'. Accordingly, I see no reason why Ermarth and Harlan cannot be combined (recontextualised out of *their* own – and maybe self-preferred – contexts) and put into the 'context' of the argument I have been running myself, 'appropriately' as it were. In which case, shorn of history and ethics, they can join Derrida *et al.* to help give us all the imaginaries we need to think the future we ought to choose to want in ironic, non-foundational ways. For in doing this, we really do stand a chance of escaping previous and pre-given formulations, and so have the opportunity to strike out for a postmodern future beyond histories and ethics.

Conclusion: Promisings

The argument I have been trying to run in this text – that we can now forget history and ethics and live in new ways of timing time and new ways of working a morality of the 'undecidability of the decision' type – might have looked pretty silly when it was first stated. I hope – though it may be a vain hope – that I have been able to make it fairly clear why such an argument has been put forward and, an even vainer hope perhaps, that some readers may have not found it silly at all. I also had a second aim, namely, to introduce history students (in an appropriative, Harlan/Rorty type way) to some of the ideas of Derrida, Baudrillard, Lyotard, White, Ankersmit, Ermarth and Harlan, and also, to Richard Evans as 'someone to forget'. The chapters are capable of being read as individual introductions to the writers in question. I hope that, even if my main thesis has been less than convincing, history students will benefit from the discussion.

But I may be being too defensive here, too half-hearted; almost apologising for arguing for the end of history in its upper and lower case modernist forms when White and Ankersmit, Ermarth and Harlan have bravely gone out on a limb to help us see history (in the case of White, Ankersmit and Harlan especially history in the lower case) as a highly problematical discourse. It is one that, caught up in the end of that experiment of modernity of which it was part, is now seriously on the defensive, Evans's mainstream counter-attack merely registering its poverty. And in the case of Derrida, Baudrillard, Lyotard and Ermarth, while their particular arguments as to the end of a certain kind of upper case, metanarrative history may also have seemed strange to some 'English' readers, the theme of the 'end of history' has been a constant one in continental thinking throughout much of the twentieth century, arguably being a dominant motif in disillusioned left-wing thought in France from the 1960s. As Derrida recalls in this connection:

> If all these themes of the end (end of history, end of man, figure of the 'last man', entry into a certain post-Marxism, and so forth), were, already at the beginning of the sixties, part of the elementary culture of the philosophers of my generation [building on Nietzsche, Heidegger, Husserl, Sartre, Lévi-Strauss, Kojeve . . .] we are not stuck today in their simple and static repetition . . . [for today] a set of transformations of all sorts (in particular, techno – scientifico – economico – media) exceeds both the traditional givens of the Marxist discourse and those of the liberal discourse opposed to it. Even if we have inherited some essential resources for projecting their analysis, we must first recognise that these [postmodern] mutations perturb the onto-theological schemes or the philosophies of technics as such. They disturb political philosophies and the common concepts of democracy; they oblige us to reconsider all relations between state and nation, man and citizen, the private and the public, and so forth.[1]

And amongst these *technics* is history *per se*. In this sense we are living in 'new times' where old times (old ways of historicising time) are *passé* and arguably have been for a while; postmodern arguments on the end of history thus being seen in this context as merely a re-articulation of the larger and quite 'normal' debates Derrida refers to. What I am saying here, then, is that, strange though it may seem to English historical sensibilities, the thematic of the end of history now has a massive literature and, indeed, a 'history' of its own that is, by Derrida *et al.*, more or less taken as read: it's just part of the accepted intellectual landscape.

It is within this intellectual context – of the 'given' of the end of history – that the arguments in this text might be best located. Although historians (and others) may say otherwise, we don't need a history in order to 'place ourselves' in present times, or for thinking about our future or (and this is the occasional position of some postmodernists) for articulating identities and programmes for a reflexive, emancipatory politics 'without foundations'. This argument is counter-intuitive in the simple sense that theorists today just do very well indeed without modernist histories, and some or most do without much of a 'traditional' historical consciousness at all. Some of the most brilliant thinkers of our current 'postist' position – Barthes, Foucault, Derrida, Baudrillard, Lyotard, Deleuze, Irigary, Kristeva, Rorty, Fish, Judith

Butler, Laclau – just are able to write book after book, article after article, on our current condition and future, emancipatory possibilities ('where we are now' and 'where we might best go to') without a *single one of them being a historian* in metanarrative upper case or professional, 'proper', lower case senses. Richard Rorty is the example that Harlan chooses as a postmodern 'historian', and he is indeed an excellent illustration of how the 'past' can be used for emancipating purposes in ways that would make most 'proper', traditional historians despair. For what Rorty does is go to texts and appropriate them to suit his own interests. Of course, we all do that, but in the context of 'proper', traditional history, Rorty's practices are almost heretical. For it is not (for Harlan's Rorty) of much concern if the book he takes off the shelf is one written in ancient Greece, nineteenth-century Japan, fourteenth-century Florence, early twentieth-century America or last week, the ideas in it are what count. So, whilst there may well be references in Rorty's own texts to Descartes and Kant, Hegel and Nietzsche, Orwell and Nabokov, Dewey and Davidson, these references are not invitations to study these writers on their own terms, in their own times, and for their own lives, but invitations to take anything you want from them to help us, today. In no way is the study of the past for its own sake, in-and-for-itself, of any concern for Rorty – and there is no reason why it should be for us.

My argument, then, is that if Derrida, Baudrillard, Lyotard, Rorty, Ermarth *et al.* can do without a historical consciousness and especially a modernist upper or lower case one, than we all can. Of course, traditional historians working in either cases, and postmodernist ones working reflexively in a differently conceived historical genre that suits them, can obviously continue to do so, as they find in their practices everything they think that they need. But in terms of emancipatory thinking and emancipatory practices, such work is, I suspect, not much to the point in a culture that is now so radically posthistorical in its postmodernity.

For if postmodernity is a phase – and if the raising to theoretical consciousness in postmodern thinking of that phase in thought is an 'actual' one – then it is easy to look back (from this postist perspective) and read the emergence and then dominance of upper and lower case histories in the nineteenth and twentieth centuries as itself the merest of 'passing phases'. It is very obvious to say so, but it perhaps needs to be said again, that we have 'obviously' never seen anything like nineteenth- and twentieth-century, Western upper and lower case history genres at any other time or place. For there has never, ever been, on any other part of the earth, at any other time, a way of historicising the past *like that*. Such histories are unique (historians like telling people that 'history' is made up of unique events) and ephemeral (historians are even better at telling us that everything is transient/temporary/temporal) and there is no need to exclude the phenomenon of modernist histories from these rather broad – but 'true' – commonplaces. Consequently, there is no need to think these phenomenal species are identical to any putative genus, or that they are instantiations of a real transcendental gesture, or that either one of them is somehow 'true'. Rather, such histories are just a part of the flawed experiment of modernity, and are now being superseded by modes of postmodern thinking that has other ways of theorising time and which speaks to our condition in ways that the old rhetorics of modernist histories do not: such histories really are now, or are now becoming, beside the point.

And the same sort of argument runs for ethics too. The power of Derrida's deconstruction; of Rorty's anti-foundationalism; of Lyotard's *différend*; of Baudrillard's indifference; of White and Harlan's sublime; of Ermarth's urgent Cronopios; of Ankersmit's reflexive post-Kantian, post-metaphorical sensibility – all these expressions bear witness to the end of metaphysical, ontological, epistemological, methodological and ethical certainties, to strong forms of realism, and to the problematic status of weaker forms of realism too. Postmodern morality – a morality of the 'madness' of the undecidability of the decision – undercuts traditional ethics (ethical systems), installing 'the madness of the undecidability of the decision'. As we saw Laclau point out, here (ethical) philosophy as a denial of this situation comes to an end and a politics of that very undecidability begins; postmodern politics is irreducibly of the *différend*, of hegemony.

It is in these changed political circumstances that we now all live. We postmodernists are people who recognise that we are finite creatures in an unintelligible, existential condition with nothing to fall back on 'beyond the reach of time and chance'. With no skyhooks, no transcendental foundations and no point, we are, to recall Rorty's remark, 'just one more species doing its best', a best that, bereft of history and ethics, we might still *choose* to articulate in emancipatory ways. And why not? For never, as Derrida puts it,

> have violence, inequality, exclusion, famine, and thus economic oppression affected as many human beings in the history of the Earth and of humanity. Instead of singing the advent of the ideal of liberal democracy and the capitalist market in the euphoria of

the end of [Fukuyama's] history, instead of celebrating the 'end of ideologies' and the end of the great emancipatory discourses, let us never neglect this obvious, macroscopic fact, made up of innumerable singular sites of suffering: no degree of progress allows one to ignore that never before, in absolute figures, have so many men, women, and children, been subjugated, starved, or exterminated on the Earth.[2]

Can a historical consciousness help here when history in the upper and lower cases has been, as Derrida suggests, part of the cause of our current, modernist-produced condition? Derrida doesn't go on to consider in this context lower case history, concentrating on the meta-narratives of yesteryear (but, of course, his omission isn't innocent), if we recall that, right from the start, his 'deconstructive procedure' consisted of 'putting into question the onto-theo but also archeo-teleological concept of history – in Hegel, Marx, or even in the epochal thinking of Heidegger'. He does not mean, he goes on, to oppose it with the idea of 'an end of history', but to show how this

> onto-theo-archeo-teleology locks up, neutralizes, and finally cancels historicity. It was then a matter of thinking *another* historicity – not a new history or still less a 'new historicism', but another opening of event-ness as historicity [contingency] that permitted one not to renounce, but on the contrary to open up access to an affirmative thinking of the messianic and emancipatory promise: as *promise* and not as ontolo-theological or teleo-eschatological programme or design. Not only must one not renounce the emancipatory desire, it is necessary to insist on it more than ever before . . . this is the condition of . . . perhaps another concept of the political.[3]

This thinking of 'another historicity', as Derrida puts it, can be expressed in many different ways. It is arguably the kind of thing Ermarth refers to as new rhythmic timings of time beyond the historical in the upper case (après Derrida) and beyond 'proper' history as such. It is, perhaps, what Baudrillard suggests as 'we transpose language games on to social and historical phenomena: anagrams, acrostics, spoonerisms, rhyme, strope and catastrophe'. It is, maybe, what Lyotard suggests we seek as we 'make up rules in the absence of rules'. It is, in effect, what lies behind White's notion of the sublime as the necessary insight for a radical, Utopian politics; behind Ankersmit's post-Kantian/post-metaphoric 'historicity'; behind

Harlan's appropriative practices that valorise moral commitments on the basis of the sublime, and behind my own argument here: that we can now live out of history but in time, out of ethics but in morality, in emancipatory ways through the imaginaries provided by the extra-ordinary intellectuality of postmodern thinking. Derrida doesn't speak for us all, of course, and how he speaks inflects *his* own idea for a new type of historicity after the 'end of history' which might better be thought of as new temporalizations (so 'radioactive', still, is the term history in our culture). With that proviso, however, and with the replacement of history/historicity with temporality in mind, we might end this discourse on the end of a certain kind of 'ethical' history (and *maybe* history *per se*) with Derrida's comment:

> In the same place, on the same limit, there where history is finished, there where a certain determined concept of history comes to an end, precisely there the historicity of history begins, there finally it has the chance of heralding itself – of promising itself. There where man, a certain determined concept of man, is finished, there the pure humanity of man, of the *other* man and of man as *other* begins or has finally the chance of heralding itself – of promising itself.[4]

Notes

Introduction

1 Although deemed to be a difficult text, Sande Cohen's *Historical Culture* (Berkeley, University of California Press, 1986) is a brilliant study of how and why *academic* history is arguably part of a 'reactive' capitalist/ bourgeois culture, and further, why and how the study of historical narratives is antithetical to present and forward-thinking critiques. For Cohen, historical narratives are a manifestation of a 'reactive thinking-about, which blocks the act of thinking-to', introducing his study as an interpretation wherein it is argued that 'critical thinking is not possible when connected to academic historical thinking' (p. 2).

2 Drucilla Cornell puts this Derridean point well – a point seen not unreasonably as being influenced by Levinas – when she argues as follows: 'For Levinas, the Good which provides the sanctity for the Other can never be reduced to a set of commandments because the Other calls me only as herself. Since her call is unique to her, how to heed it cannot be known in advance or simply through her identification with me as another moral subject. To reduce her to a set of definable categories would violate her alterity . . . My responsibility is infinite because the Other is unique and therefore I cannot know her in advance of my encounter with her through any in-place system of cognition. It is precisely because the Good is the good of the Other that it cannot be fully actualised. It is, then, as the Other that the Sovereign Good is always beyond any of our conventional systems of morality' (D. Cornell, 'Where Love Begins', in M. Felder, M. Rawlingson and E. Zakin, *Derrida and Feminism*, London, Routledge, 1997, p. 162).

Now, in this text I have *changed* the meaning of the term 'ethics' (in ways not so different from Cornell) for what I hope is a clarification.

3 For the way I have tended to use 'imaginary', see C. Castoriadis, *The Imaginary Institution of Society*, Massachusetts, MIT Press, 1987.

4 J. Derrida, 'The Deconstruction of Actuality', *Radical Philosophy*, 68, 1994, pp. 28–41. Pointing to the artificiality of all positions Derrida writes: 'actuality is indeed made; it is important to know what it is made of, but it is even more necessary to recognise that it is made. It is not given but actively produced; it is sorted, invested and performatively interpreted by a range of hierarchising and selective procedures – *factitious or*

artificial procedures – which are always subservient to various powers and interests . . . The "reality" of "actuality" – however individual, irreducible, stubborn, painful or tragic it may be – only reaches us through fictional devices' (p. 28).

5 H. White, 'Historical Emplotment and the Problem of Truth', in K. Jenkins (ed.) *The Postmodern History Reader*, London, Routledge, 1997, p. 392.

6 T. Bennett, *Outside Literature*, London, Routledge, 1990, p. 54.

7 As I go on to argue, Bennett brings to our attention the problematical nature of the past as articulated in terms of metaphysical, ontological, epistemological and ethical/moral dimensions, and I would clarify how I am using these terms as follows (further clarification appears in the text throughout).

We (apparently) live in a world that is ultimately unknowable (fabular, sublime . . .). Why are we here? What and where and how is 'here'? What could the point of existence be? I call these metaphysical questions and I don't think we can answer them or know that we had, if we ever did answer them. However, attempts have been made to in fact get an answer (*the* answer) – characterisations of the nature of God, of Being, of 'human nature' or the 'real foundation' of the social ('all history is the history of class struggle' for example) – and I call these reductions of the metaphysical to human categories and concepts (and 'interests') ontology. I use the term 'epistemology' quite conventionally as meaning 'theory of knowledge', referring to ways of thinking coherently, consistently and logically about 'things' which, when put under a description allow, say, true/false statements to be made about them, but with the proviso that such 'knowledge' is always *relative* to the description offered, and that they don't thus penetrate, as Richard Rorty puts it, to how 'things' (how Being or Nature etc.) look to themselves. By 'methodology', I mean worked up theories through which, when applied to such 'things' methodically, 'knowledge' about the 'world under description' is produced. My use of 'ethics' and 'morality', has already been given, but one point might be added here. I have found invaluable a way of thinking about 'moral relativism' (for me the outcome of thinking *aporetically*) which has not been drawn upon very much in this text; namely, the arguments for such 'moral relativism without fear or panic' as developed by Barbara Herrnstein Smith. See her *Contingencies of Value* (1988) and her *Belief and Resistance* (1997) both Cambridge, Massachusetts, Harvard University Press.

8 K. Jenkins, *On 'What is History?' From Carr and Elton to Rorty and White*, London, Routledge, 1995; see pp. 6–10 for a brief account of the 'Enlightenment project'.

9 G. Steiner, *In Bluebeard's Castle*, London, Faber, 1972, p. 13.

10 Ibid., p. 103. I have said this response may be trite, but it may also seem to undercut my own argument that, in effect, 'in a culture, culture goes all the way down', in that I may be thought to be saying (after George Steiner) that culture, in fact, doesn't 'go all the way down' because it works on something substantive that is pre-given and, somehow, knowable (for instance, my point that maybe we humans do have 'natural curiosity'). This is a tricky area few people seem to escape from with impunity, but my own position is, briefly, as follows.

It may be (for reasons we'll never know for sure) that, in a Darwinian 'theoretical' sense, humans just do want to survive and want their offspring to do so too, and that this means getting to know how to get around in a culture in ways encouraging curiosity. Now, one might imagine a culture that is so powerful in its discursive regime that questions about *why* that culture is the way it is are silenced, or that such questions are answered so totally that further questioning seems pointless. Alternatively, one might imagine a culture where questions about why that culture is as it is are so open that such questioning is never closed down. But – and this is perhaps my position – it is still possible for members in both cultures to formulate such questions as 'but why are the answers we get given total?', or 'but why must we keep all questions open?' And it is this apparent human capacity to be 'naturally' inquisitive that Steiner just takes to be part of the human condition – and I do too; I have chosen this as a reasonable hypothesis. Like Steiner, I think that no culture is ever 'total', that no settlement is ever definitively settled, and that if there is one thing to value in humans it is their capacity, their potentiality, to (to put this in a postmodern idiom) 'make up new rules in the absence of rules'. Thus, it may be that whilst culture 'goes all the way down' in that whatever it articulates (like 'nature') is culturally thought, thinking, as it were, is naturally 'given' – though we cannot 'know' we have this 'given' we call 'thinking' except culturally . . .

11 Steiner, op. cit., p. 106.
12 R. Rorty, *Contingency, Irony and Solidarity*, Cambridge, Cambridge University Press, 1989, p. 9.
13 J. F. Lyotard, *The Postmodern Condition*, Manchester, Manchester University Press, 1984.
14 R. Evans, *In Defence of History*, London, Granta, 1997, p. 9.
15 E. Ermarth, *Sequel to History*, Princeton, Princeton University Press, 1992; D. Harlan, *The Degradation of American History*, Chicago, University of Chicago Press, 1997.
16 A. Munslow, *Deconstructing History*, London, Routledge, 1997; see also his Editorial in *Rethinking History*, 1, 1, 1997, pp. 1–20.
17 Nietzsche quoted in V. Descombes, *Modern French Philosophy*, Cambridge, Cambridge University Press, 1979, p. 184.
18 B. McHale, *Constructing Postmodernism*, London, Routledge, 1992, p. 5.
19 Descombes, op. cit., pp. 182–6.
20 F. Ankersmit, 'Reply to Professor Zagorin', *History and Theory*, 29, 3, 1990, p. 96.
21 P. Jenkins, 'Dialogues', unpublished paper, presented at a University of Bristol Research Seminar in French Studies, 1997.
22 Ibid., p. 3.
23 S. Fish, *Doing What Comes Naturally*, Oxford, Oxford University Press, 1989, p. 478.
24 Ibid., p. 483. I have inserted my own comments in this quotation from Fish to make the point clear.
25 Ibid., pp. 334–5.
26 Ibid., p. 345.
27 J. Baudrillard, *The Perfect Crime*, London, Verso, 1996, p. 105.

28 R. Rorty, 'Just One More Species Doing Its Best', *London Review of Books*, 13, 14, 25 July, 1991, p. 6.
29 Ibid., p. 6.
30 R. Rorty, *Consequences of Pragmatism*, Minneapolis, University of Minnesota Press, 1982, pp. 167–9.
31 K. Jenkins, *Rethinking History* (1991); *On 'What is History?'* (1995); *The Postmodern History Reader* (1997); all London, Routledge.
32 R. Evans, 'In Defence of History: Reply to Critics', *Reviews in History – Continuous Discourse*, list@ihr.sas.ac.uk.
33 F. Jameson, *Postmodernism, or, The Cultural Logic of Late Capitalism*, London, Verso, 1991.

PART I: ON THE END OF METANARRATIVES

1 On Jacques Derrida

1 S. Critchley, *The Ethics of Deconstruction*, Oxford, Blackwell, 1992.
2 Ibid., p. 43.
3 C. Mouffe (ed.) *Deconstruction and Pragmatism*, London, Routledge, 1996. Jacques Derrida is currently Professor at the Ecole des Hautes Etudes en Sciences Sociales, Paris.
4 Ibid., pp. 85–6. In this text I have construed, relative to the 'Three Remarks', Derrida's sometime arguments in ways to suit my own purposes, my own thesis, putting Derrida, Baudrillard, Lyotard, *et al.* together here in the manner of Rorty (see David Harlan's use of Rorty in Part III). To this end, it should thus be understood that in this section on Derrida I am generally making *interpretive* and not *textual* claims about him, interpreting him for historians as I see them (which explains, for example, the use of 'square brackets' to insert my occasional comments into extracts from him). For those wanting to get a Derrida who is much more 'for himself' at the level of 'introductory' secondary texts, Geoffrey Bennington's *Jacques Derrida* (Chicago, Chicago University Press, 1993) is perhaps the best. I have also found useful (and congenial) Simon Critchley's *The Ethics of Deconstruction* (Oxford, Blackwell, 1992) and Richard Beardsworth's very different *Derrida and the Political* (London, Routledge, 1996). Tucked away in *Derrida and Feminism* (edited by E. Felder, M. Rawlingson and E. Zakin, London, Routledge, 1997) is an essay by John Caputo ('Dreaming the Innumerable: Derrida, Drucilla Cornell, and The Dance of Gender') which is so to the point that I think it can stand as a brilliant introduction to the way that, for Derrida, dissemination and undecidability are the quasi-transcendental conditions of 'moral' justice, a justice that is embodied in unending and as yet unimagined forms, forms that are innumerable.
5 Mouffe, op. cit., pp. 83–4.
6 Ibid., pp. 84–7.
7 Ibid., p. 81.
8 Ibid., pp. 76–86. John Caputo (op. cit.) makes the point very clearly that whilst Derrida is happy to commit himself to the 'grand discourse of emancipation', he has in mind an 'enlightenment', that is definitely not like the 'Old Enlightenment'; he believes that what Derrida hopes

'will come' (perhaps) is, as I say, not '"the old Enlightenment", with its sclerotic eyes frozen open in unrelenting *Aufklärung* – that would be a quite monstrous beast, the monster of panoptical law – but the Enlightenment of the *Augenblick*, of a blink of the eye, a certain postmodern Enlightenment or enlightened postmodernity'. Caputo argues that, for Derrida, deconstruction is not sceptical nihilism, 'but an openness to the beyond, a threshold of the possible, of the *mère/mehr* [more], of "the radical difference of the not yet" . . . a delimitation of the tendency of the present to close over and close off the future . . . that is why Derrida's "thought" and "desire" culminate in what is to "come", to a future *"a venir"* . . . that is why he speaks of democracy to come, or a Europe to come, of a woman or a man to come – without being able to say who or what is coming . . . but something new . . . something innumerable and unclassifiable . . . the impossible'.

9 Critchley, op. cit., p. 37. Derrida's notions of *différance* and deconstruction are often deemed to be difficult to grasp, and certainly they are not easy to summarise in a few words. But to gloss what Critchley is saying here, to put things differently re: archi-writing, *différance*, deconstruction, let me say the following.

If a word was meaningful 'in itself' it would be a transcendental signifier (i.e. sufficient unto itself). But there is no such thing as that. A signifier always gets its meaning relative to other signifiers. But because other signifiers which supplement and give the word its meaning(s) are not entailed by it, then the meaning(s) of the word depend upon which 'other' supplements it, *and* the way that that supplement has meaning(s) *vis-à-vis* its relationship with other signifiers. Thus, the meaning(s) of words are dependent on words which are different from them and which cannot be relied upon to ever be arranged in the same way in different 'contexts', so that the meaning(s) 'to come' are always deferred until the 'other' comes. The other term is thus essential in its *différance* (*différance* meaning here that the second term is both different and deferred), so that, for Derrida, this *condition* for meaning (i.e. *différance*) is irreducible: you can never get a meaning for a term without *différance* operating. Consequently, *différance* is the necessary condition for *all* meaning production (it's just the way meanings are made 'logically'), and this condition Derrida terms 'archi-writing'. Thus *différance* is not a concept or a method etc., but simply the necessary condition for meaning *per se*. Following on from this, because *différance* just is such a condition, all meaning(s) can be 'deconstructed' by showing how even the most self-evident of terms (and especially those with aspirations to be transcendental signifiers) are relatively constituted and thus capable of being de-constituted . . . deconstructed. In this part of the text, I thus try to show how attempts to fix meanings – at least in terms of binary oppositions (which attempt to 'freeze' the fluidity of meanings) are deconstructed by Derrida, mainly for political reasons. For Derrida wants to restore to words their potential always to be other than they are or have been, stressing their undecidability, their aporetic, undecidable irreducibility. For here lies the possibility of different arrangements not only of words but the actual socio-economic-political actuality that infuses them with life. Here, deconstruction serves justices and democracies 'to come'.

10 Critchley, op. cit., p. 38.

11 E. Laclau, 'Deconstruction, Pragmatism, Hegemony' in Mouffe, op. cit., p. 53. With regard to my argument as to Derrida's 'relativism', this is as much rejected by the very different Derridas of Norris and Bennington as it seems, *to me*, to be accepted by Laclau. Norris rejects relativism 'as such' and so his sometime hero 'Derrida' also does (see C. Norris, *Derrida*, London, Fontana, 1987). Bennington's readings of Derrida are regarded, by him, as pretty much the last word – no matter how playful he may 'pretend' to be – and his 'correctness' is insistent and all pervasive. Nevertheless, *contra* Bennington, I think moral relativism is a position the logic of the *aporia* gives Derrida for the reasons I discuss, and I think that Bennington's arguments as to the non-relativism of Derrida are unconvincing. A sort of mollified relativism – which turns out not to be 'relativism', at all – is outlined in Bennington's chapter ('The Rationality of Postmodern Relativism') in his *Legislations: The Politics of Deconstruction* (London, Verso, 1994), a book wherein Derrida is consistently referred to as a non-relativist: 'But in any case Derrida is neither a sceptic nor a relativist, nor simply an anti-foundationalist, and fallabilist could only be a very partial description' (p. 48).

12 J. Derrida, 'The Deconstruction of Actuality', *Radical Philosophy*, 68, 1994, p. 30.

13 E. Laclau, in Mouffe, op. cit., p. 53.

14 Derrida, 'The Deconstruction of Actuality', op. cit., p. 32.

15 N. Royle, *After Derrida*, Manchester, Manchester University Press, 1995, p. 18. Derrida discusses history particularly clearly in *Positions* (London, Athlone Press, 1981); in *Writing and Difference* (London, Routledge and Kegan Paul, 1978); in *Of Grammatology* (Baltimore, Johns Hopkins University Press, 1976) and in *Specters of Marx* (London, Routledge, 1994).
In addition to Royle, I have found Robert Young's *White Mythologies: Writing History and the West* (London, Routledge, 1990) particularly perceptive on Derrida; indeed, Young's location of Derrida *vis-à-vis* Marxist theories of history and historical theorising in general is excellent and should be on everyone's 'reading list'. At the same time, however, Young doesn't make – or doesn't work so much – the distinction I want to stress myself, between time and history, and the possibility of thinking through the end of history aided by Derrida. For Young makes the point – which might seem to critique and subvert my own argument and use of Derrida – that, for Derrida, history *cannot* end because *différance* cannot end. To clarify this possible 'tension' I will summarise Young's point and then my own.
Young argues, then, that for Derrida writing as *différance* 'determines history' (p. 65), in that it is only through the irreducible experience of *différance* that history could ever take place:

> It is only through *différance*, by which the same becomes other and produces a tissue of differences, that history could ever take place: for if full presence were possible, then there would be no difference, and therefore no time, space – or history. *Différance* means precisely that you can never get out of . . . history. It also means that if difference in its sense of non-identity sets up the possibility of history, then difference

in its sense of delay means also that it can never be finally concluded, for such deferral will always inhibit closure . . . 'History as *différance*' then means that history will itself always be subject to the operations of *différance*, and that *différance* names the form of its historicity.

(pp. 65–6)

It is in this sense, says Young, that Derrida argues that if the word history 'did not carry with it the theme of a final repression of difference, we could say that differences alone could be "historical" through and through and from the start' (p. 65). But, as Young goes on – and this distinction is registered in Derrida's remark quoted above by Young (in that *if* the word history did not carry with it the theme of the final repression of difference *then* it would be historical through and through . . .) – Derrida does indeed distinguish between the interminable play of *différance* and the *concept* of a history ending that play. And Derrida is – as Young quotes Derrida as saying – happy to see that sort of history (of that sort of historical closure) as coming to an end, an end Derrida says he has indeed always worked for: 'From the first texts I published, I have attempted to systematise a deconstructive critique precisely against the authority of meaning, as the *transcendental signifier* or as *telos*, in other words, history determined in the last analysis as the history of meaning, history in its logocentric, metaphysical, idealist . . . representation' (Derrida, in Young, p. 64).

Now, as I say, I wish to stress the difference, in Derrida, between *différance* as interminable 'writing' and the concept of history. My position is simply this. The operation of *différance* does indeed mean that 'meaning' ('the meaning of history') will never be known and that we cannot come to the end of something (history) we cannot ever finally 'define' (i.e. transform into a transcendental signifier). In *that* sense, *différance* cannot end and history cannot end because they have been made *equivalent*. But Derrida makes the point, noted above, that any particular conceptualisation/ organisation of *différance* which does claim to have found the meaning of history can – and indeed *must* – be ended; this includes, for example, history in any logocentric, metaphysical format attempting a meaning-full closure (Hegelianisms; Hegelianised Marxism's, etc.). Here I agree with Derrida – that sort of history is now clearly an untenable kind; my argument is that, in addition, 'historicising' discourses with epistemological and ontological ambitions (to know – or aim to try and know – 'the truth(s) of the past') are also untenable; I mean by this 'certaintist'/modernist histories in the lower case.

And I think that the condition of postmodernity (a condition of which deconstructionism is an element) is thus the condition of the possibility of the end of the concept of history in both these modernist 'cases' and, maybe, the possibility of the concept of history *per se* too. Thus, in this text, the argument is that time – ways of expressing temporalities – will continue without end, will continue interminably because of the actuality of *différance*, but that the peculiar and particular ways we have expressed time 'historically' need not. The concept of time and the concept of history, are *not* necessarily connected or logically entailed, but are simply contingent phenomena; consequently, time remains to be thought of in all its differences forever, but this possibility of endlessly organising time 'contingently' need not include in its organisational permutations 'history' – and certainly not 'history as we have known it'. Thus I have used Derrida here to support my argument for the interminability of temporal (and spatial) conceptualisations on the basis of *différance*, and for the desirability of ending modernist (and other) historicisations of time that would effect a definitive, meaningful closure. It is an argument for the desirability – perhaps made possible by postmodernity – of 'living in time but outside history', the point developed in this text by a consideration of Elizabeth Ermarth in Part III.

16 Royle, op. cit., p. 20.
17 Ibid., p. 21.
18 R. Evans, 'Truth Lost in Vain Views', *Times Higher*, 12 Sept., 1997.
19 Critchley, op. cit., p. 39.
20 Derrida, quoted in Critchley, op. cit., p. 39.
21 Royle, op. cit., p. 22.
22 Ibid., p. 23.
23 Ibid., pp. 30–33.
24 R. Beardsworth, *Derrida and the Political*, London, Routledge, 1996, p. xiii.
25 Ibid., p. xiii.

2 On Jean Baudrillard

1 C. Norris, *What's Wrong With Postmodernism*, Hemel Hempstead, Harvester-Wheatsheaf, 1990, pp. 164–93.
2 S. Lash and R. Boyne (eds) 'Symbolic Exchange – Taking Theory Seriously: An Interview with Jean Baudrillard', *Theory, Culture, Society*, 12, 4, 1994, pp. 94–5.
3 Ibid., pp. 90–1.
4 Ibid., p. 92.
5 J. Baudrillard, 'The End of the Millennium or the Countdown', *Economy and Society*, 26, 4, 1997, p. 455.
6 J. Baudrillard, *The Illusion of the End*, Cambridge, Polity Press, 1994.
7 Ibid., p. 1.
8 Ibid., p. 1.
9 Ibid., p. 2.
10 Ibid., p. 2.
11 Ibid., p. 2.
12 Ibid., p. 4.
13 Ibid., pp. 21–2.
14 Ibid., p. 22.
15 Ibid., p. 110.
16 Ibid., p. 114.
17 Ibid., p. 5.
18 Ibid., p. 6.
19 Lash and Boyne, op. cit., pp. 94–5.
20 Ibid., p. 120.
21 Ibid., p. 120.
22 Ibid., p. 94.

23 Ibid., p. 94.
24 Ibid., p. 120.
25 Ibid., p. 121.
26 Ibid., p. 121.
27 Ibid., p. 128.
28 Ibid., p. 91.
29 Baudrillard, *The Perfect Crime*, London, Verso, 1996, p. 105.
30 Baudrillard, *The Illusion of the End*, pp. 123–4.

3 On Jean-François Lyotard

1 J.-F. Lyotard, *The Postmodern Explained to Children*, London, Turn-around, 1992, p. 7. J.-F. Lyotard was, for many years, Professor of Philosophy at the University of Paris at Vincennes. He died in 1998.
2 Ibid., p. 7.
3 Ibid., p. 7.
4 Ibid., pp. 24–5.
5 Ibid., p. 18.
6 Ibid., p. 19.
7 Kant, quoted in Lyotard, op. cit., p. 19.
8 Ibid., p. 19.
9 Ibid., p. 20.
10 Ibid., p. 20.
11 Ibid., p. 21.
12 Ibid., p. 21.
13 Ibid., p. 22.
14 Ibid., p. 22.
15 Ibid., p. 23.
16 Ibid., p. 24.
17 Ibid., p. 24.
18 K. Klein, 'In Search of Narrative Mastery: Postmodernism and the People Without History', *History and Theory*, 34, 4, 1995, pp. 275–98.
19 J.-F. Lyotard, *The Différend*, Manchester, Manchester University Press, 1988.
20 Ibid., p. xii.
21 Ibid., p. xii.
22 Ibid., p. xii.
23 Ibid., pp. xii–xiii.
24 Ibid., p. 138.
25 Ibid., p. 142.
26 Ibid., p. 142.
27 J.-F. Lyotard and J. L. Thébaud, *Just Gaming*, Minneapolis, University of Minnesota Press, 1985.
28 Ibid., pp. 66–7.
29 C. Norris, *What's Wrong With Postmodernism?*, Hemel Hempstead, Harvester Wheatsheaf, 1990, pp. 8–9.
30 Ibid., pp. 12–15.
31 Lyotard, *The Postmodern Explained* . . . , op. cit., p. 35.
32 Ibid., p. 36.
33 Ibid., p. 40.

34　Klein, op. cit., pp. 283–4.
35　Ibid., p. 286.
36　N. Lucy, *Postmodern Literary Theory*, Oxford, Blackwell, 1997, p. 69.
37　D. Carroll, as quoted in Lucy, op. cit., p. 69.
38　Ibid., p. 71.
39　S. Fish, *Doing What Comes Naturally*, Oxford, Oxford University Press, 1989.
40　Ibid., p. 30.
41　H. White, 'New Historicism: A Comment', in H. A. Veeser (ed.), *The New Historicism*, London, Routledge, 1989, p. 295.

PART II: ON THE END OF 'PROPER' HISTORY

Introduction

1　M. Poster, *Cultural History and Postmodernity*, Berkeley, University of California Press, 1996.
2　Ibid., p. 110.
3　Ibid., pp. 112–13.
4　R. Evans, *In Defence of History*, London, Granta, 1997.
5　R. Chartier, *On the Edge of the Cliff*, Chicago, University of Chicago, 1997; G. Spiegel, *The Past As Text*, Baltimore, Johns Hopkins University Press, 1997; D. Roberts, *Nothing But History*, Berkeley, University of California Press, 1995; M. Roth, *The Ironist's Cage*, New York, Columbia University Press, 1995.
6　R. Evans, 'In Defence of History: Reply to Critics', *Reviews in History – Continuous Discourse*, list@ihr.sas.ac.uk.
7　Roth, op. cit., p. 30.
8　R. Evans, op. cit., p. 64, Evans agreeing, in effect, with E. Somekawa's and E. A. Smith's views on 'the muse'.

4　On Richard Evans

1　I object to Evans's 'jobbing historian' stance because he often quotes from a 'primary' source, references it as such, but fails to acknowledge it is taken from a 'secondary' text. For a historian of Evans's type (who often talks of going to the primary sources, to the archives, etc.) to footnote incorrectly and misleadingly is almost a hanging offence. Footnote 24 of chapter 7, referring to a quote from Tony Bennett, and cited as from Bennett's *Outside Literature*, is, in fact, taken from my *On 'What is History?'*, for example.
2　R. Evans, *In Defence of History*, London, Granta, 1997, p. 1. Richard Evans is currently Professor of Modern History in the University of Cambridge.
3　Ibid., pp. 3–4.
4　Ibid., p. 9.
5　Ibid., pp. 8–9.
6　Ibid., p. 14.

7 A. Megill, 'Grand Narrative and the Discipline of History', in F. Ankersmit and H. Kellner (eds) *A New Philosophy of History*, London, Reaktion, 1995, p. 151.
8 Evans, op. cit., p. 74.
9 Ibid., p. 87.
10 Ibid., p. 253. I have already referred (in the Notes to the main Introduction) to Sande Cohen's critique of academic 'proper' history as being part of reactive, bourgeois culture, which means that, for him, academic history is not just an unnecessary component of critiques of the present, but that its historicising positively prevents them, in that it never allows what is actually going on to be seen in its radical non-narratability, its radical non-historyness. Cohen's point is that what 'is' is not part of a narrative, and certainly not part – in its concrete, contingent actuality – of a historical narrative that purports to show such actuality in terms 'other than its own'. Because the events of the past and the present do not have in them the shapes of stories, of narratives, then any such narration can only be an artificial synoptic structuring promoting the myth that such stories, such histories, are 'the condition of knowledge' (S. Cohen, *Historical Culture*, Berkeley, University of California Press, 1986, pp. 12–13).
11 Evans, op. cit., p. 207.
12 J.-F. Lyotard, *The Inhuman*, Cambridge, Polity Press, 1991, p. 73.
13 Evans, op. cit., pp. 4–9.
14 Ibid., p. 4.
15 Ibid., p. 231.
16 See D. La Capra, *History and Criticism*, London, Cornell University Press, 1985; G. McLennan, *Marxism and the Methodologies of History*, London, Verso, 1981, see pp. 97–103 for a discussion around the 'technicist fallacy'.
17 Evans, op. cit., p. 158.
18 R. Vann, 'Turning Linguistic . . .', in Ankersmit and Kellner, op. cit., pp. 45–6.
19 G. Steiner, *After Babel*, Oxford, Oxford University Press, 1975, p. 110.
20 G. Roberts, 'Postmodernism versus the Standpoint of Action', *History and Theory*, 36, 2, 1997, pp. 249–61.
21 Ibid., pp. 252–3.
22 N. Partner, 'Historicity in an Age of Reality – Fictions', in Ankersmit and Kellner, op. cit., pp. 32–3.
23 D. Roberts, *Nothing But History*, Berkeley, University of California Press, 1995, pp. 199–200.
24 Partner, op. cit., p. 33.
25 Ibid., p. 33.
26 P. Carrard, *Poetics of the New History*, Baltimore, Johns Hopkins University Press, 1992.
27 H. White, 'The History Text as Literary Artefact', *Tropics of Discourse*, Baltimore, Johns Hopkins University Press, 1978, p. 82.
28 Ibid., p. 94.
29 Ibid., p. 98.

5　On Hayden White

1　K. Jenkins, *On 'What is History?'*, London, Routledge, 1995.
2　A. Callinicos, *Theories and Narratives*, Cambridge, Polity Press, 1995; A. Munslow, *Deconstructing History*, London, Routledge, 1997.
3　An issue of *History and Theory* was devoted to a critique of White's *Metahistory* (*Beiheft*, 19, 1980: 'Metahistory: Six Critiques'); Wulf Kansteiner has written on the general thrust of the bulk of White's work ('Hayden White's Critique of the Writing of History', *History and Theory*, 32, 3, 1993); Kalle Pihlainen has recently examined White on fictionality ('Narrative Objectivity Versus Fiction . . .', *Rethinking History*, 2, 1, 1998); Frederick Holmes has applied aspects of White to analyses of contemporary British fiction (*The Historical Imagination*, E.L.S. 1997); Richard Vann has examined White within the history of the journal *History and Theory* ('Turning Linguistic . . . ' in Ankersmit and Kellner, *A New Philosophy of History*, Reaktion, 1995); Nancy Partner has recently assessed White's influence generally on historiography ('Hayden White (and the Content of the Form and Everyone Else) at the A.H.A.', *History and Theory*, 36, 4, 1997); *History and Theory* has four essays on White by R. Vann, N. Partner, E. Domanska and Frank Ankersmit (37, 2, 1998); while White himself, in 1999 aged 71, has given some 'retrospective' interviews and is about to publish some new collections of essays.
4　One of the best clarifications of his position by White himself is 'Figuring the Nature of the Times Deceased', in R. Cohen (ed.) *The Future of Literary Theory*, New York, Routledge, 1989, pp. 19–43. It is also in his new collection *Figural Realism*, Johns Hopkins University Press, 1999. Hayden White is currently University Professor Emeritus, University of California.
5　D. Roberts, *Nothing But History*, Berkeley, University of California Press, 1995, p. 256.
6　H. White, 'Historical Emplotment and the Problem of Truth', in K. Jenkins (ed.) *The Postmodern History Reader*, London, Routledge, 1997, p. 392.
7　M. Roth, *The Ironist's Cage*, New York, Columbia University Press, 1995, p. 141.
8　Ibid., p. 143.
9　H. White, *Metahistory*, Baltimore, Johns Hopkins University Press, 1973, p. 433.
10　H. White, *Tropics of Discourse*, Baltimore, Johns Hopkins University Press, 1978, p. 99.
11　Roberts, op. cit., p. 258.
12　E. Domanska, 'Interview: Hayden White', *Diacritics*, 24, 1994, p. 94.
13　Ibid., *passim*.
14　Ibid., p. 99.
15　Ibid., p. 95.
16　K. Jenkins, 'A Conversation with Hayden White', *Literature and History*, 3rd Series, 7, 1, 1998, p. 82.
17　Domanska, op. cit., p. 98.
18　Ibid., p. 95.
19　Ibid., p. 96.
20　Ibid., p. 96.

21 Ibid., p. 97.
22 Ibid., p. 92.
23 Ibid., p. 94.
24 White, *Metahistory*, p. ix.
25 Ibid., p. ix.
26 Ibid., p. x.
27 Ibid., p. x.
28 Ibid., p. xi.
29 Ibid., pp. 428–9.
30 Ibid., p. 428.
31 Ibid., p. 429.
32 Ibid., p. 432.
33 Ibid., p. 432.
34 Roth, op. cit., pp. 113–14, 125.
35 White, *Metahistory*, pp. 423–4.
36 Ibid., pp. xi–xii.
37 Roth, op. cit., p. 145.

6 On Frank Ankersmit

1 Evans, *In Defence of History*, London, Granta, 1997. Various references in Evans's text are disparaging of Ankersmit; see also his comments on the I. H. R. Web Site, list@ihr.sas.ac.uk.
2 F. Ankersmit, *History and Tropology*, Berkeley, University of California Press, 1994, p. 3.
3 Ibid., p. 3.
4 Ibid., p. 3.
5 Ibid., p. 4.
6 Ibid., pp. 4–5.
7 Ibid., p. 31.
8 R. Barthes, 'Discourse of History', in K. Jenkins (ed.) *The Postmodern History Reader*, London, Routledge, 1997, pp. 120–3.
9 T. Bennett, *Outside Literature*, London, Routledge, 1990, p. 40.
10 F. Ankersmit, 'Reply to Professor Zagorin', *History and Theory*, 29, 3, 1990, p. 277.
11 Ibid., p. 277.
12 Ibid., p. 278.
13 Ibid., p. 280.
14 Ibid., p. 281.
15 Ibid., p. 281.
16 Ibid., p. 282.
17 F. Ankersmit, 'Historiography and Postmodernism', in *History and Tropology*, pp. 162–81.
18 Evans, op. cit., p. 8.
19 Ankersmit, 'Historiography and Postmodernism', p. 171.
20 Ibid., p. 171.
21 Ibid., p. 171.
22 Ibid., p. 175.
23 Ibid., p. 176.
24 Ibid., pp. 176–7.

25 Ibid., p. 176.
26 Ibid., pp. 177–8.
27 Ibid., p. 178.
28 Ibid., p. 179.
29 Ibid., pp. 180–1.

PART III: BEYOND HISTORIES AND ETHICS

Introduction

1 Elizabeth Deeds Ermarth is currently Saintsbury Professor of English Literature at the University of Edinburgh. David Harlan teaches history at California State University, San Luis Obispo.
2 Richard Rorty says he isn't a relativist because, there being no absolute, there is nothing to be relativist about; pragmatism isn't relativist in that all there is is a spectrum of positions. I accept this, but my position is that all such positions are then 'relative' to each other in that they are available to choose from. Thus, making a choice is relative to the other choices available – all of which are ungrounded in the pragmatic sense Rorty holds to.

7 On Elizabeth Deeds Ermarth

1 E. Ermarth, *Sequel to History*, Princeton, Princeton University Press, 1992, pp. 13–14.
2 Ibid., p. 14.
3 Ibid., pp. 6–7.
4 Ibid., p. 7.
5 Ibid., pp. 9–10.
6 Ibid., pp. 8–11; pp. 20–3.
7 Ibid., p. 18.
8 Ibid., p. 10.
9 Ibid., p. 14.
10 Ibid., p. 212.
11 Ibid., p. 26.
12 Ibid., p. 21.
13 Ibid., p. 28.
14 Ibid., p. 30.
15 Ibid., p. 31.
16 Ibid., p. 57.
17 Ibid., p. 35.
18 Ibid., p. 36.
19 Ibid., p. 40.
20 Ibid., p. 41.
21 Ibid., p. 41.
22 Ibid., p. 42.
23 Ibid., p. 43.
24 Ibid., p. 34.
25 Ibid., pp. 53, 56.
26 Ibid., p. 99.

27 Ibid., p. 85.
28 Ibid., p. 148.
29 Ibid., pp. 184, 188.
30 Ibid., pp. 210, 213, 214.
31 Ibid., p. 210.
32 Ibid., p. 140.
33 Ibid., p. 72.
34 Ibid., p. 62.
35 Ibid., p. 61.
36 Ibid., p. 59.
37 Ibid., pp. 54–72 *passim*.
38 Ibid., p. 62.
39 Ibid., p. 63.
40 Ibid., p. 63.
41 Ibid., p. 65.
42 Ibid., pp. 63–6.
43 Ibid., p. 212.
44 E. Laclau, *Emancipations*, London, Routledge, 1996, p. 123.
45 D. Harlan, *The Degradation of American History*, Chicago, University of Chicago Press, 1997, pp. 210–11.

8 On David Harlan

1 D. Harlan, *The Degradation of American History*, Chicago, University of) !
Chicago Press, 1997, p. xv.
2 Ibid., p. xix.
3 Ibid., p. xxi.
4 Ibid., p. xx.
5 Ibid., p. xxiii.
6 Ibid., p. xxiii.
7 Ibid., p. xxiv.
8 Ibid., p. xxvii.
9 Ibid., p. xxviii. In *Telling the Truth about History*, Appleby *et al.* are carrying the banner for mainstream reconstructivist history, an approach Harlan generally critiques.
10 Ibid., p. xxix.
11 Ibid., p. xxxi.
12 Ibid., p. xxxi.
13 Ibid., p. xxxi.
14 Ibid., p. xxxii–iii.
15 Ibid., p. 211.
16 Ibid., p. 212.
17 Ibid., p. 147.
18 Ibid., p. 128.
19 R. Rorty, *Contingency, Irony, and Solidarity*, Cambridge, Cambridge University Press, 1989, p. xv.
20 Harlan, op. cit., pp. 131–2.
21 Rorty, op. cit., p. 29.
22 Harlan, op. cit, p. 132.
23 Harlan, op. cit., p. 135.

24 Rorty op. cit., p. 5.
25 Harlan, op. cit., p. 141.
26 Ibid., p. 142.
27 E. Ermarth, *Sequel to History*, Princeton, Princeton University Press, 1992, p. 110.
28 Ibid., p. 110.
29 Ibid., p. 111.
30 Harlan, op. cit., p. 149.
31 Ibid., p. 151.
32 Ibid., p. 151.
33 E. Laclau, 'The Uses of Equality', *Diacritics*, Spring, 1997, p. 18.
34 Harlan, op. cit., p. 94.
35 Ibid., pp. 94–5.
36 Ibid., p. 154.
37 Ibid., pp. 155–7.

Conclusion: Promisings

1 J. Derrida, 'Specters of Marx', *New Left Review*, 205, 1994, p. 50.
2 Ibid., p. 53.
3 Ibid., p. 52.
4 Ibid., p. 51.

Further reading

This is not meant to be an exhaustive bibliography. It is an aid – with occasional comments – to some further, relevant reading. It does not list again all the works that have been cited in the text and which are already referenced in the Notes – although one or two are mentioned again as necessary. What is given here are (1) works generally not already mentioned in the text by and on Derrida *et al.* which readers might go to to further their own readings and (2) specific texts that supplement those already noted, most of which contain good bibliographies of the areas they treat and which might, therefore, provide material useful for further work.

There are very full bibliographies of works both by and on Derrida in the works already cited by Richard Beardsworth (*Derrida and the Political*), Simon Critchley (*The Ethics of Deconstruction*) and Nicholas Royle (*After Derrida*). *Jacques Derrida*, written by Geoffrey Bennington and Derrida himself (Chicago, University of Chicago Press, 1993) contains a *Curriculum Vitae* of Derrida, an exhaustive bibliography, and a 'Supplemental Bibliography' which, together, run to over ninety pages. Peggy Kamuf's *A Derrida Reader: Between the Blinds* (New York, Columbia University Press, 1991) is now a little dated – Derrida has written so much recently – but remains a wide-ranging introduction. Texts by Derrida useful for introductory purposes and areas touched upon here include *Of Grammatology* (Baltimore, Johns Hopkins University Press, 1976); *Writing and Difference* (Chicago, University of Chicago Press, 1978); *Margins of Philosophy* (Chicago, University of Chicago Press, 1984); *Limited Inc.* (Evanston, Northwestern University Press, 1988); *The Ear of the Other: Otobiography, Transference, Translation* (Lincoln, University of Nebraska Press, 1988); 'Force of Law', in D. Cornell *et al.* (eds) *Deconstruction and the Possibility of Justice* (London, Routledge,

1992); *Specters of Marx* (London, Routledge, 1994) and *Politics of Friendship* (London, Verso, 1997).

Mike Gane has provided a good 'Bibliography of Works by Jean Baudrillard' in the English translation of *Symbolic Exchange and Death* (London, Sage, 1993), containing works up to 1993. Among these (and later texts) the following are 'basic': *In the Shadow of the Silent Majorities* (New York, Columbia University Press, 1983); *America* (London, Verso, 1988); *Seduction* (New York, St Martin's Press, 1990); *Cool Memories I* (London, Verso, 1990); *II* (Oxford, Polity Press, 1996); *III* (Paris, Galilée, 1995); *The Transparency of Evil* (London, Verso, 1993); *The Perfect Crime* (London, Verso, 1995). *Jean Baudrillard: Selected Writings*, edited and introduced by Mark Poster (Oxford, Polity Press, 1988), is still a useful if perhaps now a dated general introduction. S. Plant's *The Most Radical Gesture* (London, Routledge, 1991), C. Rojek's *Forget Baudrillard* (London, Routledge, 1993), Mike Gaine's series of interviews with Baudrillard (*Baudrillard Live*, London, Routledge, 1993) and P. Petit's interviews with him *Paroxysm* (London, Verso, 1998), are all good introductions to this much misunderstood theorist. Christopher Norris tends to fit the bill here, for he has persistently critiqued Baudrillard in ways all-too-typical and all-too-hostile. See, for example, his 'Lost in the Funhouse: Baudrillard and the Politics of Postmodernism', in *What's Wrong With Postmodernism* (Hemel Hempstead, Harvester Wheatsheaf, 1990).

In 1998 James William's somewhat disappointing study of J.F. Lyotard was published (*Lyotard: Towards a Postmodern Philosophy*, Oxford, Polity Press, 1998), but it contains an interesting final chapter ('Critical Debates') and a good bibliography which includes Lyotard's major texts running from 1948; Lyotard died in 1998. Geoffrey Bennington's *Lyotard: Writing the Event* (Manchester, Manchester University Press, 1988) is a difficult but clever read(ing). *Lyotard: Political Writings* (ed. by Bill Readings and K.P. Gemain, London, UCL, 1993) is an excellent collection, as is A. Benjamin's *The Lyotard Reader* (Oxford, Blackwell, 1989). Works by Lyotard not referred to in the Notes include *Peregrinations: Law, Form, Event* (New York, Columbia University Press, 1988) and *Libidinal Economy* (London, Athlone, 1993). Though only fleetingly referred to in this text, Lyotard's *The Inhuman* is a collection of brilliant, thought-provoking essays.

Richard Evans' *In Defence of History* (London, Granta, 1997) contains 'Notes' and a 'Further Reading' section, and references to some of his own works.

I have already mentioned Hayden White's main works (*Metahistory*, 1973; *Tropics of Discourse*, 1978; *The Content of the Form*, 1987) and several recent articles on him of which W. Kansteiner's 'Hayden White's Critique of the Writing of History' (in *History and Theory*, 32, 3, 1993, pp. 273–95) and R.T. Vann's 'The Reception of Hayden White' (in *History and Theory*, 37, 2, 1998, pp. 143–61) are invaluable. The latter is especially useful when read alongside his essay on the journal *History and Theory* within which White's influence 'emerges' ('Turning Linguistic: History and Theory and *History and Theory*, 1960–1975', in F. Ankersmit and H. Kellner (eds) *A New Philosophy of History* (London, Reaktion Books, 1995)).

The two main texts by Frank Ankersmit (*Narrative Logic* and *History and Tropology*) contain his 'general' position. In addition, Ankersmit has written numerous essays for *History and Theory* and other journals/books; for example, two appear in the volume he edited with Hans Kellner (*A New Philosophy of History*) cited above.

Elizabeth Deeds Ermarth has written three books in addition to her *Sequel to History* which is concentrated on in this text; namely, *Realism and Consensus: Time Space and Narrative* (1993) with a new preface and bibliography (Edinburgh, Edinburgh University Press, 1998), *George Eliot* (New York, Twayne, 1985) and *The Novel in History 1840–1895* (London, Routledge, 1997). She has also written many essays, one of the most recent being 'Time and Neutrality: Media of Modernity in a Postmodern World', in *Cultural Values*, 2, 2/3, 1998, pp. 353–67.

David Harlan has written on early American history and on the 'linguistic turn' as applied to historiography. A major essay which appeared in the *American Historical Review* (94, 3, 1989), 'Intellectual History and the Return to Literature' (pp. 581–609), has become part of the 'postmodern debate' in 'American History', the 1989 volume being widely cited. Many of the themes developed in *The Degradation of American History* are rehearsed in this earlier essay, but the richness of Harlan's analyses can only be gained by a thorough reading of this book which I have been able to dip into in this text.

On occasion I have made reference to debates about 'the end of history', and there is a large and growing literature on this phenomenon – many connected to 'postmodernism'. The argument I have tried to run myself – though perhaps part of this 'ending' – has not drawn too directly from its main exponents, say, for example, Kojève, Niethammer and Fukuyama (writers brilliantly and critically analysed by Perry Anderson in his 'The Ends of History', in *A Zone of Engagement*, London, Verso, 1992, pp. 279–376); indeed, I have deliberately tried to come at this whole question in ways that allow a critique of lower case, academic/professional history to be made as well as the usual 'Hegelian', upper case one. Some of the texts I have found useful for this approach I give below in alphabetical order, but I mention at this point two works that I have found useful in very different ways.

I have already noted Sande Cohen's *Historical Culture: On the Recoding of an Academic Discipline* (Berkeley, University of California Press, 1988) and I just want to emphasise its value as a critique – by no means a 'postmodern' one (which Cohen thinks somewhat too 'simple' etc.) – of *academic* history as part of a reactive, conservative culture, and his view that such a history is positively harmful to radical critiques of the present. According to Hayden White, Cohen's book is the 'first thorough semiological analysis of historical discourse', and the 'most original contribution to historiographical debate since Paul Ricoeur's *Time and Narrative*', while according to Mark Poster, 'no historian who reads and comprehends this book will ever write in the same way again'. I don't suppose Cohen would much agree with the arguments I have tried to introduce here, but, for me, Cohen's text is enormously thought-provoking. Second, I have found the range of references and bibliographical information given by Robert Berkhofer in his *Beyond the Great Story: History as Text and Discourse* (Cambridge, Massachusetts, Harvard University Press, 1995) – which runs to eighty-one pages – invaluable, and for those wanting bibliographical guidance to 'postmodernism and history' Berkhofer is a must. Not only that, some of his chapters (for example his 'Narratives and Historicization') have a penetration and a lucidity difficult to find elsewhere, and the application of his argument therein to lower case history is, for me, devastating and unanswerable. All that said, a short list of other texts I have found variously useful (and which includes Fukuyama *et al.*) runs thus:

B. Cooper	*The End of History: An Essay on Modern Hegelianism*, Toronto, Toronto University Press, 1984
R. Felski	'Fin de Siècle, Fin de Sexe: Transexuality, Postmodernism and the Death of History', *New Literary History*, 27, 2, 1996
M. Foucault	*Language, Counter Memory, Practice*, (ed.) D. Bouchard, Ithaca, Cornell University Press, 1977

F. Fukuyama   *The End of History and the Last Man*, London, Penguin, 1992
B. Hindess and   *Pre-Capitalist Modes of Production*, London,
  P.Q. Hirst   Routledge & Kegan Paul, 1975
P.Q. Hirst   *Marxism and Historical Writing*, London, Routledge & Kegan Paul, 1985
H. Kellner   *Language and Historical Representation*, Madison, University of Wisconsin Press, 1989
C. Lévi-Strauss   *The Savage Mind*, London, Weidenfeld & Nicolson, 1966
L. Niethammer   *Posthistoire*, London, Verso, 1992
P. Novick   *That Noble Dream*, Cambridge, Cambridge University Press, 1988
D. Roberts   *Nothing But History*, Berkeley, University of California Press, 1995
G. Spiegel   *The Past as Text*, Baltimore, Johns Hopkins University Press, 1997
G. Vattimo   'The End of Hi(story)', in J. Hoestery (ed.) *Zeitgeist in Babel: The Postmodernist Controversy*, Bloomington, University of Indiana Press, 1991
G. Vattimo   *The End of Modernity: Nihilism and Hermeneutics in Postmodern Culture*, Baltimore, Johns Hopkins University Press, 1985

'General' texts that may be useful to refer to in order to get an understanding of some of the current debates about historiography and the status of historical knowledge, etc., can be gleaned from the following list. I would also draw attention here to Alun Munslow's up-to-date account of our current 'historiographical condition', *Deconstructing History* (London, Routledge, 1997). Munslow's text contains an extensive bibliography and a useful glossary.

J. Appleby,   *Telling the Truth About History*, New York,
L. Hunt and   Norton, 1994
  M. Jacob
W. Benjamin   'Theses on the Philosophy of History', *Illuminations*, New York, Schocken Books, 1969
R. Bhaskar   *Philosophy and the Idea of Freedom*, Oxford, Blackwell, 1991
M. Bunzl   *Real History*, London, Routledge, 1997

J. Butler	*Bodies That Matter*, London, Routledge, 1993
A. Callinicos	*Theories and Narratives: Reflections on the Philosophy of History*, Oxford, Polity Press, 1995
J. Caputo	*Radical Hermeneutics*, Bloomington, Indiana University Press, 1987
P. Carrard	*Poetics of the New History*, Baltimore, Johns Hopkins University Press, 1992
I. Chambers	*Border Dialogues: Journeys in Postmodernity*, London, Routledge, 1990
R. Chartier	*On the Edge of the Cliff*, Baltimore, Johns Hopkins University Press, 1997
M. de Certeau	*The Writing of History*, New York, Columbia University Press, 1988
G. Deleuze and F. Guattari	*Anti-Oedipus*, New York, Viking, 1977
D. Elam	*Feminism and Deconstruction*, London, Routledge, 1994
N. Geras	*Solidarity in the Conversation of Humankind*, London, Verso, 1995
G. Himmelfarb	*On Looking Into the Abyss*, New York, Knopf, 1994
G. Iggers	*Historiography in the Twentieth Century: From Scientific Objectivity to the Postmodern Challenge*, Hanover, Wesleyan University Press, 1997
F. Jameson	*Postmodernism, or, The Cultural Logic of Late Capitalism*, London, Verso, 1991
P. Joyce	'The Return of History: Postmodernism and the Politics of Academic History in Britain', *Past and Present*, 158, 1998
M. Lemon	*The Discipline of History and the History of Thought*, London, Routledge, 1995
C.B. McCullagh	*The Truth of History*, London, Routledge, 1997
L. Mink	'Narrative Form as a Cognitive Instrument', in R. Canary and H. Kozicki (eds) *The Writing of History*, Madison, University of Wisconsin Press, 1978
P. Osborne	*The Politics of Time*, London, Verso, 1995
B. Palmer	*Descent into Discourse*, Philadelphia, Temple University Press, 1990

P. Ricoeur   *Time and Narrative* (3 vols) Chicago, University of Chicago Press, 1984–8

V. Sobchack (ed)   *The Persistence of History*, London, Routledge, 1996

B. Southgate   *History: What and Why?*, London, Routledge, 1996

M. Stanford   *A Companion to History*, Oxford, Blackwell, 1994

P. Veyne   *Writing History: Essays on Epistemology*, Middletown, Wesleyan University Press, 1984

E. Wood and   *In Defence of History: Marxism and the*
J. Foster (eds)   *Postmodern Agenda*, New York, Monthly Review Press, 1997

R. Young   *White Mythologies: Writing History and the West*, London, Routledge, 1990

S. Zizek   *The Sublime Object of Ideology*, London, Verso, 1989

Numerous journals carry articles on areas pertinent to the arguments presented here, amongst which *History and Theory, New Left Review, Rethinking History* and *Past and Present* are prominent. But so widespread, nowadays, is the influence of 'the posts', that few journals are immune from some sort of position on them, and this influence shows little sign of slowing down; it's thus a matter of 'keeping reading'.

Index